THE COMPLETE
GUIDE TO
LIVING
WITH THATCH

THE COMPLETE GUIDE TO LIVING WITH THATCH

MICHAEL BILLETT

ROBERT HALE · LONDON

ISBN 0 7090 7158 2

Robert Hale Limited
Clerkenwell House
Clerkenwell Green
London EC1R 0HT

A catalogue record for this book is available from the British Library

2 4 6 8 10 9 7 5 3 1

Typeset in 10/12pt Granjon
Printed in Great Britain by
St Edmundsbury Press Limited and
bound by Woolnough Bookbinding Limited, Irthlingborough

Dedicated to my daughter
Sonia

Contents

Illustrations

LIST OF PHOTOGRAPHS

9

Illustration Credits

R.D. Megilley:1, 3, 43. S.T. Billett: 4, 63, 67. Roy J. Westlake: 6, 21, 22, 26, 31, 32. *Dorset Echo*: 8. Steve White: 9. Eileen Preston: 15, 61, 65. John Baguley: 38. Geoffrey N. Wright: 19, 24, 25, 33, 40, 45, 53, 56, 66, 68. Richard Jemmett: 11, 17, 30, 37, 39, 59, 60, 62, 64. Wales Tourist Board Photo Library: 69. Highlands and Islands Development Board: 70. Joy Wotton: 74.

All other photographs are from the author's collection.

LIST OF LINE DRAWINGS

1

Thatch Through the Ages

Little documentary evidence exists on the history of thatch through the ages. Old prints and paintings of thatched cottages from the sixteenth to the eighteenth centuries yield some hints on the varying shapes of thatched roofs in different regions of Britain. The variation shows how thatchers have always worked independently of one another, stamping their own individuality on their work. This applies today; nearly all thatchers still work as individuals or with small firms. The ridges topping the roofs shown in these old prints were invariably plain, flush and straight, with no decorative ornamentation. Raised block ridges were never used. In the Middle Ages, ridges were normally covered with clay or turfs.

Although thatch is a perishable material, it is fair to surmise that its use as a roofing material had very ancient origins. This was because Nature had made available suitable plants, which grew in most parts of the world and could be adapted into some form of roof covering.

In the broad sense, the term 'thatch' implies any roof made of matter of vegetable origin, although it usually means the stems of plants. Coconut leaves are still used in many underdeveloped tropical areas of the world for the roofs of simple hut shelters. The palmetto or thatch palm of the West Indies yields large leaves which are frequently used for thatching. The wood of the tree is also sometimes employed as a thatch material. In Scandinavia, on the small island of Laeso, between Denmark and Sweden, dried seaweed was once used for thatching. It was a readily available local material. The 3-foot (91 cm) thick seaweed roofs had a very long shaggy appearance; the thatch had a long life and was exceptionally rainproof. Examples of such buildings may still be seen at the Frilandmuseet open air museum at

Copenhagen in Denmark, where many old cottages have been rebuilt in their original forms.

In Britain, thatch in various forms has been in use throughout many centuries. The precise material used has largely depended upon its ready local availability. It may have been brushwood, turf, heather, broom, gorse, water reeds or straw derived from corn. Straw and reed were most favoured in England and Wales, whilst turf, heather, broom and gorse were used in parts of Ireland and Scotland.

Thatching is probably the most ancient building craft still practised in Britain. New houses are still being roofed with it in England but it has now become rare in other parts of Britain. It started when man first left his cave-dwelling existence and learned to grow crops and tend animals. It then became essential for him to build some form of shelter nearby for his own protection. During the Stone Age, shelters were covered with a crude thatch. The first simple outdoor shelter was probably constructed by piling cut branches around a standing pole such as a tree. The circular-shaped structure was then covered with a rough thatch made of brushwood, bracken or turf. The practice continued until the Bronze and Iron Ages, still using a crude form of thatch over upright wooden supports and wattle and daub, a network of interlaced twigs plastered with mud or clay and chopped straw. It is likely that in areas where timber was scarce, rough stone walls may also have been built to support the roof.

A simple development of the roundhouse roof construction was the cutting of a hole in the thatch, to allow the smoke from a fire on a central hearth within the hut to escape. This was an early form of smoke flue. The entrances to the huts were made as small as possible, to prevent or delay attacks from intruders, and window spaces were not provided. The roundhouses were usually built within a fortified surround; reconstructions of such buildings may be seen at Butser Hill in Hampshire. When viewed from afar, they have the appearance of large tepees, similar to those of the North American Indians. Another Iron Age roundhouse has been built at Bradford Peverell in Dorset; because of its size, two concentric rings of posts were needed to support the conical thatched roof.

In later times, in country areas, the Romans occasionally used thatched roofs on their dwellings, which were built with wood, stone and masonry and strengthened with brick courses. The Romans were possibly the first to introduce common wheat into England. But because of the fire danger, they came to prefer stone slabs and eventually flat and arching tiles, which they manufactured. The early Anglo-Saxon settlers stopped using stone and built houses in perishable materials such as thatch, timber and wattle and daub. The wood used in the wattle was probably hazel, which was traditionally preferred later. The Anglo-Saxons left the Roman towns to decay and built new villages in the countryside, usually by streams and on fertile soil, as dictated by their theory of agriculture. The need for water usually meant that the villages were built in valleys or on the lower southern-facing slopes, where spring water was likely to be available. Such locations are still common in England, in contrast to other countries of Europe, which frequently have villages sited on the tops of hills. This was only occasionally done in England, when a good vantage point was required for a strategic observation or defence purpose.

The houses of the early Anglo-Saxons were normally built in such a fashion that they appeared to be all roof with no walls (see fig. 1). In the early designs, a shallow excavation was dug approximating to the area of the proposed house. Two straight heavy timbers were bound

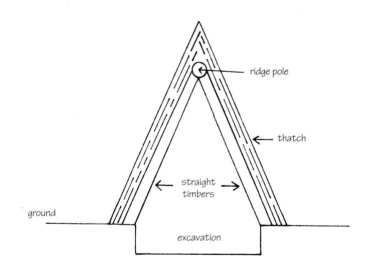

Fig. I Saxon house (cross-section)

together at their tops and the other ends set in two of the corners of the excavation. The process was repeated at the other end of the excavation. A strong timber pole was then lashed across to connect the tops of the triangular end-pieces of the house. This connecting pole formed the ridge timber support of the roof, which was made of rough thatch, possibly rushes, laid on a support of brushwood or wattle and daub, rather than rafters or battens. Later, a gorse layer was introduced under the brushwood because its waxy surface encouraged any penetrating raindrops to drip onto the earthen floor instead of remaining in the thatch to cause it to rot. A hole was cut in the roof to act as a smoke flue. The fuel used for the fires inside the Anglo-Saxon houses was either wood or turfs, and the atmosphere must have been smoky and foul. However, the fumes from the fires would have been more toxic if coal had been burned.

The 'all roof with no wall' design considerably restricted the head space within the house. Walls of timber were later constructed to raise the roof level (see fig. 2). A crude form of timber frame was also used and filled with wattle and daub, wood or stones.

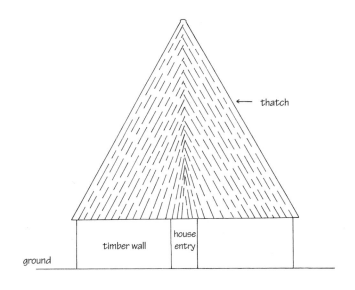

Fig. 2 Timber-walled Saxon house

Examples of thatching Anglo-Saxon style have been re-created at Bede's World, Church Bank, Jarrow, Tyne and Wear. An Anglo-Saxon farm with a variety of thatched timber buildings may be viewed there, together with a church dating back to AD 681–2 and a museum.

Eventually, curved timbers were used as the house end pieces and the early type of cruck roof construction evolved. The cruck gave rise to an arch shape, owing to the lashing together of the curved timbers (see fig. 3); cutting a curved tree in half lengthways made each cruck. The two pieces were then reversed and joined at the top of the arch shape. Sometimes, a strengthening timber was fixed across the arch to make an A-shape. The very early cruck houses were thatched and the design gave additional headroom. The thatch used would have been rushes, turf, ling, or straw, depending on the area. The Anglo-Saxons introduced rye into England, so the straw was probably of this material.

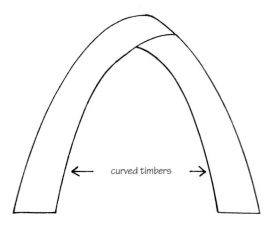

curved timbers

Fig. 3 Cruck

The Anglo-Saxon houses were of a barn-like nature and families shared them with their domestic animals and cattle, which were kept in separate bays. The building of the houses in shallow excavations led to considerable dampness and flooding, and eventually this practice was discontinued. Later houses were built on slightly sloping land and the animals kept at the lower end of the house slope, for obvious reasons of drainage. Locally available material was again used for the thatching. This was sometimes water reeds and the art of thatching with this material as we know it today probably dates back to at least the tenth century. Therefore, present-day methods of water reed thatching have not drastically altered since the later Saxon era.

During the following Norman period, stone buildings were constructed and many examples are still standing today. Although the majority of the population still lived in the countryside, the building of houses in small townships was also taking place. However, most people under the feudal system still lived in humble dwellings constructed of perishable materials such as thatch and wattle and daub.

The fire risk with thatch was always great in early times because fires were lit on an open hearth inside the dwelling and the only exit for the smoke was the hole in the roof. The problem became even more serious in the early Middle Ages when thatch and wood were used as building materials for houses in close proximity to one another in the towns. In 1212, the use of thatch in new buildings was banned in London. Stone tiles and sometimes lead were used as alternative roofing materials. It was also decreed that existing thatched roofs should be coated with a protective layer of crude lime-based plaster to reduce the risk of ignition. This practice of whitewashing thatched roofs to increase their fire resistance, spread to other parts of the country. It was still possible to see the occasional whitewashed thatched roof in parts of Yorkshire, and even sometimes in Wales and Scotland, until the latter part of the twentieth century. In 1727, the fear of fire prompted the Sun Insurance Company to introduce a substantial surcharge on thatch. Local authorities started to ban its use in many towns outside of London, where there had been many fires.

Special tools and hooks were made so that burning thatch could quickly be pulled away from the roof. The huge fire hooks were attached to rough wooden poles about 14 feet (4.27 metres) long and the implements were heavy and cumbersome to handle (see fig. 4). Later, it became the practice to fix iron rings to the eaves, so that ropes could be inserted through them to assist in pulling up and supporting the weight of the fire hook. The many fires that occurred in the Middle Ages led to the gradual development of chimneys in England. The first tall chimney stacks were introduced at the end of the twelfth century, but they were not generally used in vernacular buildings until at least the sixteenth.

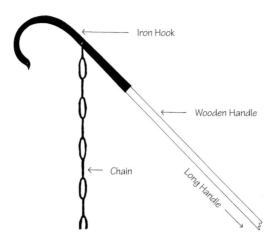

Fig. 4 Thatch fire hook

A few thatched houses still survive from the sixteenth century, with the underside of the thatch and the rafters blackened by smoke drifting upwards from an open fire of wood or peat. The smoke accumulated in the open roof space before drifting away through a makeshift chimney. Smoke-blackened thatch now provides a useful indication for dating buildings to the late medieval period. It also gives an idea of the type of straw used during this period and there-fore the type of natural corn being grown before botanists and agricultural scientists produced hybrid varieties. In Hampshire, there are only five known properties with smoke-blackened thatch. One of them is Molesey Cottage, a Grade II listed building at Goodworth Clatford, near Andover. More examples survive in Devon, where for centuries the overcoating of thatched roofs has been practised. This involved fixing a new thatch coat over the surviving thatch layer, after the decayed layer had been stripped away. The underlying thatch was therefore conserved and is now several centuries old.

In country areas, fire was not such a problem as it was in the towns because the houses were more isolated. Lightning occasionally caused thatch fires but the villagers would have had to cope alone and quickly, before the house was destroyed. Oak was frequently used, especially in later times, for the rafters. Its greater resistance to fire often meant it was merely charred after the burning thatch had been pulled away by a fire hook. Well or river water was the only other means of fire fighting before the availability of mains water. After a fire had been extinguished, the roof was thatched again. The furniture and other items inside the buildings were relatively simple, and manufactured from materials that were not as combustible as those used in modern day furnishings; there were obviously no wallpapers, curtains, synthetic paints and varnishes. The general fire risk was therefore much less. On the other hand, much wood was used in the house construction, in addition to the wattle support for the under-thatch on the oak rafters.

Timber was much used for walls in the twelfth and thirteenth centuries, even in areas such as the Cotswolds where large quantities of limestone were available. This was because wooden houses were easier and cheaper to build. The combination of wood and thatch therefore always presented a potential fire risk. (It was not until the end of the thirteenth century that local stone was used widely to replace timber in the Cotswolds.) In the following centuries and even after limited quantities of fired bricks became available in certain areas in the seventeenth century, local materials continued to be used for the walls of thatched buildings. Country areas could not easily obtain building materials from other regions and construction still used established methods.

Cob, a mixture of clay, straw and gravel, or sometimes mud, straw, animal dung and horsehair, was much used for wall construction, particularly in Devon and also in Cornwall, Somerset and parts of Dorset. The walls were built up in a series of layers, each being allowed to dry before the next was applied. This process was carried out 'by eye', with the result that cob walls were not straight but undulating and with the corners rounded rather than sharp. The walls also tapered from about 4 feet (1.2 metres) at the base to 1 foot (30 cm) at the top. A very large number of these cob houses, white or colour lime-washed, can still be seen today. Many date from the sixteenth and seventeenth centuries. It was found that the material was prone to deteriorate if exposed to damp but if adequately protected it would last for centuries. Cob walls were therefore constructed on the top of a sturdy thick stone foundation to lessen the effect of rising ground dampness. Pitch was also sometimes used at the base of cob walls to prevent damp. The overhanging eaves of the thatched roof adequately protected them from rain. This led to the old Devon saying, 'All cob wants is a good hat and a good pair of shoes.'

Stone and chalk ashlars, materials cut into the shape of large building blocks, were much used in Dorset and Somerset for wall construction in cottages and barns. Chalk ashlar also lasted for centuries if adequately protected from water attack. Again, this was found to be particularly so if the walls were covered with a thatched roof to keep them perfectly dry and prevent water gaining access into the tops.

Local stone was often used where it was available in various parts of England, but if timber was more abundant, then it was preferred. Combinations of timber and local stone were also employed. In Lincolnshire, thatched cottage walls were often built in the seventeenth century with 'mud and stud'. This was a crude form of timber-framing, using a slender frame of vertical rough wooden staves plastered with mud. The walls were only 4–9 inches (10–23 cm) thick. Unlike half-timbered houses, exposed studs did not divide the storey and bay widths. About 400 mud and stud cottages still survive in Lincolnshire, some of which are thatched. Many of them now have their walls completely encased in bricks and other strengthening materials, so they are not easily identifiable.

The thatch materials were always those most readily available, and included marsh water reeds, ling, straw or sometimes turfs, depending upon the region. Thatch was therefore predominantly used in the country areas where these materials were abundant. If stone was more readily to hand, then stone tiles would be used. In the medieval era, a newer, better type of thatched house was being built for the yeoman farmers who were owners and cultivators of small landed estates. They, and the various craftsmen of the time, wanted houses that were better and larger than those inhabited by the tenant farmers, who rented land from a landlord. However, the yeoman houses were not as grand as the manor houses. During this period, thatch was also used as a roof covering for churches, especially those constructed in East Anglia and, to a lesser extent, in the West Country. There are still approximately thirty thatched churches surviving today.

In early Tudor times, farmers built their houses in the villages and not on the sites of their farm buildings. It was only later that thatched farmhouses could be built in the centres of the farms, with the enclosure of land from 1760 to 1820. There are many of these thatched farm and yeoman houses still surviving and being lived in today. They are normally much larger than those constructed for the farm workers. During this era, it was also popular to build the type known as the medieval long house. As the name implies, these houses were extremely long in comparison with their width. It was the practice to support the thatched roof over many huge timbered beams and to build large fireplaces. At this time, thatch was not frequently used for manor house roof construction because the wealthy started to consider it an inferior material.

In Elizabethan times, during the second half of the sixteenth century, the population of England stood at approximately 4 million, of whom three-quarters lived in villages rather than towns. However, the rough pattern for the typical English village had been set before this, in medieval times. Particularly in southern England, there was the church, the manor house, farms, thatched dwellings and often a village green and pond. Many villages were still on the original Anglo-Saxon sites. It was during the Elizabethan period that the village really developed into a self-sufficient unit. There was an impetus to expand food production to feed the country's increasing population. Many more simple thatched cottages were therefore built in the countryside, especially where corn was being produced which yielded straw for thatching. A few more elaborately thatched houses were also being built during this period, the timber-framed house, with various in-fillings, also became popular. The box framework transmitted the weight of the roof structure to the ground; such houses became common in Norfolk and Suffolk but also in parts of Warwickshire and Worcestershire.

The houses built in the sixteenth century were predominantly oblong and narrow. When they were thatched, it became the custom to lay the thatch over all the four walls in a hipped fashion, with eaves all around the house (see fig. 5). The thatch was swept around the four corners of the house, as it was difficult to construct a satisfactory gable end in the thatch (see fig. 6). The thatch under an exposed gable end was thought to be prone to being lifted by the

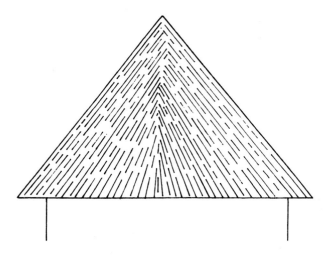

Fig. 5 Hipped roof end

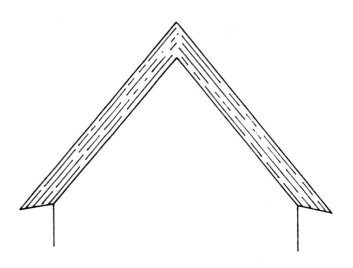

Fig. 6 Gabled roof end

wind, with possible deterioration of the roof. In England, thatched roofs had always been made steep, mainly to shed snow so that its accumulated weight would not damage the thatch. However, this meant that headroom in the houses was restricted, especially near the walls (see fig. 7). Most thatched houses in the country areas were of single-storey construction with no entrance to a loft, which accentuated the space problem. In order to increase the headroom, therefore, it became the practice to build houses in the medieval long house style with the roof steeply thatched (see fig. 8). In the second half of the sixteenth century, those people who were able to afford something better had a top storey built to obtain additional space. These Tudor-type buildings were sometimes built on restricted sites and the upper storey was given an overhang, by cantilevering above the one below; this also protected the ground floor walls from rain. Again the roofs were steeply thatched and hipped, although by this time satisfactory gable ends could be made. A further variation later appeared in the south-east of England with the development of the Sussex hip (see fig. 9). This allowed the thatch to be swept upwards around an attic window space in an end wall. Many examples of thatched houses of this type can still be seen.

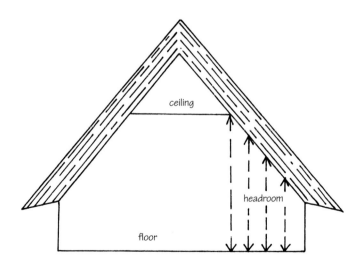

Fig. 7 Roof inclination

Fig. 8 Long House

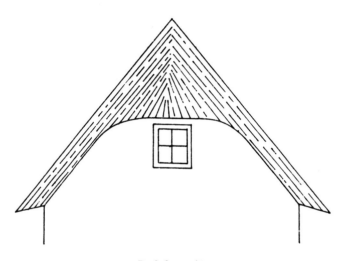

Fig. 9 Sussex hip

It was during the late seventeenth century that the use of glass for windows became popular. Before this time, any window spaces in houses had been kept as small as possible to retain warmth. In earlier times, animal skins covered window openings. Later, oiled parchment sheets or diagonal lattices of twigs were substituted. In 1696 a window tax was introduced in England, owing to the increasing areas of window glass being used. The early form of glass resembled the bases of bottles, fixed in a latticework of lead. The tax had the effect of reducing window spaces again, as people blocked up some of their windows to avoid the tax. All inhabited houses paid 2 shillings (5p) a year, with exemptions for those not paying church or poor rates. An additional tax of 4 shillings a year was payable on properties with ten to nineteen windows. The 1840s brought the mass production of sheet glass and then even the humbler thatched cottages could have simple and larger windows. The tax was repealed in 1851 and replaced by a tax on inhabited houses, similar to our present-day council tax. It was also during the seventeenth century that the dormer window was introduced into house designs. With thatched buildings, a wall section was often raised to allow the construction of a dormer, so that the window could be placed vertically in the sloping roof. The thatch was then gently swept around the top of the window, assuming the shape of an eyebrow (see fig. 10).

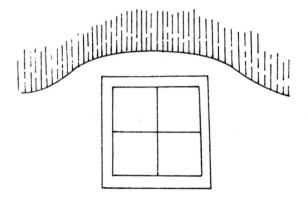

Fig. 10 Dormer window – eyebrow

In 1662 a hearth tax was introduced and as with the later window tax, those not paying church or poor rates were exempted. The tax was imposed at the rate of 2 shillings (10p) for each hearth or fireplace in all houses, whether in town or country. This encouraged a reduction in the number of hearths and in turn the number of chimneys, as the parish constable counted chimneys to check the tax due. Eventually, the unpopularity of the tax forced the authorities to repeal it in 1689. The idea of a hearth tax was not new; the Anglo-Saxons had introduced a similar tax on smoke, which was levied on all hearths except those of the poor. Many early cottages were constructed with chimneys projecting from the gable wall to keep them well clear of the thatch (see fig. 11). This was done to reduce the fire risk but later the chimneys became incorporated into the gable wall. With hipped roofs it was also the practice to position chimneys so that they projected from the wall, to avoid the thatch at the eaves. However, this design badly affected the ability of the thatch to shed water at the chimney junction and therefore it became customary to build chimneys that passed through the ridge. Examples of the siting of chimneys in the middle area of the main slope of the thatch, to avoid passing through the ridge, are rarely found because this grossly interfered with the shedding of water from the roof. Water tended to gather at the thatch interface with the chimney.

From the seventeenth to the early nineteenth century, the use of manufactured tiles for roofs became popular in England. Thatch was then predominantly found only on the more humble dwellings. It was used for these because it was cheap and also because it was relatively light, so it could be used over walls constructed of cheap locally manufactured materials such as cob. The walls were built directly on a stone layer on the ground without dug foundations.

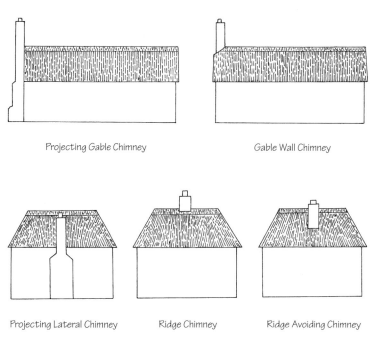

Projecting Gable Chimney   Gable Wall Chimney

Projecting Lateral Chimney   Ridge Chimney   Ridge Avoiding Chimney

Fig. 11 Chimney types

27

As it was not fashionable in those times to live under a thatched roof, people went to great lengths to pretend that they did not, such as having the front roof, which could be viewed from the road, tiled and the back one thatched. The situation changed in the first half of the nineteenth century when slates were introduced from Wales. The quarrying of slates in large quantities eventually became just as important an industry in North Wales as coal mining in South Wales. With the growth of the railways and canals, it was possible to distribute them widely throughout the whole United Kingdom. Thatch became comparatively more expensive and therefore fashionable again with many classes of society. Wheat straw, in particular, became relatively expensive as a result of shortages during the earlier Napoleonic wars.

The wealthy now built whole country estates of thatched buildings. Many integrated villages were built consisting of nearly identical thatched cottages. Thatched dwellings in the *cottage ornée* style also became popular during the Regency decade, 1810–20. This term denoted a small building deliberately built to capture the careless rustic style of the vernacular. It was thought to be a manifestation of the picturesque as most appropriate to England. The thatched roof was often built at several different levels for decorative effect and the over-hang of the eaves from the walls was always made extremely wide. Larger country houses were also designed in a *cottage ornée* style, as were the lodges guarding the entrances to the estates. In such designs, vertical heavy timbers supported a steeply inclined thatched roof structure. The supports were ornamentally set around the outside of the house, in front of the main wall structure. There were normally thatched verandahs around the perimeter of the house and also thatched porches sheltering the doors. Tall chimneys often towered over the thatch. This type of thatched building, with rustic pillars, was especially favoured in the Isle of Wight. The *cottage ornée* style also became popular in fashionable areas near London, such as Richmond and Roehampton. Seaside towns, such as Brighton and Sidmouth also became favoured locations. In the early part of the nineteenth century, it also became fashionable to build rather ornate arch-shaped doorways in some thatched farmhouses. However, this practice did not remain popular for long because it clashed with the aesthetic appeal of the thatched roof.

Preferences for certain shapes and styles of roof in different areas gradually became more pronounced. In Norfolk, and generally in

A cottage ornée lodge, Morden, Dorset

East Anglia, the roofs were very steeply pitched with wrapped and sharp-edged gables. In the West Country, a more rounded, chunky appearance evolved, with reduced pitch. In Essex, it became the fashion to shape the gable ends with a rounded or barge effect. In the Cotswolds, the development was normally towards gable-ended rather than hipped roofs. This was in contrast to Kent and also to parts of Buckinghamshire and south and south-west England, where the hipped shape became very popular.

Preferred roof shapes were not just confined to specific regions of England. For example, in the south and south-east of Ireland there is still a predominance of thatched hipped roof houses. In contrast to this, the northern and western parts of the country incline mainly to the gable

29

type of roof. As in England, old farmhouses with thatched roofs can still be seen throughout Ireland. They are normally single-storey long buildings with whitewashed stone walls, although they are sometimes colour lime-washed. Two-storey thatched houses are more rarely seen.

In country areas, thatch was used for many centuries for the protection of buildings other than inhabited dwellings. For example, thatched barns were commonly built, and some of these had huge thatched roofs, especially those in the south-east of England. The use of thatch on barns sometimes presented problems, however: the thatched roof was able to cope adequately with wind pressure on the outside surface but if the barn door was left open and the wind hit the inside of the roof, then parts of the thatch were likely to be lifted and carried away. Thatched barns are still found on farms and remain a magnificent feature and a reminder of the old method of storing grain. The architecture of barns has remained fairly simple through the centuries and the exposed timber interiors of many look very impressive. The earliest were often cruck built to support the roof and walls; later ones used a crown-post frame, whilst a post and truss construction became popular in the seventeenth and eighteenth centuries (see fig. 12).

The large sizes and roof areas of barns now make them a very expensive proposition to maintain and re-thatch. Many farmers may face expenditure of several thousands of pounds to preserve even medium-sized barns, but it would be a pity if such buildings were allowed to disappear from the English countryside because of lack of finance. Fortunately, many are now listed or scheduled buildings and therefore it is sometimes possible, although difficult, to obtain financial assistance towards maintenance with a government or local authority grant. There are also many old thatched tithe barns scattered throughout England. These were originally used to store the contributions of grain that each parish had to donate to maintain the church. These large old tithe barns usually had two doors at the opposite ends of the building. Wagons could then readily enter a barn to unload the grain and then leave by the other exit, thus avoiding having to turn in the middle of the barn. In Dorset, thatched roof corn-stores were often built close to the farmers' barns. These stores had timber walls and were raised off the ground by placing them on a number of stone legs (see fig. 13). The straight legs shown did not prevent mice and rats climbing up and reaching the grain, and mushroom-shaped staddle stones were therefore substituted.

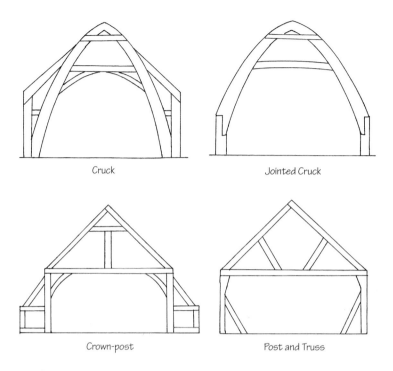

Cruck

Jointed Cruck

Crown-post

Post and Truss

Fig. 12 Barn roof designs

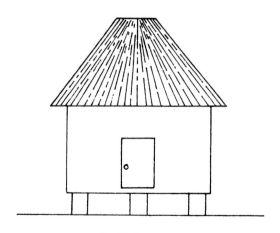

Fig. 13 Corn-store

31

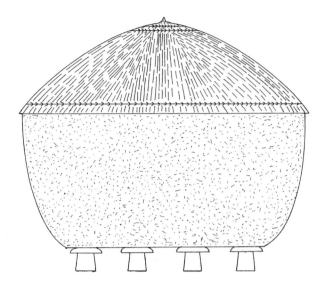

Fig. 14 Thatched rick on staddle stones

It was also common practice in England to thatch ricks and haystacks (see fig. 14). It was not a practical proposition for the local thatcher to thatch a very large number of ricks on his own, as all the farmers wanted his services at the same time, at the end of the harvest season. This thatching was therefore often done by the farm workers, as well as by the thatcher, because the quality of the thatch was not so important, as it did not need to be as durable as a house roof. Speed was also essential in rick thatching, in order to beat the weather. The thatch on the ricks was normally secured by plaited straw ropes and twisted hazel spars.

The top of the thatched rick or haystack was often ornamented with a corn dolly, which was usually made in the shape of a bird or animal. These were used for many centuries as good luck charms for the future harvest. They were traditionally made from the last sheaf of corn of the final wagonload of the harvest. They were kept throughout the winter and the grain obtained from them was sown the following spring to ensure a bountiful harvest during the coming months. The idea was later modified so that the corn dolly was placed on the rick or haystack roof.

These finished ricks and haystacks were very pleasing to the eye. However, for many years now, with the advent of the combine harvester, Dutch barns with arched metal roofs have replaced them. A modern Dutch barn, consisting of a metal roof on sturdy pillars, gives not only a rainproof cover but also perfect ventilation for straw and hay, but it lacks the aesthetic appeal of an old thatched barn, rick or haystack.

Thatchers and farm workers often made straw ropes for securing thatch from a standing straw rick, using an instrument called a whimmer (see fig. 15). It consisted basically of a metal hook, a holding handle and a turning handle. The hook would be pushed into the straw rick, so that when it was withdrawn it would bring with it a small amount of straw. The person holding the whimmer would then walk slowly backwards (see fig. 16). He would clasp the holding handle with one hand and turn the end handle with the other, in the manner of a carpenter's brace. The twisting and pulling action had the effect of making and drawing out a straw rope from the rick. The rope could be made to any desired length, depending on the distance the operator walked back from the rick.

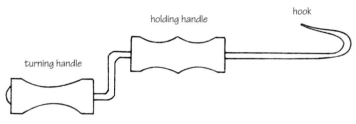

Fig. 15 Whimmer

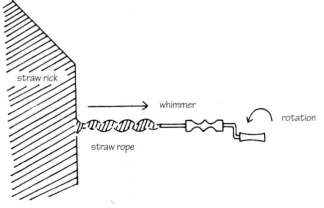

Fig. 16 Making a straw rope

Thatched wall at Coombe Bissett, Wiltshire

Thatch was once used to protect milk-stands and platforms from the rain. These used to be a familiar sight along many country lanes, keeping the milk cool whilst waiting for collection. Little thatched roofs or canopies were also often built over village notice boards to protect the paper and prevent the ink from running in the rain. Country privies were also frequently protected with a thatched roof as, later, were some bus stops. Another use for thatch in the past was to protect boundary walls from the rain. During their construction, the tops of the walls were also sometimes capped with a temporary thatch layer as protection against frost damage, as they were built up in layers. The fairly unusual sight of a

Thatched wall, Winterborne Zelston, Dorset

thatched wall can still be seen in Dorset, Wiltshire and also parts of Berkshire and Hampshire.

Originally, these walls were made by pouring a mixture of water, chalk, flint and other ingredients such as horsehair and dung into two pieces of parallel wooden formwork. Sometimes, for farmyard walls, a mixture of straw and clay was used instead of chalk and flint. The formwork or shuttering acted as the mould to maintain the wall shape, until the water had evaporated from the mixture, after which the formwork was removed, leaving the wall. The materials used to construct the walls were not stable under adverse weather conditions and therefore a permanent covering of thatch was constructed over their entire lengths. The walls were fairly narrow and it was difficult to attach thatch to the top of them, as there was no timber. It was therefore necessary to fix tightly bound bundles of reed along the top of the wall. This gave a firm base for the thatcher to secure the top sloping layers of thatch. If the walls had not been protected in this way, they would have disintegrated long ago and would not still be an occasional feature. The type of thatch used for wall protection was not usually of the best quality, but the thatchers or farm workers always gave it a very neat, attractive appearance.

Thatched wall, West Kennett, Wiltshire

Thatched cottages can be found scattered throughout the whole of Britain but English counties lying south of Yorkshire and Lancashire possess the greatest number. There are today an estimated 50,000 thatched dwellings in England, of which 24,000 are listed. This is a huge decline from the 1 million peak reached in 1860 (see fig. 17). This peak was reached after a steady rise in thatched cottage numbers during the previous decades. The decline since 1860 is partly due to many of the more poorly built cottages being allowed to deteriorate and eventually to be demolished to make way for new housing. Also, a few previously thatched buildings were covered with galvanised iron roofs, whilst others had their roofs strengthened to support a slate or tiled roof instead of thatch. Certain counties have a higher proportion than others; East Anglia, and especially Suffolk, have a high number, no doubt owing to the ready availability of the locally grown Norfolk water reed, much favoured as a thatching material. The West Country also has a high proportion; it is estimated that Devon has approximately 8,000 thatched homes in its area of 2,591 square miles (6,711 square kilometres) and the smaller county of Dorset 4,000 in 1,024 square miles (2,652 square kilometres).

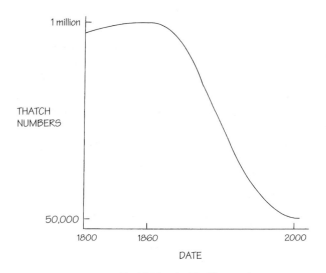

Fig. 17 Thatched building numbers

The West Country boasts an exceptional number because it has always been largely agricultural and a producer of corn from which straw and wheat reed could be derived for thatching. The exception is Cornwall, where there are fewer, mostly situated on the south coast, away from the Atlantic gales. Other counties of England that have traditionally produced large quantities of corn also have a big proportion of thatched buildings; the long corn straws were the most widely used thatch material. These counties are predominantly found in the south of England and the Midlands. The term 'corn' covers wheat, oats, barley and rye. However, thatch is not so abundant in Kent, Surrey and East Sussex because of the popularity of local tiles.

The north of England has a relatively small number of thatched houses because of its lack of large-scale corn production. For example, it is estimated that Yorkshire, the largest county in England, now possesses less than fifty thatched homes and Stoke-on-Trent, in Staffordshire, has only one surviving thatched cottage.

The type of people living in thatched properties has changed over the centuries. In the past, with the more wealthy, the position was largely dictated by whether thatch was in or out of fashion at a particular time. However, farm workers, tenants and yeoman farmers occupied the vast majority of thatched properties in the countryside. During the last few decades, there has been a large decline in the numbers of agricultural workers living in the old thatched cottages, as mechanization has made the agricultural industry much less labour intensive but at the same time more productive. The population has now changed due to the influx into the villages of a new type of occupier. Many thatched dwellings have now been purchased, extensively renovated and modernized by city- and town-dwellers, who buy the country cottages as idyllic second homes for use at weekends or holidays, with a view perhaps of one day retiring to them. Property developers have played a role in restoring and modernizing such properties before placing them on the market. Also, owing to modern transport, many new owners can drive each day from their country cottages to jobs in cities and towns. Others are able to work at home as a result of information technology advancements. The majority of these new owners are usually wealthy enough to maintain their properties in good order. The dwellings have thus become much more readily resaleable and expensive than they used to be.

The migration of new types of people to the countryside has also changed the nature of the old village concept. Many of the former inhabitants and especially the younger ones, have drifted away from agriculture to find work, often more financially rewarding, in more industrialized regions. Their replacement by people from the towns results in a new type of mixed community with the few remaining agricultural workers and farmers. However, English villages still retain much of their original charm, despite the closures of many village pubs, post offices and schools; luckily, thatched cottages still provide a permanent distinguishing feature. At the present time, it is true to say that the aesthetic appeal and the charm of a thatched roof remain irresistible to a great number of people. Thatch can therefore be found covering not only some of the more humble cottages in rural England but also some of the most expensive and exclusive homes, most of which are several centuries old. In addition, new homes are now being built roofed with thatch, despite the fact that there is a shortage of long straw for thatching because combine harvesters chop the stems into small pieces. Obviously, people still yearn to recapture the former styles of England's rural heritage.

2

Thatch Materials Old and New

Most old houses that were thatched were covered by materials grown in the surrounding areas because it was easy and economic to do so. For example, *Calluna vulgaris*, commonly known as heather or ling, is still on rare occasions seen in Scotland on the roofs of crofters' cottages and outhouses. However, its present-day use is mainly restricted to the roofs of pavilions and summer-houses. Heather was originally used because it grew to a considerable size in the Highlands and yielded a readily available thatching material. The plant formed very tough, wiry stems on a bushy base and for thatching purposes it was cut into lengths of about 3 feet (91 cm). It was harvested during the autumn when still flowering and laid to dry with its roots uppermost. It was sometimes shaved with shears to give it a trim finish. Heather was also once widely used in Northumberland, Durham, Yorkshire and Dartmoor because in the persistent damp conditions found in moorland regions, it was less likely to rot than straw. In parts of Kent, Surrey and the New Forest in Hampshire, it was sometimes used as a base coat, beneath a top coat of long straw.

Broom was available as an alternative material. It also has stiff, long, wiry branches and grows to a height of between 3 and 5 feet (91–152 cm). It is found on dry heathlands and open sunny downs throughout the United Kingdom. It was thus a widely distributed material for the thatcher. It is sometimes confused with furze or gorse, which grows in the same areas and has similar yellow flowers. The main difference between the two is that broom is not prickly, whilst furze has sharp spikes.

Another material freely available for thatching was turf. This was frequently cut and used either alone or together with any water reeds which were found growing locally. The turfs were normally lifted in lengths of about 20 feet (6 metres), about 2 feet (61 cm) wide and about 2 or 3 inches (5–8 cm) thick. They were preferably cut from ground that had never been ploughed, in order to ensure that the grass roots had not been severed and therefore were still well entangled. The area of each turf was kept as large as could be conveniently handled. This reduced the number of joins when they were laid and sewn on the roof purlins. The turfs were always fixed to the roof with the grass side upwards facing the weather and the root side in contact with the under-roof. Turf was frequently used in Ireland and to a lesser extent in Scotland. It was also favoured for ridge construction in England. It was still used until the end of the nineteenth century for finishing reed roofs, especially in Wales and the border counties of England. They provided a watertight seal for the ridge, being fixed so as to cover 2 or 3 feet (61–91 cm) down on either side of the apex.

A much rarer form of thatching material was wood chips made from hazel in lengths of about 2 or 3 feet (61–91 cm). The lengths of wood were slightly tapered and were bundled with all the thick butt ends gathered together. The bundles were next tied to the roof with the thick ends facing downwards on the roof slope. As the roof was covered, these ends were pushed upwards, so that they became firmly wedged together. The end result was a tightly packed thatched wood-chip roof. It formed a variation on the shingle-clad roof, which consisted of thin, tapered, overlapping wooden tiles laid in rows. Although now rarely seen in Britain and Europe, shingle roofs are still fairly popular in the United States of America and Canada, where cedar or cypress woods are favoured. Another uncommon material that was used for thatching was chestnut shavings.

A much more common form of thatch in England was sedge (*Clodium mariscus*). This is a razor-edged grass-like plant, found in bogs and ditches and it is still very occasionally used for whole roof areas in the fens. However, it is now more frequently used as a ridge material for roofs constructed with Norfolk reed, which is difficult to bend over the apex because of its toughness. Sedge under favourable soil conditions can grow as high as 6 feet (1.8 metres). Although it can be cut at any time of the year, it can only be harvested every seven years. It is very pliable and easily bent when in the green condition, but its sharp edges often cause cuts on a thatcher's hands. With age, it becomes brown and less resilient. It has a life of approximately thirty years when used on the ridge and blends well with the dark golden brown of a Norfolk reed roof. The long life of a sedge ridge means it will outlast the hazel spars fixing it to the roof and they will have to be replaced on occasions.

Most thatched roofs in England are now made of either reed or straw. The most common reed materials are Norfolk reed and combed wheat reed. Long straw is used for straw roofs. These cultivated natural products have been used for a very long time, although long straw has had the widest and longest use. The best-known thatching water reed is *Phragmites communis*, the tallest reed found in the United Kingdom. It grows up to 10 feet (3 metres) in height, with hollow jointed stalks. The dried stems have been used to make arrows, basketry and pens, and have even been incorporated into musical instruments. However, the reed is normally only suitable for thatching when obtained from certain areas, where it has been semi-cultivated to encourage a straight and strong tapering structure. The reeds need wet conditions for growth and they then grow vigorously, forming dense clusters on the edges of fresh or brackish water. They are perennial and spread by creeping. They can be seen in dark purple flower during August and September. They grow on a single main stem and the seed heads are brown and feather-like. The leaves are large and pointed, with the appearance of spears. An area such as Norfolk, which has many rivers and waterways, is ideal for their propagation, as they need wet conditions.

Many of the waterways in Norfolk were originally made by turf-cutters, when the excavations they left behind became filled with water. Some are fresh and others brackish. The intensive turf and peat digging took place over many centuries, from Roman times until the end of the fourteenth century. They remained as marshes until reclaimed during the seventeenth to the nineteenth centuries.

Without doubt, Norfolk reed is the most famous, tough and durable of thatching materials. Its reputation was firmly established by the skill of the Norfolk thatchers, especially in the early nineteenth century. The reeds are sometimes called by the alternative name of Norfolk spears. For maximum strength, the reeds should be cut low on the stem, after the frost has killed off the leaves. The regular cutting of the beds produces reeds that are straight and strong and taper well. They flourish best in standing water but they have a tendency to build up the soil level as they die back each year and create debris, although burning old growth helps to destroy both the debris and the weeds. It also creates potash to encourage the growth of new straight reeds. Depending upon the weather conditions, the best harvesting time is normally between January and March. At this time of the year, flat-bottomed boats loaded high with bundles of reeds can still occasionally be seen on the Norfolk Broads. Some of the harvest was once exported to the United States of America. Neglected reed beds rapidly deteriorate and the reeds yielded are no longer of the right quality for thatching. In general, the 'wilder' the reeds the weaker will be their basic stem structure.

Reeds cut by hand are often stronger than machine-cut ones. This is because the former method is more gentle and the material is subjected to less stress than when machine cut. However, modern machine development has overcome the problem to a great extent. It is now possible to obtain machines such as power-driven scythes which cut and bind several hundred bundles of reeds per day. This innovation has saved the harvesters from the extreme hardship of wading and working in ice-cold water during the winter months. Other modern aids to the marsh reed farmers include sledges towed by tracked vehicles such as Snowcat-type tractors. These haul the reeds away from the cutting area, across the marshy ground, to reach lorries parked on firmer ground. Unfortunately, from the thatching point of view, many of the open marshlands in East Anglia are now nature reserves or bird sanctuaries, which has led to a shortage of supply. In the past, nearly the whole area from Norwich to the Wash was managed as reed beds.

As would be expected, many examples of Norfolk reed roofs can be seen in East Anglia. However, the *Phragmites communis* reed is found in many other parts of the United Kingdom, though it is only called Norfolk reed if it originates from that area. A little is established in Dorset, in the Radipole and Abbotsbury areas. The use of Abbotsbury reed was once quite widespread in the south of England but its use is now restricted to local thatching. *Phragmites communis* is also found in coastal areas of Wales, Hampshire and many other marshy regions on the east coast of England, such as Suffolk. All these areas have the correct environmental conditions for its growth, but, as with Norfolk reed, the beds must be semi-cultivated to produce the high-quality reed suitable for thatching. Many of these local marsh reeds were used by thatchers in the areas where they grew and are called by their local names, such as Hampshire or Dorset marsh reeds. Sometimes, even the name of the local town was used, for example Weymouth marsh reed and Abbotsbury reed. However, all these supplies have now drastically dwindled.

Other types of water reeds are frequently found growing alongside *Phragmites communis*. Typical of these are bulrushes *Typha latifolia*, also known as cat's tail and great reedmace. This plant grows up to 8 feet (2.4 metres) in height and flowers in July. It can spread very rapidly. Another intruder in marshlands is *Iris pseudacorus* or yellow flag, which normally grows to a height of about 4 feet (1.2 metres) and flowers in June and July. These varieties of marsh reed are occasionally used blended in minor proportions with *Phragmites communis* for thatching.

The main alternatives to Norfolk and other marsh water reeds are combed wheat reed and long straw. These are the same material when growing in a field; they are just harvested differently, combed wheat reed being combed out while long straw is threshed. At one time, long straw was the most commonly used thatch material in the majority of English counties, but it is not possible to harvest thatching straw with a combine harvester because it threshes the corn at the same time as it reaps, pouring the grain into sacks and scattering the straw stalks, which are usually broken into short pieces, on the ground. So the advent of the combine harvester, although greatly improving the world's grain harvest, has at the same time reduced the amount of good length straw available for thatching. In order to obtain long unbroken straw stalks suitable for thatching, it is essential to harvest the wheat with a reaper and binder. This machine does not thresh as it reaps but just cuts the wheat and binds it into bundles. However, the process is costly, labour-intensive and very dusty. Also, the farmer takes a greater risk growing long stem wheat, as the crop is more easily damaged by bad weather.

The shortage of suitable wheat straw for thatching has been further aggravated by the improved varieties of corn that are now planted to optimize grain yield. These varieties are shorter and stiffer than those grown during the first half of the twentieth century. Farmers prefer the shorter varieties of wheat, barely 18 inches (46 cm) high, because they can tolerate much greater levels of nitrogenous fertilizers to increase their yields. They are also less likely to become flattened by wind and rain. However, farmers sometimes grow a limited number of segregated acres of a long wheat variety such as Red Standard, Maris Huntsman and Maris Widgeon especially for the thatching trade.

To ensure an extended growing period, the wheat must be autumn sown; spring wheat does not produce the height and strength required for thatching. The thatchers buy the crop and make arrangements with the farmer for it to be harvested in the summer with a reaper and binder, before being allowed to dry and ripen fully in stooks. Normally there are four to six sheaves in each stook. The wheat will then probably have to be placed in a rick before eventually being either combed out for reed or threshed in a special drum for use as long straw. Before a rick is dismantled, a wire fence must first be erected around it to contain any vermin living in it, so that they can be trapped and killed. Special care is taken during the harvesting and later handling of the long wheat, to ensure that the stems are not bent or crushed. Some thatchers even grow and harvest their own crop. After drying, instead of using a rick, some store the sheaves in rat-proof steel bins until required for threshing.

The wheat from which the straw is derived should ideally be harvested when still slightly green, as this gives a stronger, more durable straw. The length required for good thatching is about 2½–3 feet (76–91 cm). Straws that are allowed to grow naturally have a greater strength than those that are artificially forced, and fertilizers tend to make the straw grow brittle. Wheat was originally combed by hand to remove the grain and leaves without damaging the stalks. This was a laborious but necessary process to obtain a wheat reed suitable for thatching. Combed wheat reed is now obtained by attaching a special reed-comber to the threshing machine. The sheaves of corn are fed into the machine, all the same way round, and a comb removes the leaves and grain but does not allow the stalks to enter the threshing drum to which the combing machine is attached. The straw is therefore not subjected to mechanical stress and the unbroken stalks are kept parallel, ready for tying into bundles with the thicker butt ends together.

Combed wheat reed is classified as a reed from the thatcher's point of view and is laid into a roof using a similar technique to Norfolk reed or other marsh water reed. It is predominantly used in the south-west of England and is sometimes known as Devon reed. Many examples of houses thatched with this material can be seen in Devon, Dorset and Hampshire. The development of combed wheat reed processing was probably initiated by the wetter climate of the West Country, which often resulted in a shortage in the local wheat supply. The processing method involved less wastage than with long straw.

In contrast to combed wheat reed, long straw is separated from the wheat grain by itself undergoing a threshing operation. In past times, the wheat was cut by hand and then threshed as gently as possible to remove the grain. Nowadays, the threshing is still carried out as carefully as possible to minimize damage to the stalks, but the straw delivered from the threshing operation is in a more broken and tangled state. This necessitates a tedious procedure to straighten it by hand. The butt ends are also not gathered together with their stalks parallel. Therefore, long straw has to be laid into a roof using a different technique from that employed for Norfolk reed, other water reeds and combed wheat reed.

Rye straw was once commonly used for long-straw thatching as well as wheat straw, but it has become scarce because few farmers now grow it. The decline in rye production in England started in the 1930s when it decreased by over 40 per cent. Production received a slight boost during the Second World War, when government incentives sometimes made it more profitable for farmers to grow it on lighter, poorer soil than wheat. However, production has steadily declined since then. Rye straw was an ideal material for thatching, as the straw stalks were extremely strong and long, up to 6 feet (1.8 metres) and less brittle than wheat straw. It was once very popular in Lancashire, where incidentally ferns were also used at the end of the eighteenth century. Barley and oat straws were once used for long-straw thatching but the stalks were less tough than those of wheat straw.

Long straw derived from wheat is used as the main thatching material in most of the counties of England where large quantities of corn are grown. It is thus predominantly found in the south of England and the Midlands. In particular, many examples of long-straw-thatched roofs can be seen in Cambridgeshire and Bedfordshire. However, cottages thatched with combed wheat reed and water reeds have now sometimes intruded into these areas.

Many different terms have been used to describe and measure harvested quantities of reeds and straws for the thatching trade. For example, bundles are sometimes known as 'thraves', and in certain areas 'boultings'. For reeds, the term 'bunch' is often favoured, and 'yealm' for long straw. A yealm of long straw is normally reckoned to be approximately 16 or 17 inches (41–43 cm) wide and about 5 inches (13 cm) thick. A bundle of combed wheat reed is known, particularly in Devon, as a 'nitch' and weighs 28 pounds (12.7 kg). Norfolk reed is not calculated by weight; it is traditionally measured in fathoms. A fathom of Norfolk reed means a tight bundle with a circumference of 6 feet (1.8 metres), or 1 fathom, around the butt end of the bundle. This large bundle is made by gathering together five smaller tied bunches known as 'bolts'. These smaller bunches would probably have a circumference of about 2 feet (61 cm).

It has often been said that a well-constructed, good-quality Norfolk reed roof can be expected to last, under England's fairly temperate weather conditions, for a period of thirty to sixty years. This compares with approximately twenty to forty years for a combed wheat reed roof and ten to twenty for a long-straw roof. With the latter type, the life was even less when barley or oat straw was used but a little longer with rye straw. Other factors affect the lives of roofs. For example, it should be borne in mind that in East Anglia, where Norfolk reed gained its reputation, the weather is much drier than in the West Country and the Lake District. Also, steeper roof pitches are used than in the west, which helps to shed water. In addition, the higher average temperature, humidity and rainfall experienced in the west, together with the generally less polluted air, encourage the multiplication of minute fungi and biological growths which lead to the thatch decomposing.

However, Norfolk reed roofs have a good mechanical stability, when their surfaces are exposed to the rigorous forces of nature. This is due to their dense, thick stems with strong cell walls. In practical terms, this means that the tough, hollow reeds are less likely to break or be crushed when repeatedly buffeted by strong winds and rain. The reeds therefore retain their original cross-sectional areas for longer. This stability prevents the thatch compacting, which can result in biological degradation and rot, with pieces of rotted thatch being carried away in the wind or by birds. Straws have more oval-shaped cross-sections than water reeds and are more likely to become crushed. This can easily be demonstrated by squeezing a piece of wheat straw in the fingers and comparing its relative lack of toughness with that of a Norfolk water reed. On the other hand, combed wheat reed has a better mechanical stability than long straw, which has been weakened by threshing.

An important factor which also affects the lives of roofs in the different materials is the particular method of thatching. Reed roofs are constructed in a different manner from long-straw roofs. The reeds have all the butt ends together and can be packed more tightly, without the danger of fractures occurring. The finished reed roofs are denser, with more material to give additional strength and durability for combating the ravages of the weather and birds. They have only their butt ends, or the last inch or two of their length exposed. A long-straw roof has more of the stems exposed to the weather because they are more loosely packed.

Unlike Norfolk reed, many roofs constructed of long straw and wheat reed are never completely renewed but have a long history of patching and coating with fresh materials as the need arises. Roofs that have been constantly well maintained offer little trouble. With repair coating, a complete new layer of material is secured over the roof surface after any rotted material and moss have been removed. A worn roof is always taken down to such a level that a secure base is ensured for the fixing of the new layer on top.

Other factors that determine the relative lives of thatched roofs include the nearness of trees, whether the roof is in shade or sun, whether the property is in a sheltered or exposed position and whether repairs are carried out immediately. This is especially so when birds have damaged it when searching for nesting or feeding materials. However, despite all these influences the skill of the original thatcher is of the greatest importance, and can considerably enhance the life of a roof, especially if the thatch material has a low nitrogen content and has been carefully harvested and processed.

The influence of extreme weather conditions shortening the life of a thatched roof can be seen in areas where persistent gale-force winds are encountered. It is then essential to use ropes to hold down the thatched roof. Cottages along the entire west coast of Ireland, the western Highlands, the Scottish islands and the Isle of Man are all exposed to very fierce winter gales. In these regions, and especially the western coast of Ireland, the roofs will be found to be covered with a network of weighted or pegged ropes to withstand the gales. Unfortunately, the ropes drastically decrease the life of the roofs, as they interfere with the free flow of the rainwater from them. The thatch therefore has to be constantly renewed.

Unlike other products used in the building trade, there is no British Standard or specification to cover the quality of straws and reeds used for thatching. However, thatchers have always thought that a high nitrogen content in a thatch material plays a significant role in causing degradation. It is therefore best grown organically, without the use of nitrogenous fertilizers to boost growth. Modern analytical techniques allow nitrogen contents to be fairly easily assessed. The water content, water absorption characteristics and water capillary movement within the thatch stems also have an effect on rates of decay. The drier the product, the less decay. Density measurements give an indication of whether a thatch material has enough bulk and strength to withstand mechanical stress on a roof. However, it is difficult to specify precise parameters for the various factors.

Since the 1980s, there has been an acute shortage of both traditional long straw and reed suitable for thatching in Britain. As we have seen, the long varieties of straw are now more rarely grown and the reduced acreage of the Norfolk reed beds can no longer supply all the demand throughout the year. This has led to an importation of foreign reeds and it is estimated that about 75 per cent of all water reeds now come from Europe. If this trend continues, then more areas will eventually have imported water reeds on their roofs rather than home-grown thatch. Water reed will thus intrude still further into traditional straw areas and blur regional differences. A secondary effect will be that farmers may be less inclined to grow wheat suitable for thatching, which is grown for its straw rather than its grain. The situation has caused much controversy between conservationists, local planners and the many thatchers who want to meet their customers' wishes to put the best available material on their roofs, whether it is British or foreign.

The imported materials come from a variety of countries, and include Turkish, Hungarian, French, Austrian and Danube delta water reeds, Polish rye straw, South African veld grass and triticale straw. Thatchers suggest that the quality of the water from which the water reeds have been harvested plays a significant role in the quality. Some favour Austrian reed when it comes from unpolluted water, although, others report that a few roofs thatched with it deteriorate after only about twelve years and need patching. Others prefer the Turkish water reed, the best of which originates from Anatolia and certain inland lakes. It is harvested after a hard frost has killed off the leaves. Polish rye straw has also gained a good reputation for its consistent quality, as has some Hungarian water reed. However, thatchers hold different views on the merits of South African veld grass. It has been widely used on thatched roofs in Germany and some thatchers suggest that it should be very durable, which augurs well for a long life under British climatic conditions. On a finished roof, even the experts find it very difficult to distinguish it from combed wheat reed, and it is cheaper. Other thatchers cast doubts on its longevity, owing to its rather pithy solid structure. It dries less quickly than hollow wheat straw and has a capillary action which takes up moisture. Triticale straw is also now used as a substitute for wheat reed. This is a hybrid cereal, a cross between wheat (*Triticum*) and rye (*Secale*). Only time will tell which of the many new imported materials will perform the best on a roof. A true evaluation will only emerge after several decades, when the thatch has endured the varying weather conditions encountered in Britain.

Items other than the thatch itself are, of course, essential parts of a thatched roof. These additional materials include the various items used to secure the thatch to the roof, such as spars, sways, liggers, cross rods, straw ropes, crooks or iron hooks, wired screws, tarred twine and withies. Thatching spars are usually made from split pieces of hazel. Hazel is the preferred wood because it is readily available, and is soft and easily split but at the same time tough and flexible. Less frequently, spars are made from willow. This also splits easily and is flexible. It can also withstand blows and general compression of the wood. The quality of the wood used for securing thatch is important to ensure a long life, comparable with that of the thatch material. Hazel (*Corylus avellana*) was formerly grown on a large scale in coppices throughout many southern counties of England, to provide the type of wood required for thatching and hurdle-making. The wood was always of good quality because the shrubs were carefully tended. Today, coppices are declining and those that remain are generally less well tended. Hazel is a spreading shrub, and unless it is satisfactorily coppiced every seven years, it will not produce the straight, pliant branches required. A coppice needs to be well protected, otherwise deer, in particular, spoil the wood by eating the young shoots and the shrub then branches out into a bushy form, like a gooseberry bush. The decline in the number of coppiced hazel woods has led to an increase in their cost, to between £1,200 and £1,500 an acre. As a result, some thatchers buy cheaper imported wood from European countries, such as Poland, for spar-making.

A thatching spar is made by first splitting in half down its length, a hazel rod of approximately 2 inches (5 cm) diameter (see fig. 18), using a spar billhook (see fig. 19). It needs skill to ensure that a true central cut is obtained through the middle of the hazel rod from top to bottom. The two halves are then split further down their lengths, usually into two or three pieces but sometimes even four, so that four, six or eight pieces of split hazel are obtained. Each will have two flat white sides and one rounded one with the bark still on it. Thatchers either make the spars themselves or obtain them from a supplier or spar-maker. They are normally tied up in bundles of a hundred or more so that they can be easily transported. Large quantities are used: for example, each thatcher's basic square, or 100 square feet (9 square metres) of roof surface, requires about 300 spars. The spars are pointed at each end, by the thatcher if the supplier has not already done so, and then twisted in the middle, by revolving them in reverse directions and doubling over into a U-shape. The twisting action must not break the fibres in the wood, or the springy nature will be lost. To avoid this the spars need to be twisted within three months of the wood being cut. They must grip and remain firmly secure when pushed into the thatch during roof construction. The 'legs' may be up to 2 or 2½ feet (61–76 cm) in length. One leg is often made shorter than the other. Thatching spars are known by numerous names in various parts of England. Typical examples are 'brawtches', 'brooches', 'brotches', 'buckles', 'roovers', 'prickers', 'scollops', 'sparrods', 'sparrows', 'spears', 'spics', 'spikes', 'splints', 'tangs', and 'withynecks'.

The U-shaped spars are driven by hand into the thatch to hold adjacent bundles tightly together on the roof. They are also driven over the

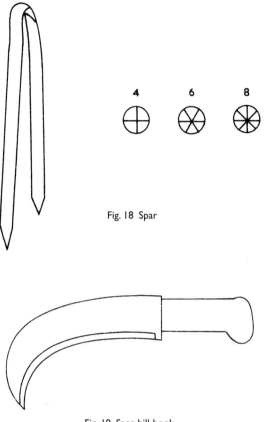

4 6 8

Fig. 18 Spar

Fig. 19 Spar bill hook

liggers, which are placed over the thatch to secure it. These liggers are the long lengths of hazel that can always be seen on the exterior surfaces of thatched roofs, at the eaves and gable ends. They are approximately 5 feet (1.5 metres) long and are usually made by splitting hazel or willow branches in a similar way to that used for spars (see fig. 20). Cross rods are also made of hazel and are often used in a herringbone or diamond shaped ornamentation on a thatched roof, when they are secured between two parallel fixed liggers. Scuds, twisted ropes of straw, were sometimes used in conjunction with spars for the decorative securing of thatch material.

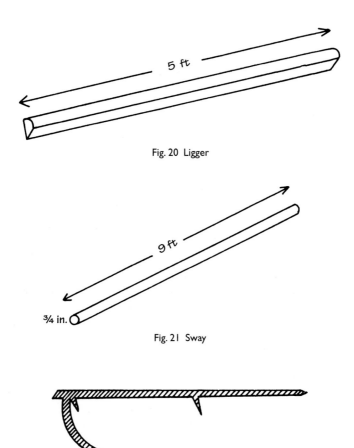

Fig. 20 Ligger

Fig. 21 Sway

Fig. 22 Iron hook

Unlike the liggers, which can be seen, the sways, which are used for securing the underlying layers, are never visible because they are covered by the top layer of thatch. A sway is a length of hazel rod approximately 9 feet (2.7 metres) long with a diameter of about ¾ inch (1.9 cm) (see fig. 21), and it is used for holding down all types of thatch. Steel rods now often replace the traditional hazel sways. The sway is placed horizontally across the thatch course, and is permanently secured to the rafters beneath by iron hooks (see fig. 22). These hooks vary in size and length, but they all consist basically of a pointed end, which enables them to be driven into a wooden rafter and a hook end that can grip over the wooden sway and hold it firmly against the thatch bundle underneath. Stainless steel screws and wires are sometimes used as an alternative to hooks, as they cause less damage to the rafters.

Thatch material is also sometimes sewn to the roof battens with tarred twine, which is normally composed of jute or sisal, as these are natural, strong, coarse textile fibres ideally suited for the work. The twine is tarred to make it water-repellent and therefore rot resistant. This ensures a long life when the twine becomes an integral part of the roof construction. At one time, withies were used for tying bundles of thatching straw to the roof rafters, especially in Somerset. The withies were obtained from the young shoots of pollarded willow trees that had been planted on a large scale in the ditches of Sedgemoor during the nineteenth century. They were tough and flexible and were used not only for binding thatch bundles but also for basket-weaving. Pollarded willows had their tops cut to encourage the growth of a close, rounded head of young shooting branches. The cut was made above the reach of browsing animals, which left a stump between 6 and 15 feet (1.8–4.6 metres) high. Osiers were the same as withies, but were cut from particular species of willow. They were whippy and were also used for basket-making and wickerwork as well as thatching. In thatching, they were threaded through and over thatch bundles, and then lashed to the roof purlins or rafters with tarred twine.

One other material sometimes used on the surface of a thatched roof is wire netting. The net which is of ¾ inch (1.9 cm) or 20 standard wire gauge mesh size, is always galvanised to prevent rusting and to lengthen its overall life. Despite this, it will still probably need replacing every fifteen years or so, as it is very exposed and a lot of water passes over it. It is also subjected to corrosive smoke from chimneys. It may cover the whole of the roof, in long straw, or it may be placed in strategic areas over reed roofs. It is not an essential part of roof construction and it is used mainly to protect the thatch against bird attack. Sometimes, netting made from synthetic fibres is used. This has the advantage of being completely resistant to corrosion. Heavyweight nylon netting is useful in coastal regions, where the salt spray in the air attacks galvanised wire. However, it is more difficult to fix to the roof than wire netting. It also lacks rigidity and offers less protection against bird, wind and vermin damage. One advantage of synthetic fibre netting is that it can be made to look fairly inconspicuous and therefore more attractive to the eye. Plastic spars are now also sometimes used as an alternative to the wooden variety.

3

The Craft of Thatching

Thatched roofs are designed to shed snow and rain fast. The longer the thatch surface remains wet, the greater the prospect of rot. To assist the process, the angle or pitch of a thatched roof should always be considerably steeper than that of a conventionally tiled or slate roof. A pitch angle of about 50 degrees is normal in a thatched roof, which means that there is a rise of 16 inches (40.6 cm) to each span of 12 inches (30.5 cm) (see fig. 23). This compares with 45 degrees with a tiled roof and 30 degrees for a slate roof. As a general rule, the smaller the individual components used in a roof covering, the more irregular their shape and the more absorbent they are, the greater is the pitch angle required. There are, of course, many exceptions to this generalization and slate roofs may sometimes be seen with equivalent pitch angles to thatched or tiled roofs.

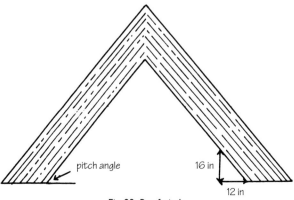

pitch angle   16 in

12 in

Fig. 23 Roof pitch

The reeds or straws of a thatched roof are open-ended hollow tubes filled with air. The roof is thus relatively light in comparison to its thickness, or to one constructed of most alternative roofing materials. The rafters in most old thatched cottages are not usually robust enough to take the weight of tiles. Moreover, they are much more widely spaced than those in a tiled roof and their finish is also much rougher. Sometimes the roof purlins were originally made from ash poles directly cut from a copse and then fixed across clefted oak rafters. The basic wooden construction was therefore fairly light, but the strength was quite adequate to support a thatched roof. In some very old cottages, it may be possible even to see the original wattle work built to support the thatch secured on top of it. In a few instances, purlins or roof battens may not have been used but instead a thick mat, woven from straw or reed, supported and attached the thatch bundles when they were laid.

Because of the differences of pitch angle and weight, it is not usually practical to replace a tiled or slated roof with a thatched one or, conversely, a thatched roof with another type. It can be done but the operation usually involves a great deal of expense and the timbers usually have to be changed or altered. Replacing thatch with slates may also involve raising the walls to reduce the pitch angle. Unfortunately, in some cases sheets of corrugated iron are used to cover the roof, in order to avoid the expense of thatch renewal, especially with old barns, because of the huge expanse of their roofs.

end view

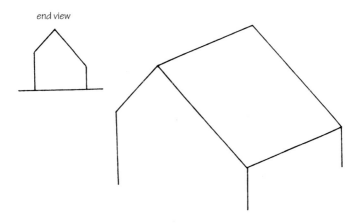

Fig. 24 Outshot roof

56

A great advantage of thatch is that it can be laid to fit the contours of any shape of roof. However, to be a practicable proposition, as I have said, pitch must be steep. In addition, to the conventional gabled, hipped and Sussex hipped types, there are many other roof designs which can be satisfactorily thatched. The outshot type, in which one side of the roof extends to below the bottom level of the other side, (see fig. 24) is often seen thatched. The catslide, in which one section of roof extends below an adjacent section on the same side, (see fig. 25) is also commonly thatched. Lean-to roofs (see fig. 26) are sometimes thatched for appearance's sake when they form a small extension to an existing thatched house. Thatched winged and E-type roofs, in which the cross-wing meets the main roof structure at right angles, (see fig. 27) are also found.

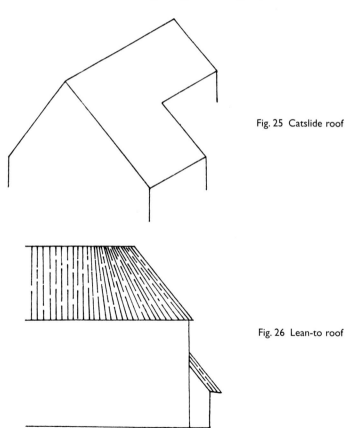

Fig. 25 Catslide roof

Fig. 26 Lean-to roof

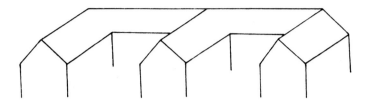

Fig. 27 Winged roof

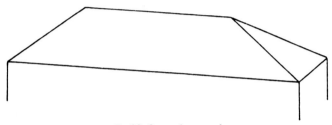

Fig. 28 Queen Anne roof

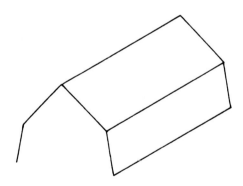

Fig. 29 Mansard roof

Queen Anne roofs (see fig. 28) cannot be thatched satisfactorily because of the low-angled pitch. The Mansard roof (see fig. 29) is also impractical because of the arrangement of the double slope on each side of the roof; the bottom slope is steeper than the top slope. With a thatched roof, the section at the top of the ridge area should be the steepest part to ensure that water is shed rapidly. The gambrel roof (see fig. 30) would present difficulty and is unsuitable for thatching because of the reduced inclination of the end roof section.

A finished thatched roof, whatever its shape, always has beautiful smooth contours. There are no sharp corners and roof valleys are given a swept appearance, so that no hollows are left where water could accumulate. The thickness of the thatch layer depends on the quality of the roof, the type of material and the pitch. The thickness may vary between 10 and 17 inches (25–43 cm). The overall thickness of a combed wheat reed thatch is usually slightly greater than that of a long straw or a water reed one. The eaves of a thatched roof are always artistically constructed with a good overhang, so that the water shed from the roof is kept well clear of the walls (see fig. 31). The eaves normally project about 18 inches to 2 feet (46–61 cm) from the walls.

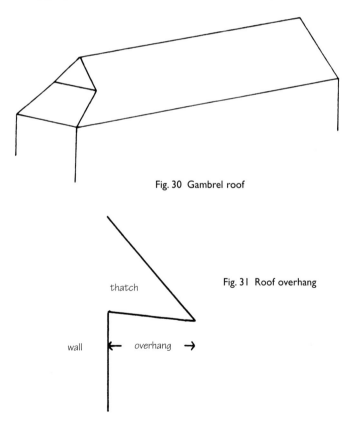

Fig. 30 Gambrel roof

thatch

Fig. 31 Roof overhang

wall ← overhang →

The craft of thatching requires that the reeds or straws in the roof are arranged in thick, overlapping layers in a parallel fashion, pointing downwards with the slope of the roof (see fig. 32). Water droplets can then rapidly cascade over the outside surfaces of the straight reeds or straws, finally running off the eaves. Water should never penetrate below about the top inch (2.5 cm) of the thatch surface. In order to ensure this, it is very important that no bent straws or reeds are used in the thatch bundles, as these would be liable to turn water into the body of the roof.

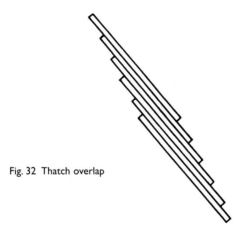

Fig. 32 Thatch overlap

Some preliminary treatment on the ground is necessary with long straw after the threshing process to make it more flexible and resilient before it is used as a thatch material. This consists in slightly but uniformly wetting a bed of straw. This is normally done by damping the layers of straw as they are heaped on top of one another, making no effort to align the straws. The damping process allows bent straws to be straightened without causing fractures. The prepared bed is left to soak for several hours and the layers are then thoroughly but carefully turned and mixed together to ensure that the dampness is equally distributed over the entire surface area. This treatment is known as 'yealming'. The tight, wet bundles of straw, when they are drawn out from the front of the pile and gathered together for thatching, with the ears and butt ends of the straw lying both ways in the bundles, are known as 'yealms'. The ends of the individual straws in the yealms are made as level as possible.

Far less wetting is needed to make combed wheat reed suitable for thatching. Water is normally just dripped into the ends of the bundles, which are stacked vertically after their straw butt ends have been levelled by tapping them down on a flat board surface. The wetted bundles are then placed horizontally on the ground and left to steep for a short while before use.

Norfolk reed requires no preliminary damping treatment. The reeds are simply dressed by the thatcher on a dressing-board to level the butt ends. The tops of the reeds may need trimming by cutting off any feathery tips still present.

Fortunately, thatched cottages are only one or one and a half storeys high, although the occasional two storeys may be seen (see fig. 33). The roofs can therefore be reached fairly easily by ladder. Individual thatch bundles are sometimes carried up under the thatcher's arm or on the shoulder. However, several yealms or bundles are often brought up at the same time. A simple carrier may consist of a piece of an ash tree

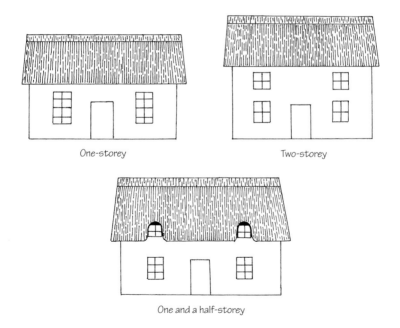

One-storey

Two-storey

One and a half-storey

Fig. 33 Cottage types

branch in the shape of a two-pronged pitchfork (see fig. 34). After the thatch bundles have been placed in the fork, a loop of rope is passed over the top of the two prongs; the prongs can easily be compressed, which allows the loop to be slipped over. The natural springiness of the prongs allows the thatch bundles to be held gently but firmly. The carrier may have a hook on it to allow it to be hung on the roof, so that it cannot slip and the thatcher can work unimpeded. Sometimes, the thatch bundles may be transferred to another holder, which has already been installed on the roof, to stop them rolling down the thatch slope. This type of holder would probably also have been made by the thatcher out of ash or hazel wood. It would be large enough to hold and retain several bundles of thatch material.

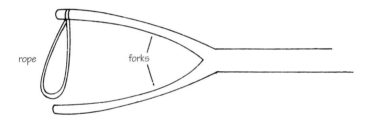

Fig. 34 Thatch carrier

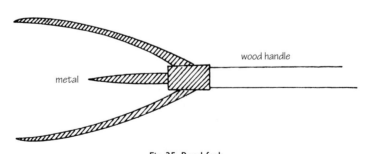

Fig. 35 Reed fork

Fig. 36 Thatcher's spear

A three-pronged reed fork may also be used to lift reed bundles from the ground to the roof (see fig. 35). This type of fork has two long prongs and one short one. The same type is often used for the careful handling of reed or straw material on the ground, so that the stalks are not damaged. When thatch material has been transferred to the roof, it may sometimes be held near at hand with a thatcher's spear (see fig. 36), instead of using a holder. The total overall length of this spear is around 4 feet (1.2 metres), with a metal spear section fitted to a wooden handle. It is used to hold the thatch bundles until they are required by spearing them to the roof.

The material must obviously be tightly secured to the roof, so that it will be able to withstand the ravages of the weather. Thatchers use many different methods for this, but basically they all consist of combinations of various fixing devices made mainly of hazel. Some of them are fixed over the thatch to the underlying rafters with iron hooks. Sometimes the hazel lengths may be used, in conjunction with spars, to secure a top coat of thatch to a thatch undercoat which has already been sewn to the roof timbers. At one time, the first layer of thatch was commonly tied to the roof purlins with such materials as split brambles, stripped of their thorns and outer skins to make a strong flexible cord. Straw ropes or withies were also used, but later it was more usual for tarred twine or spun yarn to be substituted.

In the case of long straw and combed wheat reed thatching, it is the usual practice for the thatcher first to spread and also sometimes tie straw bundles horizontally to the roof purlins before laying the actual thatch layers (see fig. 37). This gives a neat appearance to the inside of

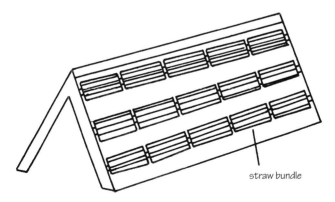

straw bundle

Fig. 37 Roof purlins

the roof when viewed from the loft area. This preliminary operation is not done with Norfolk reed, which is always attached directly to the rafters. However, with Norfolk reed it is usual for the thatcher to push in a back filling of reed behind the reed bunches after several of them have been laid and fixed. This helps to increase the tension on the reed bunches after they have been secured to the roof.

After any preparatory work has been carried out, the thatcher normally starts to construct a new roof by first fixing a large thick yealm or bundles of thatch material to the angle formed between the gable and the eaves at the bottom right-hand side of the roof (see fig. 38). Horizontal layers, called 'courses', are then gradually built along the corner, together with vertical layers, called 'lanes', which eventually extend from the eaves to the ridge of the roof. Lanes are normally in widths of approximately 2½ feet (76 cm). In each completed lane, there is no appreciable weight to hold the thatch down other than the overlapping material from the course above. An extra yealm or bundle is normally used at each bottom corner of the roof to give additional strength and thickness and to achieve better weatherproofing.

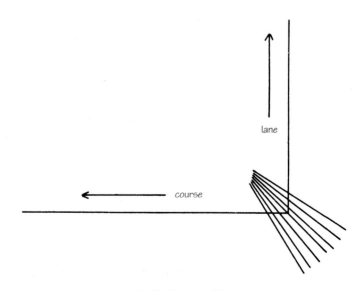

lane

course

Fig. 38 Course and lane

The thatch is securely fixed along its full width as it is laid, by a variety of techniques which depend upon the material being used and the preference of the thatcher. A common method, especially with Norfolk reed, is to place a sway across the top halves of several thatch bundles as they are placed side by side on the roof. The bundles are normally held temporarily in position by iron hooks, until the sway can be permanently fixed across them by driving iron hooks into the rafters. The exact position of the rafters is found by probing with a needle. The top parts of the hooks grip the sway and hold it firmly down on the thatch bundles, which are thus securely fixed to the roof. The iron hooks that were used temporarily to hold the thatch bundles in position are then removed. Norfolk reed is therefore usually secured directly to the timber structure of the roof and closely follows its underlying contours. It is rarely sparred over an existing coat of thatch. When a roof has been rethatched several times on a centuries old cottage, the timbers eventually deteriorate and split owing to the repeated nailing in of the iron hooks.

As I have said, an alternative method involved sewing the under-coat materials to the roof battens with tarred twine or spun yarn. This was particularly favoured for the construction of combed wheat reed and long straw roofs but the use of sways and thatching hooks is now more usual. During the sewing procedure, it was usual for the thatcher to have an assistant in the loft area who could push the needle back through the thatch. During this process, the twine was looped around the thatch bundle and the supporting roof batten underneath. The twine was pulled tight when the stitch loop had been completed.

As the layers of thatch are built up in a lane from the bottom to the top of the roof, they are placed and secured to overlap the previously laid ones considerably. The layers on top therefore eventually hide from view the sways, spars and other fixing devices on the thatch layers underneath. This means that the sways are never visible on the exterior surface of the finished roof. In theory, on the very top course of the roof the sways would remain exposed because there would not be a further thatch course to cover them. However, in practice these are also eventually covered by the ridge.

As each lane is completed, the thatcher moves to the left to start the next, although some thatchers lay two lanes at a time. Thatchers always work from right to left along the roof. As the horizontal courses become longer, temporary needles are thrust in at the ends of the courses to keep the material tightly packed and square.

In the case of reed laying, a wooden tilting fillet is usually placed at the eaves level, so that the first course laid is tensioned at an angle to the rafters (see fig. 39). This helps to ensure that the final exposed surface of the roof will consist predominantly of the butt ends of the reeds. As each bunch is laid, it is worked upwards as it is fixed, so that the reeds become slightly staggered as the face is tightened. The larger butt ends are always at the lower end of the bundle when it is placed on the roof and the slimmer ends are always at the top. The continual working of the reeds upwards tightens and packs them close together (see fig. 40). This ensures that only the last inch or so of the butts will eventually remain exposed to the weather. This method is used for all types of reeds, whether they are Norfolk, imported water reeds or combed wheat reed.

The tool used by the thatcher for this reed dressing is commonly called a 'leggett', also known as a 'leggat', 'leggatt' or 'legget' (see fig. 41). It looks like an oblong wooden block fitted with a handle. It is frequently made of poplar because it is more fibrous and less likely to split than other woods. The base of the block is either grooved or patterned with a series of raised horseshoe nail heads, to help push the reeds into position.

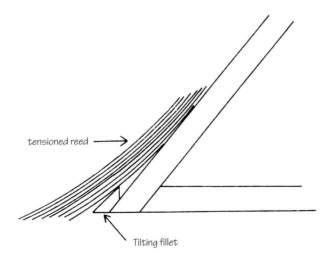

tensioned reed ⟶

Tilting fillet

Fig. 39 Tilting fillet

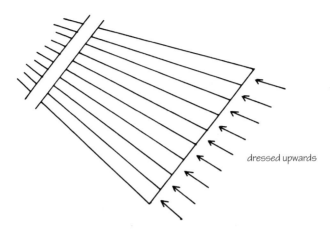

Fig. 40 Bunch tightening

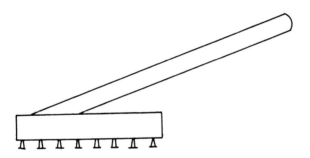

Fig. 41 Leggett

The precise type of leggett used depends on the thatcher and the reed material. The raised nail variety is popular in Norfolk and Suffolk for Norfolk reed, while the diagonal wooden groove type is preferred in the West Country for combed wheat reed. The wood groove is usually in the form of a diagonal corrugation (see fig. 42). The grooved type is also commonly known as a 'beetle', or in Dorset, a 'beater' or 'pomiard'. In Somerset, the term 'flatter' is frequently encountered. Leggetts vary in size and some are made quite small for use in restricted corners and awkward places. The small variety is also sometimes called a 'moulding-plane'. A different shape of wooden tool, called a 'Dutchman' (see fig. 43), is used to form valleys and also to dress and round off corners of 'eyebrow' thatched windows. Most leggetts are fitted with hooks on their back surfaces so that they can be hooked into the thatched roof when not in use so that they do not fall to the ground.

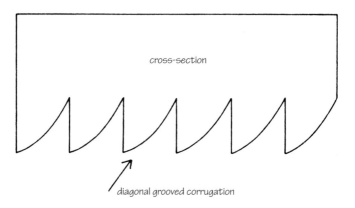

Fig. 42 Leggett base

Fig. 43 Dutchman types

Leggetts, like so many tools, are normally individually selected to suit the thatcher's requirements. In the past, the local blacksmith frequently helped in making tools, which would often be assembled from various odd spare parts from other implements. Items such as knives, sickles and scythe blades were adapted with different types of handles and then used for the shearing and cutting of the straight edges of straw thatched roofs. They were known as 'thatcher's hooks' (see fig. 44). Similar tools are now manufactured commercially. Sheep shearers' clippers are sometimes adapted as hand-shears for trimming thatch ends (see fig. 45).

Thatchers used many designs of needles when sewing thatch to the roof. They varied considerably in length and size, but most had a harpoon- or spear-shaped head and a large base eye for threading the tarred twine or spun yarn (see fig. 46). Rakes used for the downward

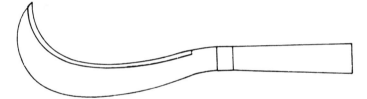

Fig. 44 Thatcher's hook

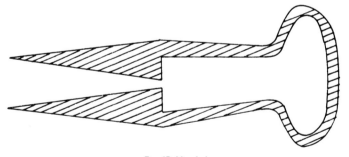

Fig. 45 Hand shears

Fig. 46 Thatcher's needle

combing of long straw roofs are also frequently handmade to an indi-vidual thatcher's design. A simple thatcher's comb may be made by driving a series of long nails through part of the length of a 3 foot (91 cm) strip of wood (see fig. 47). The protruding nail points form the teeth and the nail-free wood section is used as the handle. Another tool sometimes used by thatchers is a guillotine, which is used for trimming spars, sways and liggers. The wood is placed in the U-shaped recess of the implement and the blade then squeezed shut (see fig. 48). Thatchers also use wooden mallets for tapping spars into position and metal hammers for driving iron hooks into rafters. Most of these tools are also used for long-straw roofs, with the exception of the leggett.

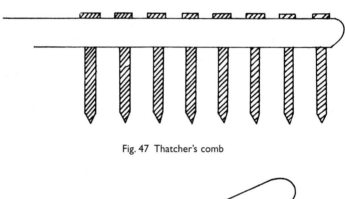

Fig. 47 Thatcher's comb

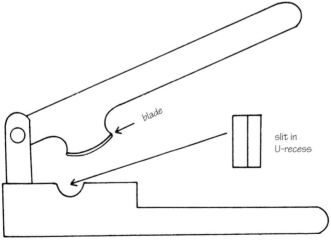

Fig. 48 Guillotine

As I have said, the technique for laying a long-straw roof is different from that for a reed roof. This is because the straws in the yealms are of different sizes and all the butt ends are not lying together in exactly the same direction. The straws are also not as tough as reeds and the long straw is therefore not packed so tightly. A long-straw roof has a much looser appearance than a reed roof because it is laid in place rather than dressed. Also, the long straw is not laid at an angle to the roof rafters, so no tilting fillet is used. With long-straw thatching, as each lane is finished, it is combed downwards and beaten to remove small pieces of straw. This helps to arrange the long straws in the desired direction and to improve the overall appearance. This downward combing operation is in direct contrast to the upward dressing and beating with a leggett in reed laying.

During the construction of a course, the long-straw yealms are fixed by pushing spars into the undercoat of thatch. Spars are also used to tighten and fix the individual yealms to the ones laid alongside, after any bent straws between them have been straightened by hand. Spars are also driven in over sways to fix the courses, which overlap one another, together. Obviously, many spars are used, set close together, in the construction of a complete long-straw roof. During the laying operation, the yealms are tightened in such a manner that the ends of the straws tend to face slightly outwards towards the weather. This gives the finished thatch extra durability. The roof is then finally raked and given a press down with the back of the rake. After the ridge has been completed, the whole roof area is sometimes sheared down and trimmed with a thatching knife or shearing-hook, and the eaves clipped to shape. Long-straw roofs are always finished with a decorative securing arrangement of spars, liggers and often cross rods around the eaves and the gable verge (see fig. 49). The thatcher drives the spars horizontally or slightly upwards over the external fixings which are placed over the thatch to secure it. The liggers are always fixed before the thatcher finally cuts the gable verge and eaves. This is necessary to ensure a neat edge because of the looser nature of the long straw thatch.

Combed wheat reed and Norfolk reed roofs are not finished in this manner because they are more rigid. They require no external fixings, other than on the ridge. It is thus easy to distinguish a long-straw roof from a reed one by its additional decorative securing arrangements.

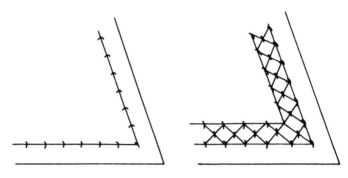

Fig. 49 Long straw finish

Long-straw roofs always have a less stiff, looser 'poured on' appearance than those constructed of reed, which always have the texture of a short-cropped hard brush.

Combed wheat reed produces a roof of similar texture to Norfolk reed. However, it will be seen on close study that the eaves and gable have been cut with a knife and trimmed to the line and form required (see fig. 50). This is not the case with a Norfolk reed roof, where the reeds have only been dressed into position to form the desired shape and line. A further distinguishing feature is that Norfolk reed roofs assume a dark golden-brown colour on ageing, in contrast to the more greyish colour of an aged combed wheat reed one.

Considerable care is taken with all the types of thatch materials to ensure that waterproof junctions are made at the chimney flashings and also at any roof valleys, where appreciable water flow will occur during rainstorms (see fig. 51). The thickness of the thatch layer is increased at valleys, so that the smooth-swept appearance of the thatch is maintained. This also has the effect of spreading the rainwater flow over a larger surface. A fairly wide concrete ledge is usually built immediately above the chimney flashing to overlap the thatch material and cover the chimney/thatch junction area. The use of vertical pipes such as flues, which would pierce the thatch, is always avoided.

It is essential during construction that the whole area of thatch is evenly compacted throughout, so that sagging is avoided. It is thus imperative that a thatch is laid firmly, which is the reason for all the beating or dressing during the thatching process. If sagging occurs, then over a period of time rain will be channelled along that area,

Fig. 50 Cut and uncut reed

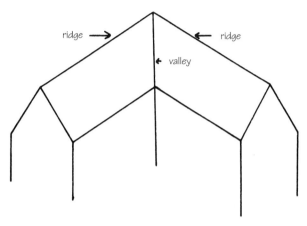

Fig. 51 Roof valley

which will then require immediate repairs, or the life of the roof will be much reduced.

The thatch over windows has to be skilfully dressed, or trimmed and cut, to ensure that the maximum light is obtained in the upstairs rooms. The shaping has to be done without affecting the overhang which will carry the water well away from the windows and walls. It must also be done without detracting from the finished appearance of the roof or interfering with the opening of windows. Dormer windows are always given a swept appearance in the shape of an eyebrow. However, some restriction in the opening of upstairs casement windows is sometimes unavoidable. Considerable skill is also required in obtaining clean, straight edges to the eaves and gable verges. Gable ends must be exceptionally strongly made because their sides are usually exposed to wind pressure and lift.

To ensure maximum water-shedding ability, the inclination at the top or ridge of a thatched roof is always extremely steep and the thatch material is closely packed into a near vertical position (see fig. 52). This near vertical top layer is firmly secured by thatching spars to an underlying horizontal roll of thatch, which has been previously fixed along the apex or summit of the roof (see fig. 53). The underlying roll acts as a secure base for the spars to be pushed into and it also gives some compressibility below the top course of thatch. During laying, the thatch straw ends at the top are arranged much higher than the roof summit, so that they can later be bent over the apex. Material from each side of the roof is then interlocked and sewn into position with tarred twine on the opposite side. A series of apex rolls of decreasing diameters may be laid progressively over one another as the ridge construction proceeds (see fig. 54). This ensures that the final apex is very narrow.

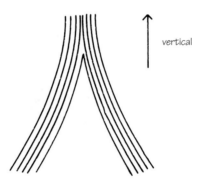

Fig. 52 Ridge top cross-section

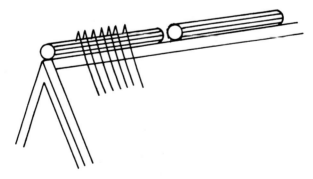

Fig. 53 Apex thatch rolls

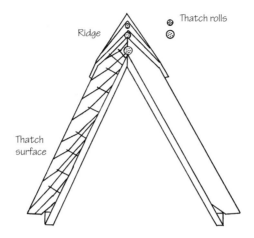

Ridge

Thatch rolls

Thatch
surface

Fig. 54 Apex rolls

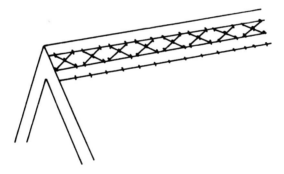

Fig. 55 Level ridge

The ridge work is done with straw in a long-straw roof to make a completely watertight seal. In the case of Norfolk reed, which is relatively inflexible, it is common practice to use sedge. If it has been allowed to become hard and dry before use, damping with water softens it. This process enables the sedge to be manipulated and bent. The ridge may be constructed at the same surface level as the thatch material on the main roof (see fig. 55). A more expensive method involves building up a thick ridge layer, up to 4 inches (10 cm) above the surface level of the main roof (see fig. 56). This type of block ridge is more frequently found with a water reed thatch that has been secured directly to the roof timbers rather than sparred in as a coat. The bottom edge of this raised ridge may later be cut into various artistic shapes, such as crescent-shaped scallops and points, or decorated in other ways (see fig. 57). The extra material needed to build up the thick ridge layer and the time taken in its artistic construction make the work expensive.

The liggers and spars which are used on the exterior surfaces of both types of thatch ridges to secure them, are always visible. The spars are driven into the thatch close to each other over the liggers. They may be arranged in an ornamental fashion with decorative cross-pieces, which are also secured by spars between the liggers. The spars are always driven into the thatch with enough slope to prevent any water being turned into the thatch when it rains. All finished ridges must be firm and solid. A narrow apex is also essential, from both the water-shedding and artistic points of view. If a chimney stack is in the middle of the apex of the roof, then the thatcher will often start at each side of it and work outwards towards the hips or gable ends.

It is always advisable, after about five to seven years, to have a thatched roof cleaned and patched. Regular inspection and maintenance will prolong its life. In the long term it is also the most economical approach, because if the whole roof is allowed to deteriorate grossly, then the only solution will eventually be its complete renewal, which will be expensive. It may also involve the replacement of some of the roof timbers, which may have rotted if they have been in contact with

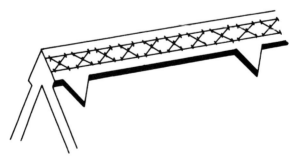

Fig. 56 Raised ridge

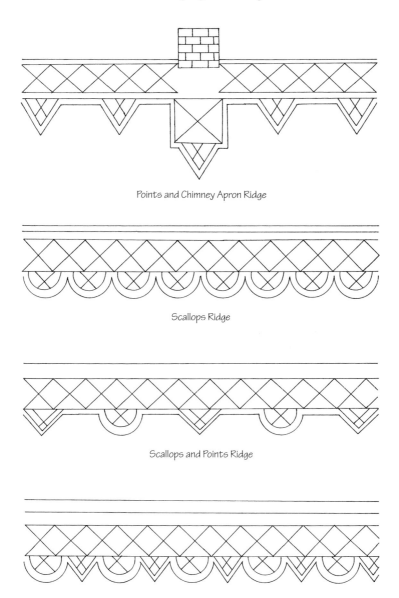

Points and Chimney Apron Ridge

Scallops Ridge

Scallops and Points Ridge

Scallops and Points Variation

Fig. 57 Thatched ridge ornamentation

damp compacted thatch for a long period. Sometimes repairs and renewal will be needed more frequently on one side of the roof than the other, because it may be more exposed to the weather and receive less sunshine.

During repair work, the thatcher will pay special attention to the ridge and also to the eaves and gable ends. A good ridge is the essential primary requirement for a waterproof roof. When patching or repair work is carried out on long-straw or combed wheat reed roofs, the new thatch material is frequently dressed as a layer or coat over the old, after any decayed thatch and moss have been first removed. The stability of the new thatch coat can only be as good as the strength of the underlying layer to which it is attached. The new material is secured to the old by the use of thatching spars and these are driven into the underlying thatch over the sways placed on top of the new coat. Isolated patches of new thatch look yellow, but the appearance soon changes and blends with the darker colour of the original material. When bird holes are first noticed in a thatched roof, it is advisable immediately to fill them by pushing straw into the holes, provided of course they can be reached without causing other damage to the roof. This prevents birds enlarging the holes still further, before a thatcher can do a permanent repair.

As I have said, wire netting is sometimes used to discourage birds from pulling out straws from thatched roofs. In the case of long straw, the whole roof area may be covered with wire netting, as its looser nature makes it more prone to bird attack. With combed wheat reed and Norfolk reed, it is normal practice to cover only the ridge, gables and eaves sections. When netting is fitted, it is done in such a way that the joins in the wire mesh lengths and the net ends where they are secured at the eaves and gables can be released quickly and the whole netting can be more speedily removed in the event of a fire.

Some thatchers will not recommend the use of wire netting because it imposes an additional strain on the roof. Strong winds have a slight tendency to lift the material and the restraining wires then exert a frictional force on the surfaces of the reeds or straws, with the possibility of some stem breakages occurring. The thick broken ends may become trapped under the wire and these may eventually turn inwards as they cannot escape. This may allow rainwater to seep below the top layer and cause the thatch beneath to rot.

Even when straw or reed breakages have not occurred, the presence of a wire mesh lying in contact with the thatch surface impedes the flow of rainwater as it cascades down the roof. There is thus more chance of water penetration below the top inch (2.5 cm) of the surface thatch layer. Many people also consider that wire netting spoils the look of the thatched roof. One then needs to weigh up the advantages and disadvantages of using wire netting. A thatcher will normally never recommend wire netting if the roof is near trees, as it tends to trap leaves and twigs on the roof, further impeding water flow. The presence of rotting leaves also encourages the thatch underneath to rot.

4

Thatchers

In the past, thatchers were always local men and the craft was usually handed down from father to son. Owing to a lack of transport, they seldom travelled outside their particular area. Nowadays, with the availability of modern transport, thatchers can travel longer distances. However, most still remain local men and originate from the areas in which they work. Many have learned their trade from their fathers and the sons have continued to operate the small family business. Most thatchers are therefore self-employed and have retained their originality and individual methods. Many employ apprentices, who are also often local young men keen to learn the trade and eventually set up in business on their own.

Thatchers have always taken pride in their craftsmanship and, of course, they still do. Besides financial reward, most obtain great satisfaction from artistically working with nature's materials and using old-established techniques. The type of craftsmanship involved cannot be hurried. The renewal of a fairly large roof may

Thatcher at work,
Ringwood, Hampshire

take a skilled thatcher and an apprentice five weeks or more. A similar roof area could probably be tiled in a few days. Even a medium-sized cottage roof may take three weeks to thatch. The slow, artistic nature of the work ensures that master thatchers are much in demand and it is usually necessary to book their services well in advance. Some thatchers may already be booked with enough work to last them a year ahead. It will therefore never be easy to get a thatcher of your choice at short notice.

Thatchers enjoy working in the open air but it is a fairly solitary occupation. Most of the day is spent in isolation on the roof. Even when a thatcher has an apprentice, they are frequently apart. The apprentice may be on the ground preparing the thatch material and carrying it up the ladder, or perhaps in the loft space, assisting in sewing but still separated from the thatcher on the roof. Large uninterrupted roof expanses present the easiest and quickest areas to thatch, but most master thatchers find this boring and prefer the challenges presented by dormer windows and other more complicated features.

The narrow streets of old villages were obviously not designed for modern traffic, which can be hazardous for a thatcher, perched on the top of a ladder. The bottom of the ladder has frequently to be placed precariously in the road, as often there will be no pavement or front garden to the cottage. It may have to stay in the road during the whole of the thatcher's working day and also over a period of several weeks, as the construction process cannot be hurried. Operating in a constricted space, such as a village street, also hampers the progress of the work. It is difficult to unload considerable quantities of straw or reed just outside the cottage. Also, each evening the site outside the cottage will have to be tidied, so that no hazards remain during the night for motorists or the general public. Most thatched cottages are only one, or at the most two, storeys high so long ladders can easily reach the top of the roof when laid flat on its surface. With larger projects, such as a cluster of houses or a barn roof, scaffolding is often erected.

Thatching is very hard on the hands and elbows, owing to the constant need to handle wet straw and manipulate tough, scratchy, sharp reeds. Some thatchers wear a special leather glove to protect the palms of the hands, which are particularly prone to damage, as they are often used in the dressing of the thatch material into the desired position. The twisting of spars and the general labour of securing thatch to the roof are also abrasive to the hands, especially during winter. Despite the harshness of the work, however many women, as well as men, enjoy the life and have been working as thatchers for many years.

Severe winter weather greatly curtails a thatcher's work and the elements play an important role in determining the best time for thatching. Rain will cause the thatch material to become too damp and handling it is even more unpleasant on the hands. Moreover, frost has the effect of stiffening straw and making it unworkable. Working in high winds is also to be avoided wherever possible, because the thatch material is blown about and generally becomes unmanageable. The ideal conditions for thatching are therefore windless, dry and warm days. However, thatchers cannot always wait for ideal weather; they have to compromise and work when they consider the conditions reasonably tolerable. In the past, a thatcher would normally never remove more of the old thatched roof than he knew he could replace with new before he finished work for the day. Securing thick poly-thene sheets over the roof overcomes this problem nowadays and is also useful in emergencies, when the weather suddenly becomes bad.

Thatching is also hard on the knees, as they are in constant contact with the roof and ladder and inevitably rub against them. Some thatchers protect their knees by strapping on knee pads; in the past, these were normally made of tough leather and were frequently felt lined to make them more comfortable. Many thatchers also use a special type of ladder, with the rungs made flat and wide. This avoids having to kneel on a sharp edge, as frequently happens with a conven-tional ladder, where the surfaces facing the user are normally fairly narrow. This also helps to spread the weight over a larger area of the roof, when the ladder is leaning against it and stops the thatch being excessively compressed.

The type of thatching material used in a certain region will still largely be determined by its local availability. For example, water reed will be the predominant type in Norfolk and Suffolk, combed wheat reed in Devon and Dorset and long straw in the Midland counties. However, all the three types are now used to some extent outside their main regions of traditional use. Thatchers will often specialize in either reed or long-straw thatching, depending on the local preference and tradition in which they operate. However, most thatchers are nevertheless adept at working with most types of materials. In addition, they occasionally use suitable marsh water reeds that may still be cultivated in their areas. Others use imported water reeds.

Some thatchers also specialize in the art of ornamental ridge construction. These elaborate, fancy-cut and decorative finishes to a thick raised roof ridge are expensive and time-consuming to complete, but the end products are delightful to look at. In addition to ridges, raised ornamental thatched apron areas are also often constructed below window spaces in the main body of the roof surface. These aprons further enhance the overall beauty of the completed roof. Thatchers who do specialize in particular types of thatching sometimes make this apparent in their advertisements in the Yellow Pages. It is best to look for a member of the local Master Thatchers' Association or a member of the National Society of Master Thatchers.

In addition to the many thatched dwellings that are a century or more old, a fair number of new houses are now being built with thatched roofs. This ensures that thatching remains a healthy and thriving craft, which is undergoing a mini-boom. In the late 1950s and early 1960s, there were only about 300 thatchers, and many were in their seventies. Now the numbers have risen to about 1,000 and the majority are in their thirties. Young men and women are still being attracted to the craft, so the total number may even increase slightly in the future. As there are approximately 50,000 thatched buildings in England, this means that each thatcher has the potential to find plenty of work maintaining and rethatching them. There are hundreds of inns with thatched roofs, as well as many thatched farm buildings, thatched roofs require much more regular maintenance than tiled and slated ones. British thatchers also sometimes obtain work in Europe, the United States of America and even Japan. The work in America mostly involves the creation of vernacular or picturesque neo-vernacular houses, although there is also work on barns, restaurants and museums. There are, however, few thatched cottages, unlike in Japan, which has as many thatched cottages as England. Most are found in country areas, where they blend into landscaped gardens. Many are several centuries old, with a single storey. Rice grass reeds constitute the main thatching material in Japan and it is applied to the roof using a similar technique to combed wheat reed, which it also resembles in appearance.

During the twentieth century the number of thatchers waned with the general decline in the number of thatched buildings. Also, many experienced craftsmen lost their lives in the two world wars and the future of thatching was placed in jeopardy. The Rural Industries Bureau, as it was then called, helped to create local county associations to assist in the training of new craftsmen in 1947. Subsequently renamed the Council for Small Industries in Rural Areas (COSIRA), it continued to encourage the thatching craft and held courses in the art of thatching for many years. In 1960, it published its manual, *The Thatcher's Craft* and a revised edition was issued in 1977. COSIRA merged with another body, the Rural Development Commission (RDC) in 1988 and ceased to operate as a separate entity. The RDC is now part of the Countryside Agency.

The RDC has for many years run training courses, backed by the Government, for young apprentice thatchers to learn their craft, at Knuston Hall, near Irchester in Northamptonshire. Most classes are held during winter, when their employers, the master thatchers, are less busy. In order to attend a course, apprentices must have worked for a master thatcher for at least six months and whilst on the course their employers pay their wages. The RDC pays the cost of tuition and accommodation and some of the travelling expenses. The courses are spread over two years and during this period, each apprentice has to attend on twelve separate weekly occasions. They have to specialize in two of the three most commonly used materials, long straw, combed wheat reed or water reed. Success at the end of the course leads to a National Vocational Qualification (NVQ) in thatching and a City and Guilds Apprentice Certificate. An apprenticeship with a master thatcher normally lasts five years (it used to be six). However, ten years is considered the minimum time to gain enough expertise to call oneself a master thatcher. Membership of Master Thatchers' Associations is normally restricted to thatchers who have submitted their work to a standards committee.

Unfortunately, anyone can call himself a master thatcher, even if he has never attended a course or worked with a master thatcher. Further confusion arises, as there are twelve different county Master Thatchers' Associations in England, all with their own appointed secretaries. In addition, there are two national bodies, the National Council of Master Thatchers' Associations and the National Society of Master Thatchers. The picture is further complicated by the fact that fewer than half the thatchers operating in the country have ever joined any of these trade organizations. In view of this, English Heritage believes thatchers should come together as a single self-regulating body that would be generally acknowledged by the industry and capable of enforcing standards. This idea is not new; as long ago as 1977 the National Society of Master Thatchers proposed that a register of qualified thatchers should be compiled. It was suggested that only those who could perform to the high standards demanded of the profession and the craftsmanship associated with it should be included and allowed to operate officially as thatchers. It was thought that such a register would protect not only the reputation of the master thatchers but also the general public against the increasing numbers of unqualified thatchers.

It is interesting to recall that it was precisely these two points that led to the institution of the craft guilds during the Middle Ages. At the time, a craft guild consisted solely of the skilled workers of an individual trade or craft, working together in close co-operation within a town or region. There were three types of members of a craft guild; masters, journeymen and apprentices. The length of service of an apprentice was often left to the whim of the master, but in 1563 a law was passed to specify a seven-year apprenticeship. At the end of this period, an apprentice was considered to be adept at his craft. He could then practice in his own right – but first as a journeyman. The name derived from the French word *jour*, meaning 'day'; a journeyman was paid for work on a daily basis. He would continue to work for his previous master until he could establish that he was an exceptional craftsman. This was done by the making and submitting for approval a piece of his work that he considered to be of a very high standard, a *master*piece. On acceptance of the work, the journeyman could then become a master of the guild of his chosen craft and trade. The system became unacceptable when it was found that many highly skilled journeymen were unable, or could not afford, to be their own masters. They had no alternative but to continue working for an employer. Journeymen therefore formed their own guilds and by the seventeenth century these were established alongside the companies of masters. Only skilled workers were members of the old craft guilds.

Nowadays, an increasing number of unqualified workers undertake craft tasks in the thatching trade. Unqualified thatchers may offer apparently cheaper rates for general thatching work, but in the long term they will usually prove more expensive than employing a recognized master thatcher. Even if the initial finished artistic appearance of the thatch is not taken into consideration, the passage of time may reveal faults. For example, heavy rain may cause sagging in certain areas and this will entail costly repairs. Weak ridge construction will eventually result in a leaky roof. Badly made eaves and gable ends will encourage bird damage. Also, a few semi-skilled thatchers have become itinerant workers and it may be difficult to get them back to correct faulty workmanship. Another consequence may be a decrease in the use of long-straw thatch, in areas where traditionally the material has been employed for many centuries. The handling and preparation of long straw on the ground entails more time and trouble, which put itinerant workers off. They may suggest a change to combed wheat reed or water reed. Another reason for the intrusion of combed wheat reed into established long-straw regions is the fact that this reed is more robust and easier to transport. The same, of course, applies to water reeds, which are even tougher and are often taken into traditional combed wheat reed areas. A good general guide to the ability of thatchers can often be obtained from people who have used them, or by contacting the local Master Thatchers' Association.

A thatcher at work at Cockington, Devon

Thatchers in different counties adopt their own individual distinctive finishes, particularly for ridges and often for gable ends. The thatchers of East Anglia, for example, normally make extremely high-pitched roofs with steep, sharp gable ends. This is because when a house is rethatched, the entire old reed is normally removed before putting on the new roof and the shape tends to be angular and sharply defined. Also, dormer windows are gabled and thatched. Another distinguishing characteristic is that the bottoms of the block ridges are frequently finished with a number of large scallops and points (see fig. 58). In contrast, the thatchers of Devon often make roofs of a more chunky nature with a lower pitch, because when a roof needs renewing, another thatch layer is sparred on the top of the old. This gives rise to more rounded gable ends.

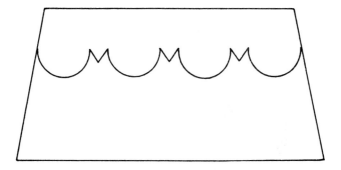

Fig. 58 Scallops and points

Unfortunately, regional differences have become blurred during the last few decades. The intricate block ridge roof patterns that were traditional in East Anglia have become fashionable in the West Country and the Midlands, especially since the 1960s. The shortage of long straw has also reduced the number of neat flush ridges on roofs and encouraged the use of imported water reed in counties where traditionally it was completely alien. For example, it has spread to Devon where combed wheat reed once thrived, to the exclusion of most other types. Water reed itself was traditionally found only in Norfolk, Suffolk and Abbotsbury in Dorset. Whatever the reason, an alternative type of thatching material, especially a change from long straw, gives a cottage a completely different appearance and with an old building that is listed, it requires listed building consent.

Besides the major regional differences, individual thatchers also make their own characteristic minor changes of detail. Instead of plain scallops and points, some may employ decorated versions (see fig. 59). This involves fixing hazel lengths, spars and cross-rods on the scallop and point surfaces to make patterns. Others may cut the occasional rectangle or square, rather than a point, along the traditional design at the bottom ridge edge. For instance, rectangles are frequently used directly below the areas of chimneys. A few may fashion a pattern in the bottom ridge edge consisting of alternating long and short points, mixed with the occasional scallop. The cutting of alternating long and short curved tongue shapes in the bottom edge of the ridge is sometimes favoured rather than points. Along the complete central area of the ridge, some thatchers build elaborate diamond-shaped patterns, using horizontal hazel liggers and cross-rods (see fig. 60). There are many other variations, such as patterns made in the shape of dogs' teeth and also herringbone (see fig. 61). Other thatchers may use some form of ornamentation around the chimney apron area, in addition to that on the main roof ridge. At one time, the use of stripped brambles interwoven around the spars was a popular decorative finish. Straw ropes were also often used to make various individual ornamentations to roof ridges and chimney areas.

Thatchers also have their own characteristic methods for trimming, shaping and finishing the eaves and gable thatch edges. For example, they may be cut or dressed at different angles on the under-face. The type of trimming around the area of the window spaces is also often the individual preference of the thatcher. In the case of long straw, the

ridge

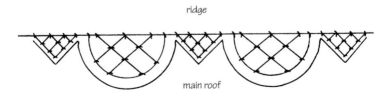

main roof

Fig. 59 Decorated scallops and points

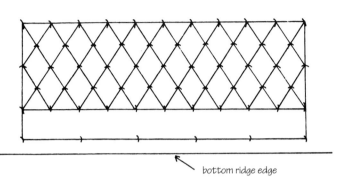

Fig. 60 Ridge diamond pattern

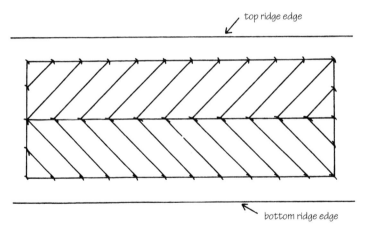

Fig. 61 Ridge herring-bone pattern

whole roof area may be severely trimmed down to give a tidier and more distinctive appearance. Other thatchers consider a drastic trimming reduces the overall life of the roof by the unnecessary removal of material.

The type of finish on the very top or pinnacle ends of the ridge is also often a characteristic of the individual thatcher. Similar designs are often also used to finish the pinnacles of house porches. Some may be finished with a very pronounced tuft (see fig. 62). Others may be ornamented with a more gently curved one (see fig. 63). Some roofs may have a long tuft with a zigzag end (see fig. 64). In Essex, exceptionally sharp tufted ends are popular. There are a host of other variations in different regions. It was once common for some thatchers to hide a small tool or souvenir in the thatch layer, so that the next thatcher would discover it at some future date. Inhabitants of thatched cottages also sometimes tucked a message in the underside of the thatch in the roof space. A girl called Jenny once left the following poem, entitled 'Star' in her cottage thatch:

> We have slept side by side
> Peacefully, deeply, trustingly
> And walked together
> Dreaming a landscape of silver and black shadows
> But you are nowhere now
> And I have removed myself to that shadow world
> Where I can float and fade and dream again
> Hoping always to find you
> And curl up into your softness
> And sleep again, side by side, so content...
> Will you come to me soon, love?
> I wait here shrouded in mist
> Pale and forlorn
> The elder sheds flowers and they fall
> Like a thousand tiny stars stranded on the bare earth
> Their brother stars that hang in the sky
> Are all around me here,
> I shine with them now.

Distinctive straw corn dollies are also often placed as finials on the tops of thatched buildings to decorate them. This is intended to bring good luck to the occupants, an extension of the original concept of ensuring good harvests and the later use of corn dollies on hayricks. However, corn dollies are also placed on buildings to show the thatcher's pride in his handiwork. They often indicate that a roof was thatched by a certain thatcher, acting as a thatcher's signature. Most corn dollies used

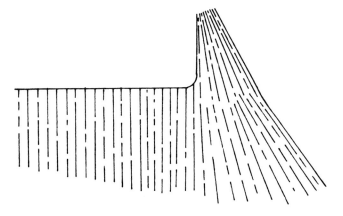

Fig. 62 Large tuft pinnacle

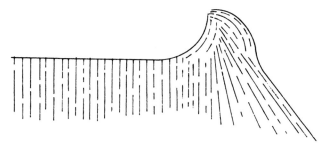

Fig. 63 Curved tuft pinnacle

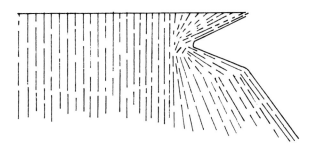

Fig. 64 Zig-zag tuft pinnacle

for this purpose resemble animals or birds. Pheasants are popular on rooftops in the south and west of England. Peacocks are sometimes seen and foxes are popular in many country areas. Corn dollies representing fishes, squirrels, horses and lambs are occasionally spotted, together with cats and dogs, and farm tractors and deer may be sighted, but they are fairly rare.

Horse and jockey finial over the weighing room, July Racecourse, Newmarket Heath, Suffolk

The straw used for making corn dollies, like that employed for thatching, must ideally be derived from the long-straw wheat varieties; the straw produced from the wheat harvested by a combine harvester is not suitable. Many types of wheat also have too much pith in their centres. Rye and oat straws are satisfactory if they can be obtained, but barley straws are considered inferior. Skill is required in the making of a corn dolly, as the hollow straws have to be bent, twisted and shaped without causing them to fracture. If the straw has become dry in storage, it is essential to wet it before use. This procedure can be avoided if the straw is used within about a week after it has been cut. Ideally, the wheat should be harvested when nearly ripe. In this state, the straw joint immediately below the grain ear will be green. The straw may be plaited, woven, folded and knotted during the construction of the corn dolly.

The technique used for making an individual type of corn dolly varies considerably. Some thatchers may encase a rough outline body in a wire mesh and then mould the outer wire case into the desired finished shape. Others may adopt more elaborate procedures, which are extremely time-consuming. These may involve the building of a basic skeleton shape in wire and hazel wood for a perched bird and then skilfully dressing the skeleton frame with tied and shaped solid straw sections. The final contours of the bird are obtained by trimming the straws into the various shapes required for the wings, tail and other body parts. Animals are normally built on a basic wire frame body. The rough shape of the straw animal is first constructed and this is then encased in a wire mesh and finally shaped to the desired finished form. Some thatchers purchase the more elaborate and unusual finials from specialist craftsmen. A thatcher who is using thatching straw will sometimes quickly construct a corn dolly while standing on the top of his ladder, after finishing the ridge section of the roof. The finished product, which would perhaps look crude on a close inspection, will appear perfectly satisfactory when viewed from the ground below.

Thatchers have always had to be versatile and to possess skills outside their own craft. On occasions, they have to turn their hand to basic structural repairs, such as replacing a rotted roof timber. Additionally, it may sometimes be necessary to repair brickwork at the bottom of a chimney-stack before covering it with new thatch. They are thus often called upon to use their own initiative and impro-visation skills as snags and unforeseen problems occur during their routine work.

Thatchers are also called upon to work on other things as well as houses and cottages. These may range from a huge listed tithe barn to small thatched table umbrellas for garden use, which are very popular in hotel and pub gardens. These umbrellas have a short life however, as children – and many adults – are unable to resist touching and pulling out the straws from the bottoms. Synthetic thatched canopies are also sometimes seen over bars in pubs and hotels. It is, of course, essential that the material in these 'thatched bars' are fire resistant, as many smokers congregate beneath them.

Thatchers usually have to buy their materials from the grower. For example, a farmer may advertise that he is offering to sell a certain acreage of long wheat specially grown on his land for the thatching trade. The price paid by the thatcher will depend on market forces and the quality of the crop. The thatcher may occasionally grow and harvest the crop himself. When harvested, an old-fashioned reaper and binder has to be used, which entails high labour costs because of the additional handling required during drying, stacking and later combing and tying the bundles. These factors mean that the thatcher has to pay a fairly high price for his basic raw material. In some cases, the price will be even higher when transported a long distance away from the producing area.

Because of the high costs of materials, thatchers have to be much more cost conscious than their predecessors. Thatch was once a relatively cheap material, but today the thatcher is dealing with a much more expensive commodity which is in short supply, and the market for his craft is approaching the luxury category. The time required for thatching and the cost of the material make a thatched roof an expensive proposition, and it is therefore important for a thatcher to be able to estimate the exact quantity of material required for each job before quoting a price to a customer. An accurate measurement of the roof area to be thatched has therefore to be made. Some thatchers will quote a price for thatching without supplying the thatch material, a farmer who can supply his own material, for example, may prefer this.

Other material costs have to be estimated, such as the number of thatching spars, liggers, sways, etc. that will be needed, and possibly a protective wire netting. There are also the transport costs, general equipment and miscellaneous overhead expenses, together with the labour charge.

The estimated time needed for a job will depend upon the design of the building. It will be influenced by such factors as the number of valleys and dormer windows which will require additional time. Labour charges vary and the more skilful and better the reputation of the thatcher, the more he is entitled to charge. Customers will find that the best thatchers are normally the cheapest in the long term. Although the initial price may be higher, later maintenance and repair

costs will probably be much reduced. The various thatchers in a particular area will usually have well-established reputations and there will
normally be more than one in the area, giving a degree of choice.

It is difficult to put an exact price on a thatcher's skill, but like all
workers, they must receive an adequate return for their efforts, with
an additional reward for their expertise and the artistic nature of the
work involved. Much of the craftsmanship involved depends on the
judgement of the thatcher's eye and hand. They use few scientific
measurements and instruments and no exact lines are predetermined.
A good thatcher knows instinctively what is right to obtain a good,
practical, waterproof roof that at the same time has a form pleasing to
the eye.

5

Living Under Thatch

There are several advantages to living in a property with a thatched roof, in addition to its pleasing appearance and charm. Most thatched dwellings are old and have relatively large gardens. They were mostly built on the best possible locations which, in days gone by, could be selected from a wide area. The original sites were probably chosen because of their nearness to a natural water supply, together with their aspect and the shelter from the weather that could be obtained from the contours of the surrounding land. The buildings would usually have been built on slightly sloping ground to avoid or reduce damp problems. This wide choice of sites contrasts with the availability of building plots today, which are often not in ideal locations and have only small gardens.

However, there are also sometimes disadvantages with the siting of old properties. They may have been built for convenience near a track or road, long before the advent of the motor car. These tracks may now have developed into fully fledged roads, along which busy holiday traffic may pass. A few thatched cottages may be situated in very remote areas, away from villages, and they may not always be connected to a supply of mains water. The sole water supply to many such homes is frequently wells. Sometimes, several houses may share one well. However, this problem is not too serious, as the water can be purified with a small chlorination unit or a suitable filtration system. The main point to check is whether the well has a high yield value, to ensure that it will not dry up.

Another disadvantage of a remote property may be that it is not connected to a mains sewage drainage system; it may have a cesspit or septic tank. Septic tanks are less trouble than cesspits and are therefore preferable; cesspits will require frequent emptying, while septic tanks will require little attention, provided that they are situated well below the house level and are buried in well-drained soil. It is also prudent not to allow strong doses of disinfectants or detergents to go down the sink, in case they affect the bacterial colonies which make the septic tank function efficiently. A further disadvantage of a remote rural property, especially for former city- or town-dwellers, will be the intense darkness outside because of the absence of street lighting.

Among the many advantages to be gained by living in a thatched property is the fact that the thatch layer has an excellent sound-deadening effect, a decided advantage in these modern days of overhead aircraft noise. The clatter of vehicles and farm machinery is also effectively masked. Moreover it is a good insulator, keeping the house warm in winter and cool in summer. This insulation is due primarily to the very large numbers of hollow tubes, filled with air, which make up the layer. As a high proportion of the heat in a house is normally lost through the roof, there will be a saving in fuel costs during winter. There is also no need to insulate the loft floor with a blanket of fibreglass or rock wool, as is normally a necessity in the conventional tiled house. Without insulation about 25 per cent of a house's heat is estimated to be lost through a tiled roof, whereas the loft of a thatched house remains at a reasonably constant temperature level and the danger of any water pipes or storage tank situated there freezing in winter is much reduced. Of course, it is still advisable to lag any pipes in the loft as an additional safeguard against severe frost.

Heat is also lost through the windows. In modern homes, with large windows, the heat loss may be as high as 25 per cent, hence the need for double glazing. Thatched properties, on the other hand, are generally old and were built with much smaller window spaces than modern houses.

Most old thatched houses have solid or thick rubble-filled walls, frequently constructed of stone, chalk or cob, whereas modern houses have cavity walls. These are designed to prevent the inner wall becoming damp when the exterior one is wet. In practice, the two walls are not entirely isolated from each other. Metal wall ties are usually inserted between them as a support, but these are designed not to conduct water from one wall to the other. However, sometimes during the construction of the brickwork, a little mortar is inadvertently dropped into the cavity between the two walls and this can adhere to the metal ties. The small pieces of mortar can then act as bridges and allow a small amount of water conduction between the walls, which can result in a few damp spots on the interior wall. The greater thickness of a solid wall, provided it is dry, will normally be better in terms of heat loss than a cavity wall. The rate of heat loss through a solid wall will depend upon the relative temperatures of the room and the outside air, or in other words the temperature gradient across the wall. The thermal conductivity and the thickness of the wall will also affect the heat transfer rate. The heat is lost through the wall by conduction in one stage (see fig. 65). With a cavity wall, the heat is lost in three stages; the small effect of the metal ties and mortar bridges which may be present between the walls, can be ignored. First, heat is transferred through the inner wall to the air gap, then through the air gap itself and finally through the outer wall to the atmosphere. However, as the combined thickness of the interior and exterior walls is normally much less than that of a solid wall construction, the heat losses will, as I have said, normally be greater with a cavity wall.

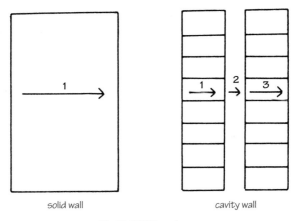

solid wall   cavity wall

Fig. 65 Wall heat losses

For this reason, it is common to insulate cavity walls to reduce heat loss. Inert heat-insulant foam is pumped into the cavity, which displaces the air in the gap. Great care has to be taken in filling the cavity to ensure that all the air is displaced and the entire space is filled. Alternatively, cavity walls are sometimes packed with mineral wool. It has been estimated that cavity wall insulation can help to save 20 per cent of the heat loss from a house.

In the summer, the reverse applies – the thick solid walls usually found in old thatched properties and the thick layer of thatch slow down the rate of heat flow into the house from outside; the house therefore remains cool. The smaller window spaces again help. It will be noticeable that any water stored in a tank in the loft under a thatched roof remains cool during hot summer days. With a tiled roof, it quickly becomes warm.

Unlike new houses, many old solid-wall thatched cottages will not have damp-proof courses or significant foundations. The interior of the walls may therefore become damp through moisture rising slowly from the ground. A damp-proof course prevents this occurring in modern houses. A damp-proof course is a water-impervious layer of material placed in the brickwork course, approximately 6 inches (15 cm) above ground level around the entire building (see fig. 66). Unless the damp-proof course is short-circuited in some way, it is not possible for the dampness to rise above it in the walls and the house is kept dry. Some new houses have suspended wooden ground floors, allowing air to circulate underneath the floors through air-bricks. Old thatched cottages frequently have solid floors and are built directly on the earth without a damp-proof course, so water can rise slowly through the floor, as well as up the walls. Modern building materials and techniques, however, allow vast improvements to be made to reduce damp in solid walls and floors, even in buildings which, at first glance, appear to be in a derelict condition. Many different methods are available. For example, it is possible to have a completely new ground floor installed. This can be done by excavating and removing the existing ground floor material and then laying hardcore. The excavation also gives a useful opportunity to gain some additional headroom, as old cottages are noted for their low ceilings. The hardcore is then covered with sand, on which a membrane layer of a tough thick-gauge polythene sheet is bedded down (see fig. 67). This waterproof membrane, which acts as a damp-proof course, is then covered with concrete and finished with a cement and sand screed to receive the new floor finish. Provision is, of course, made for the laying of service pipes and drains in the concrete layer. The edges of the polythene membrane are turned up to form a waterproof joint with special damp-proof corrugated lath sheets which are fixed on the surfaces of the interior walls. These sheets are then plastered over to make a new interior wall surface. Unfortunately, the flat new surface may not be as attractive as the quaint unevenness of the original walls.

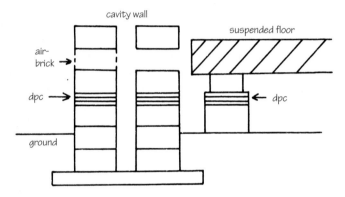

Fig. 66 Damp-proof course

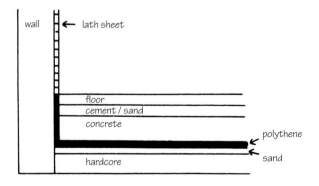

Fig. 67 Solid floor and wall

The situation can also be improved by digging soil away from the exterior walls. Soil has a tendency to build up slowly over the years, around the house. Laying a concrete apron around the walls to make a fall-away channel to carry rainwater which drips from the thatched roof to gullies leading to drains or soakaways further improves the situation.

A thatched roof which is maintained in good condition provides a very good weatherproof cover to a house. It can withstand gale-force winds if they are not sustained over a long period. It rarely leaks and, unlike conventional roofs, there are no tiles or slates that can slip to let in water. It is very rare for leaks to occur with thatched roofs. For example, it may happen when one of the wooden spars used in the ridge is broken and turns into the thatch and penetrates it. This can then create a channel to allow water penetration through the thatch layers. Old thatched roofs very occasionally develop leaks after a prolonged spell of dry weather, as small compacted patches tend to open up or breathe slightly under these conditions. When rain falls again, a few drops might trickle through the thatch. However, this fault is normally self-healing, as the compacted thatch closes up again when it becomes damp. Another potential leak-point is at the junction between the thatch and the chimney, where the thatch is likely to compact and shrink away from the brick or stone work. Birds may also have pulled some of the thatch material away in this area. As a temporary measure to prevent further damage, it is advisable to fix some wire netting over the affected area. However, if a leak occurs, it is best dealt with immediately by a thatcher. He will renew the thatch by lapping under the chimney flashing.

Thatched roofs are designed to shed water fast, so that the dwellings they cover are kept very dry. Yet strangely, perhaps one of the main disadvantages of a thatched roof is during and after rain. Water cascades down the roof and drips around the perimeter of the eaves for a considerable time, even after the storm has passed. A caller can become drenched waiting at the door, unless a porch is provided. Attractive porches can be built, and they are best thatched to blend with the main roof. It is even better if the architecture of the house allows the thatch to sweep down to form a small canopy over the porch.

This dripping is accentuated because rainwater gutters and downpipes are rarely used, for two main reasons. First, the steep roofs are designed to allow water to be shed very fast, and this would rapidly overwhelm standard gutters during heavy rainfall. Secondly, gutters are not normally needed, as the roof has a good overhang at the eaves, to throw the water well clear of the walls. Moreover, thatch was used for roofs long before gutters developed, and their use today could considerably detract from the appearance of the roof. On the rare occasions that gutters are used, they are much wider than the standard rainwater collection gutters seen on tiled or slated roofs. These special gutters can be either V-shaped or box-shaped and are often made of wood because of their large width. They are lined with lead or zinc (see fig. 68). A big disadvantage of this type of guttering is that it has to be taken down when the roof is rethatched, otherwise the thatcher will find difficulty in getting a ladder to lie flat on the roof. Of course, the absence of downpipes and gutters has one advantage in that it obviates the chore of cleaning, maintaining and painting them. A disadvantage, however, is that the rainwater cascading from the eaves splashes onto the bottoms of the walls. If the walls are white, then the resulting mud spots will soon mar the appearance. Some people overcome the problem by painting the bottoms of the exterior walls black. Constant water splashes can also encourage the growth of patches of green mould, which can be overcome by occasional washing with a commercial bleaching agent diluted with water.

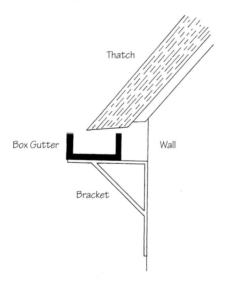

Fig. 68 Box gutter

If snow should accumulate on a thatched roof it is best left alone; trying to scrape it off is liable to cause damage.

The open-tube structure of reeds and straws ensures that they do not self-ignite, as can sometimes occur, for example, with hay. Obviously, thatch will burn if ignited by an outside source and insurance companies consider the fire risk with thatch to be greater than with other roofing materials. They will thus inevitably charge higher premiums. Some thatchers doubt whether there is a greater fire risk, especially when a modern chimney design is used. Old-time thatchers were sometimes known to pour a bucket of red-hot coals or roll a burning log over the top of a newly thatched roof, to demonstrate that there was no exceptional fire hazard, and the available statistics suggest that the percentage of fires with thatched roofs is not greater than with other roof types. However, if a fire does break out then the potential damage to the property and contents is much greater than with a tiled or slated roof. Most thatched cottages have stood for centuries and more are demolished than burned down. Some thatch fires are caused by sparks from extraneous sources but it is unusual for the sparks from the house chimney to cause a roof fire. More likely are fires that are started inside the roof space due to an electrical fault or a grossly overheated chimney-stack. Many chimney fires are caused by soot and resin accumulation.

If a thatched house is attached to another, it is considered essential that a raised brickwork ledge separates the two roofs (see fig. 69). The

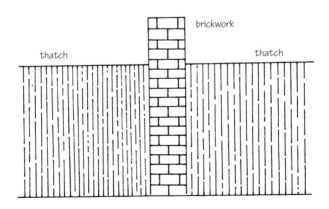

Fig. 69 Roof separation

position of the chimney will also have an influence on the potential fire risk. It is best if the chimney is tall and situated at the highest point of the roof. It is recommended that chimney flues be at least 32 inches (81 cm) above the roof level. Open fires in the house are then safer, as any sparks emitted from the chimney will have been extinguished before they can fall on the thatch. It is important to remember, during a rethatch, not to increase the thatch thickness and so reduce this recommended safety level. If a chimney height has to be increased, then the flue must be extended, rather than installing a taller chimney pot. The latter may cool the combustion products too much and cause condensation problems. It is also considered safer if the chimney-stacks are constructed with walls at least 9 inches (23 cm) thick. Before changes in Building Regulations in 1966, the usual flue was a single brick chimney, which was unlined. Most thatched cottages built before this date will probably therefore be of this design.

Spark-arresters are frequently found in industry as fire safety devices when fitted, for example, to chemical plant chimneys, funnels and industrial engine exhausts. They contain a fine corrosion- and heat-resistant wire mesh and are designed to stop any large solid sparks from escaping into the atmosphere. Such devices are also commercially available for fitting to thatched house chimneys to reduce the fire risk and at the same time provide a rain and bird guard (see Useful Addresses for details). However, it is possible to find the occasional company prepared to make a spark-arrester to an individual's own specification. This will be manufactured to suit the particular interior diameter of the chimney-pot and, when fitted, will look like an inverted wire-mesh bucket (see fig. 70), with legs fitting into the top of the chimney-pot. However, it may be difficult to obtain a suitable type, which will not cause a smoky fire, owing to the gradual clogging of the mesh, and it may be necessary to clean it regularly. An ordinary fine wire mesh fitted directly over the chimney would quickly become clogged with soot and create a smoke problem in the house by affecting the drawing of the flue, and there would also be a danger of carbon monoxide build-up in the house.

It is always advisable not to use paper to light or draw fires in an open hearth but to use fire-lighters and wood tinder instead. Paper can easily be sucked up the chimney with the draught and fall, still alight, onto the thatch, although this type of accident is avoided if a spark-

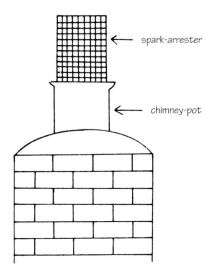

spark-arrester

chimney-pot

Fig. 70 Spark-arrester

arrester has been fitted to the chimney. It is essential to have chimneys swept regularly in order to reduce the risk of chimney fires. Once a year is recommended for smokeless fuels and twice a year for wood and bituminous coal. Coal produces a different type of soot from logs. It is softer and fluffier, and can be brushed off the surfaces of the inside of the chimney relatively easily with a sweep's brush. Logs produce a much more adherent type of soot, which normally has to be removed with a scraping tool rather than a brush or vacuum sweeper. Certain types of wood soot can be much more inflammable than coal soot, especially if unseasoned woods are burned. These have a high moisture content, which causes condensation in the flue, leaving deposits of tar. The best logs to use to get a cheerful and hot fire are ash and oak. They are much improved by storage and weathering. If possible it is best to avoid pine and other conifer woods. Some people burn a mixture of coal and logs; coal is used to create a good initial heat before the logs are added.

Many old thatched cottages have chimneys that were deliberately constructed to lean slightly inwards, so that the alignment appears wrong. This was done to ensure that in the event of the chimney falling, it would topple inwards and land on the roof rather than outwards, where it would fall on the ground or worse on the head of a passer-by. Most old chimneys have also not been lined or sealed efficiently with a fire- and smoke-impervious layer throughout their entire lengths. This means that when an open fire is burning, traces of smoke fumes may escape into the upper rooms. This is especially so if the brick or stonework inside the chimney has become badly cracked with heat and age. The acidic combustion gases from the fire can also penetrate and stain the plasterwork and wallpaper in the areas surrounding the chimney breast. This is more likely if the chimney is damp, owing to rain entering the porous stack. However, much more serious is that any missing or decaying mortar in the chimney flue could allow sparks and hot gases to reach the thatch, with a risk of fire. These faults can be overcome by having the chimney lined, but this is normally fairly expensive, as the refractory lining material has to be both chemically inert and fire resistant. If wood is burned it is advisable to have the chimney flue lined and if a wood stove is used the flue should also be insulated.

It is worth remembering that if there are any exceptionally high buildings, trees or hills in the immediate vicinity of the thatched property, then there is a possibility that an open fire may smoke more than usual. They may create turbulent air and cause a down-draught in the chimney and some smoke can be pushed down into the room (see fig. 71). The wind direction will have an important bearing, but it is possible to alleviate the problem to some extent with a suitable chimney cowl.

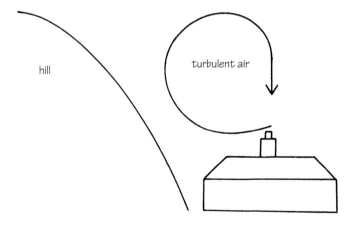

hill

turbulent air

Fig. 71 Chimney down-draught

Thatch fire at night, Briantspuddle, Dorset

It is important with a thatched roof to be extremely cautious when lighting bonfires, or to avoid them altogether. Great care should also be taken to ensure that the wind is blowing away from the house when burning rubbish in an incinerator. It is also preferable to light bonfires early in the morning, when the roof is still covered with dew. If this is not convenient, it is best to wait until it has rained and the roof is wet. Fireworks should, of course, never be lit in the vicinity of a thatched roof. Great care must also be taken if a blowlamp has to be used by a plumber; this is exceptionally dangerous in the loft area. Blowlamps should never be used for burning off old paint from windows or doors of thatched buildings.

Smoke alarms should always be fitted and it is wise to keep a fire blanket or a fire extinguisher, containing dry powder, in the kitchen. In the event of a fire, always leave the house promptly, after telephoning the Fire and Rescue Service. Tell them if anyone has been trapped or injured, so that an ambulance can be sent. If the cottage is remote, try to give a precise location and the best way to reach it. If possible, it is best to ring the Fire and Rescue Service on a mobile phone outside the cottage. When leaving the property try to shut all doors on the way out and never re-enter the building. No attempt should be made to remove burning thatch from the roof before the arrival of the Fire and Rescue Service. This would allow air to penetrate below the thatch and rapidly increase the rate of spread of the fire. If there is a neighbouring thatched house, a garden hose can be used to spray the roof, assuming that sufficient water pressure is available. When the fire officers arrive they will as quickly as possible remove any wire netting on the thatch. They will pull the sections apart at the apex and then down the seams. The individual lengths of netting would have been laid so as not to overlap at their edges. They are joined every 9 inches (23 cm) by special pull-apart hooks.

It is possible to obtain special chemical solutions for treating thatch to improve its fire resistance. They contain fire-retardant salts, which cut down the oxidation rate of the material. This has the effect of slowing down the rate of spread of fire. However, the material must be thoroughly impregnated with the salts, otherwise their action will not be long lasting. The solutions have to be applied to the straw or reed before the roof is constructed and must be allowed ample time to soak in and to dry thoroughly. In the case of straw thatch, the thatcher always wets the straw before fixing it to the roof and he can conveniently substitute a water solution of fire-retardant salts for this purpose. The solution cannot be applied after construction, because the overlapping layers would prevent it reaching the underlying thatch. Moreover, because of the roof's propensity to shed water, the solution would quickly run off. A disadvantage of the use of fire-retardant chemical solutions on thatch is that they may shorten its life and encourage the growth of moss and moulds. Also, the application may only last about five years and the ridge area in particular is very prone to the salts being leached out.

To assist fire fighting, a long, perforated water pipe can be fitted along the ridge of the thatched roof. It is also possible to have an automated pop-up sprinkler system, with heat sensors buried within the thatch. These devices can be used only if the building has a mains water supply to which the pipe can be connected. Sufficient water pressure is essential to reach the top of the roof, preferably from an outside mains water source and stopcock. The sprinkler device is also a preventative measure as it can be used if there is an imminent risk of fire. However, a disadvantage is that it has to be drained in winter to prevent freezing pipes.

It is important to keep small pieces of straw in the loft space away from electric junction boxes, in case they have faulty covers. It is also prudent to use bulkheads to protect electric light bulbs from direct contact with fallen straw debris, and to protect electric cables from rodent damage. As a safety precaution the lights should always be switched off when the loft is vacated. Fitting heavy-gauge aluminium barrier foil under the thatch prevents debris falling and acts as a fire-retardant barrier in the event of a fire. It also functions as a thermal reflective insulator. An alternative is to screw or nail sheets of plaster-board to the roof timbers if they are robust enough.

Most old thatched buildings have fairly draught-free roof spaces, as the eaves are virtually closed off. This is advantageous as regards potential fire risk, and the lack of ventilation also makes the loft warmer and prevents the condensation problems that would occur in a cold roof space. To reduce draughts further in old properties, some thatchers recommend a traditional lime plaster that is spread directly onto the underside of the thatch. It has to be supported and keyed with wooden laths to prevent it falling off when wet. In the early seventeenth century, it was quite common to use inner linings beneath water-reed thatch. They often consisted of a 2-inch (5 cm) layer of reeds bonded together by plaster. The reeds were used as a key for the plaster and the lining was also frequently covered with several layers of lime-wash. This no doubt also served as a fire-retardant.

It later became fairly common in East Anglia to place woven mats of reed on the rafters below water-reed thatch, especially when the roofs were not fully battened. They gave a neat appearance to the inner surfaces of roofs with exposed rafters, such as barns. The ceilings of the thatched verandahs of lodges and houses were also often given a decorative underlining of reeds arranged in elaborate radial patterns, with added designs made in fir bark attached to the underside of the reeds. In the West Country, wattle hurdles sometimes supported the thatch. All these methods are similar to the medieval practice of using oak laths to support thatch. The laths were made by splitting the oak rather than sawing it. They were also sometimes crudely plastered.

It is possible that the use of any barrier or underlay under thatch may shorten its overall life, especially if it is not permeable to air, so that the thatch cannot 'breathe'. This encourages condensation and possibly rot. New houses normally have roofing felt as an underlay to keep the building waterproof. It is fixed loosely to allow ventilation at the eaves, as required by Building Regulations.

Many new thatched houses are now being built with fire preventive features already incorporated in their design. Wooden sheets completely shield the rafters and counter battens are fixed to them, on which the thatch is laid. This gives a small air gap under the thatch, allowing it to breathe and dry (see fig. 72). The wooden sheets provide a thirty-minute barrier, in the event of fire, to protect the main structure of the house, including the roof timbers. The method, known as the Dorset Model, was developed in Dorset, as the name suggests. It has since been adopted in many other counties where new thatched houses are being built. Some owners further reduce the fire risk by installing lightning conductors at the highest point of the roof. Others, who have wire netting on the thatch, connect it to a sound earth. To be efficient, the earth strip should have a diameter over ⅜ inch (1 cm).

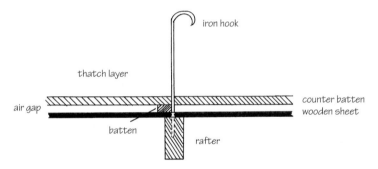

Fig. 72 New roof fire barrier

The Royal Institute of British Architects can provide a list of their members who specialize in the design of thatched properties. New thatched buildings must adhere to current planning law and Building Regulations and these frequently change to account for new technology. They are mainly concerned with the possible spread of fire, and so restrict the building of new domestic thatched properties to detached or semi-detached houses with a total capacity not exceeding approximately 53,000 cubic feet (1,500 cubic metres). Furthermore, no part of the main thatched roof must measure less than 40 feet (12 metres) from any point on the property's boundary. If a thatched porch or bay window protrudes from the house then this small area is usually exempted, so long as its total area does not exceed 32 square feet (3 square metres). It must also be separated from the main roof by at least 5 feet (1.5 metres) of non-combustible material and no part of the protuberance must be less than 20 feet (6 metres) from the property's boundary. These precautions are designed to prevent the spread of flames to a neighbouring building. Very occasionally, a local authority may relax the 40 feet (12 metres) from any point of the property's boundary but most are not amenable to easing the regulation.

In new thatched buildings the structural members of the roof must conform to the mandatory requirement of the appropriate Schedule of the Building Regulations. It is essential that the rafters are always more than 2 inches (50 mm) thick, so that they can securely hold thatch hooks. The size of the wooden scantlings selected, appropriate to the span, must be able to bear a thatch load that is no less than 5 pounds per square foot (25 kg per square metre), and preferably up to 8 pounds per square foot (40 kg per square metre), which is the weight of the heaviest material reed. As thatch is fairly light compared to alternative roofing materials, it needs relatively little sophisticated carpentry for the underlying roof structure. The size of the battens required for thatching is usually 1½ inches (38 mm) x 1 inch (25 mm) or 1½ inches (38 mm) x ¾ inch (20 mm). They should be treated against rot and woodworm attack before being nailed to the rafters. Master thatchers are always willing to offer advice on builders' timberwork, both old and new. They can also help by providing useful suggestions on new proposed extensions to existing thatched houses.

The popularity of thatched homes has increased enormously. With its snug look, thatch appeals to many people, especially those who wish to live in a house with an 'olde worlde' exterior, but with all modern conveniences inside. New thatched houses come with National House-Building Council (NHBC) warranties and have damp-proof courses and cavity-wall insulation. Owners will therefore have no rising damp to deal with, and no fungus and decay, as is sometimes experienced in old houses. However, all surviving period thatched properties with their quaint uneven walls, floors and ancient gnarled patinated beams were built to last several centuries; only time will tell if the lifespan of the new ones matches that.

Nearly all the modern thatched houses being built copy the relevant local exterior vernacular design, so that they blend unobtrusively with the older cottages and properties in their neighbourhood. In some areas, this may involve building alternating courses of flints and bricks in the walls. In other areas, bricks may be cut in half and laid in a pseudo-Flemish bond style, so that stretcher bricks are viewed alternating with header-type bricks, which gives a more traditional look. As the original uses for thatched barns have vanished, so conversions to make homes have gained momentum and become fashionable. Barn conversions form a 'half-way house' for those wishing to live in a modern home in a genuine period property in the countryside. It often proves difficult to retain the original exterior image but modern architects have made a lot of progress in placing windows, for example, in unobtrusive positions. A very high percentage of barns have now been converted and many people are willing to pay substantial sums to live in one.

As I have said, thatched roofs are prone to attack by birds, especially when they are searching for nesting places or materials. They also cause damage searching beneath the eaves for insects or seeds left in the wheat straw. The problem appears to have increased as more trees have been felled and hedgerows replaced, thus reducing the insect population, seeds and other food sources available to them in the countryside. Sparrows, in particular, are a nuisance and in the past country folk called them 'thatch birds'. Holes appear in the thatch, as if caused by a punch.

To keep repair costs to a minimum and if one cannot get a thatcher quickly, it is wise to repair these holes as soon as they are noticed by pushing straw into them. Otherwise, the birds will concentrate on the holes and enlarge them still further. This temporary repair should be done only if the holes are fairly accessible and can be reached without damaging the rest of the thatch. If a ladder is used, it is essential that it is positioned accurately, so that it lies absolutely flat on the surface of the thatched roof to spread the load (see fig. 73). If it is placed at an angle to the roof, it will cause severe damage by breaking down the eaves. Window cleaners and painters also have to be careful.

To fill a bird hole, gather a bundle of long straw or reed together big enough to make a good, tight fit. Tie the bundle loosely with a rot-proof tarred twine, roughly at the middle and about a third of the way down from the 'ears' end. Push a 20-inch (50 cm) length of willow or hazel, about the thickness of a pencil and with one end sharpened, down the centre of the bundle, with the sharp end protruding from the 'ears' end of the bundle; half the length of the stick should be left protruding. Tighten the twine around the bundle and push the bundle

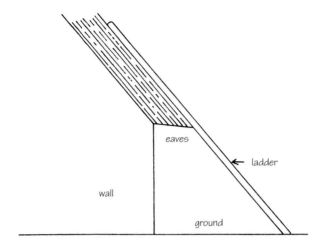

Fig. 73 Ladder on roof

(protruding stick end first) into the hole. With a flat surface such as a bat or spade, gently tap the bundle more firmly into the hole. Trim the ends to the same level as the surrounding thatch surface. It is also advisable to push in any isolated reeds or straws that may have been partially pulled out by the birds. These can normally be easily reached, where they are most noticeable, along the eaves and around the window spaces. However, it may not always be possible to push individual straws or reeds back into position, because of the tightness of the thatch layer.

Birds enjoy seclusion and shelter and usually attack the thatch at places where they can hide from view. Favourite spots are under the eaves and gables and at junctions of the roof and chimney, where the thatch sometimes compacts. Some roofs are wire netted at these strategic points to prevent bird damage, and as I have said, long-straw roofs are completely covered with wire netting for protection. There are some bird-scarers on the market, but their usefulness is doubtful. They also need to be changed frequently so that the birds do not become familiar with them and lose their fear. Some bird repellents are available, but they remain active for only short periods. Several bizarre ways of dealing with the problem have been recorded over the years. One amusing Irish country method dates back to 1885, when whiskey could reputedly be purchased at 36 shillings (£1.80) for a dozen-bottle case. The technique involved gathering together several large handfuls of wheat and soaking them in whiskey for twenty-four hours and placing them at strategic points on the thatch. It was reported that after five to ten minutes the birds became helpless and could easily be collected and removed. In 1264, Simon de Montfort, Earl of Leicester, envisaged a different form of bird attack! In an attempt to overthrow the throne he planned to release hundreds of chickens with flaming brands tied to their legs in London. He hoped they would flutter about in panic and destroy most of London, which still had a great number of thatched buildings, despite the ban on thatch in 1212. The plan did not succeed!

As well as birds, rats, mice and squirrels are occasionally attracted to thatched roofs to find shelter, warmth and food. They cause damage by chewing rather than pulling out the thatch. Rats climb walls fairly easily and once established in a roof space they are difficult to dislodge. It is essential to destroy any female rats because of their breeding potential. Most pest controllers attack the problem by placing rat poison safely at strategic places. Wire netting also helps to keep them out, but care must be taken to check that they are not already in the thatch, as they will then be trapped underneath the wire and create even more havoc trying to get out.

The growth of trees and bushes near a thatched roof must also be carefully watched. Pruning must be carried out at regular intervals to prevent branches rubbing against the thatch and causing it to deteriorate. The close proximity of trees may also give rise to leaves and twigs falling on the roof; if this is the case, it is not advisable to have the roof covered with wire netting as it traps them. Trees also cast shadows and cause additional water to drip on the roof. Lime trees are a special nuisance because they deposit a sticky honeydew on the thatch. This sugary substance may originate from the excrement of aphids and other insects and can be a catalyst for fungal growth.

Damp conditions favour the development of moss, which reaches the roof area, when spores are dispersed during dry conditions in May, and the prevailing wind direction is therefore important. Moss and lichen are often found on the north side and when there is little air movement, but although the northern side stays wetter longer, thatch decomposition is slower, as the temperature is lower than on the southern side. The formation of moss will also be affected by the nearness of hedgerows and the amount of sun that can shine on the roof. Mosses have no true roots and are attached to a roof by hairlike threads called *rhizoids*. Large areas of well-established moss on a thatched roof can greatly interfere with its water shedding ability and prevent it drying out. It also spoils the appearance. An advantage of a thick moss layer on a roof is that it may make it slightly more fire resistant and forms an extra coating to the thatch. Moss can be gently removed by hand but this may do more harm than good, as it will disturb the thatch underneath. Moss killers will destroy the growth but not remove it. Some thatchers try to prevent moss formation by fixing a length of bare uninsulated copper wire along the underside of the ridge. Rain normally has a pH value below 7 and this slight acidity slowly reacts with the wire to form traces of copper salts and hydroxides, which cascade over the thatch surface and help prevent moss formation. Unfortunately, during rainfall the drips from the eaves may prove toxic to any delicate plants below.

On some very old thatched roofs that have grossly deteriorated, grass may also be seen growing on small areas. If ivy is allowed to grow up the wall of a thatched building, it is advisable to cut it below the eaves level to stop it spreading to the thatch and so prevent the accelerated deterioration of the roof and interference with water shedding. It is advisable with old properties, especially those without damp-proof courses, to cut the ivy only below the eaves level and not to remove it completely from the walls by severing the base of the plant. This is especially important if the ivy is well established over the whole wall area, as the aerial roots of the ivy absorb moisture, which assists in keeping walls dry. The mass of ivy leaves also prevents rainwater from directly hitting the wall. These processes may prevent moisture penetration to the interior walls of the house.

A thatched roof has a tendency to release small pieces of straw and dust, which descend into the loft area of the house. This is a nuisance when a water-storage tank is situated in the loft and great care should be taken to ensure that it is adequately covered. This also denies any rats which manage to get into the roof space a source of water.

Thatch also attracts spiders, which make their homes in it. Many cobwebs will be formed in the loft and will be also noticed around the outside of window areas and under the eaves. Fortunately, all the spiders in Britain are non-poisonous.

Lofts were originally rare in thatched cottages and spaces that have been incorporated later are usually very cramped, with little head-room. They are also very poorly ventilated and this should be remembered when treatments such as woodworm killers are applied to roof timbers. These products are dissolved in volatile low-viscosity solvents to facilitate penetration of the wood. However, in a restricted space, vapour may accumulate that can be dangerous to inhale. The hydrocarbon mist can also present a fire risk. Work such as wood-worm treatment is therefore best done in small stages to allow the vapour ample time to disperse. Light switches should not be used for a considerable time to avoid sparks causing a possible fire.

It has been seen that the eaves of a thatched house always overhang the walls by a wide margin but this can restrict the amount of light in the upper rooms. It is therefore worth considering carefully what colour schemes to use for interior decoration in upstairs rooms, in order to optimize the light available. The rooms of a thatched house are also usually fairly narrow, because the steep pitch of the roof can be obtained only if a relatively narrow span is used. Long houses over-come this problem to some extent by increasing the room length.

Thatched buildings will inevitably have higher maintenance costs than modern conventionally roofed properties; moreover, older prop-erties generally require much more attention than modern ones. It is worth repeating that it is advisable to have a thatched roof inspected by a thatcher every five to seven years and to have any necessary clean-ing and patching repair work carried out. This will, in the long term, be the most economical method of prolonging the life of the roof.

It may appear that the disadvantages of living in a house with a thatched roof outweigh the advantages. However, the disadvantages are relatively minor and the advantages are considered by many people to outweigh them, especially those who prefer charm, quaintness and snugness. The warmth and aesthetic appeal of a thatched roof are of inestimable value to many people. This alone is enough to justify the minor disadvantages, which can all be comfortably lived with.

6

Costs and Insurance

Most old thatched cottages cost little when they were first built. Labour and building materials were both cheap. Some people therefore view them with scepticism, as many were constructed with cheap local materials obtained from the earth. They sometimes associate them with the simple mud buildings with grass roofs which they may have seen during their travels in other parts of the world. They perhaps forget that many of our thatched cottages were constructed robustly enough to have survived several centuries. Also, like all good antiques, they have considerably matured in value with the passage of time. Many of these once humble farm labourers' cottages are now highly desirable residences, especially those that have modernized interiors to make them comfortable and luxurious homes.

Most people who live in thatched properties take great pride in the appearance of the thatch and its aesthetic appeal, and most can afford to lavish attention on keeping their properties in immaculate order. This is one reason that thatched houses generally demand a good market price. In fact, estate agents report that they command a considerable price premium (10 per cent or more) over homes of the same period in similar condition and location with tiled or slated roofs. The market may be more specialized than for conventional houses, but estate agents encounter little difficulty in finding prospective purchasers. This preference for living in a snug thatched home, outweighs the extra expense of maintaining and insuring it.

However, it is only prudent to buy a thatched property if one can afford this extra expenditure. There are few sights more forlorn than unkempt thatch that has become bedraggled by neglect. If the property is old, it is obviously wise to have a full structural survey done before purchase. This may well reveal damp in the walls or floors. The structural soundness of the building will also be revealed during the survey, but remember that period houses are completely unlike modern ones; they were constructed long before the introduction of modern Building Regulations. Despite this, many have survived several centuries. If possible, it is best to employ a surveyor who has had experience in assessing period houses, and thatched ones in particular.

It is also possible, and advisable, to arrange for a local thatcher to survey the state of the roof on a property before making a final decision to purchase. It will be best in the long term if the most skilled thatcher in the area is employed to carry out the survey and also for any future work if the house sale goes through. Newly built houses, of course, come with a ten-year NHBC guarantee.

At one time, many mortgage lenders were hesitant about lending money on a thatched house, not only because it would require more maintenance than a tiled or slated one, but also because most thatched properties were old. Walls, for example, may have been made of such materials as cob or chalk ashlar, and if there had been a leaky roof, water might have penetrated the tops of them. This water could have frozen during a cold spell in winter and the walls would then have suffered deterioration. They were also concerned that the beams and timbers might have been subjected, over a long period, to rot because of the absence of a damp-proof course and perhaps a roof in disrepair.

The picture has changed considerably today. Most mortgage lenders will now lend money on older thatched properties, especially if the borrower agrees to undertake any stipulated repairs or improvements, which may include the improvement of the damp-proofing of the house and repair or, in extreme cases, renewal of the thatched roof. The mortgage lender may withhold a portion of the money until suggested alterations have been satisfactorily completed.

Solicitor's searches will establish whether the property is listed as being of historical or architectural importance. Listed buildings include all those built before 1700 that have received little alteration. This has now been expanded to cover the majority of houses before 1840 that have not been subjected to significant alteration. All buildings of national importance are always included, irrespective of their age. Only about 1 per cent of listed buildings receive a Grade 1 rating; the rest are Grade 2, although some in the latter category are considered more important than others and are given a signifying asterisk, Grade 2*. Living in a listed building offers both advantages and disadvantages. For example, it may sometimes be possible for financial assistance to be obtained towards the maintenance of the building, with a local authority grant. On the other hand, considerable delays must be expected in obtaining permission to make any alteration to the building; indeed, permission may be refused.

When applying to the local authority for listed building consent, it is usual to submit a sketch map or plan to identify the location of the property exactly. It is desirable to include a drawing of the external or internal elevations affected by the proposal. In addition, it is considered helpful to submit a drawing of the property before and after the requested alterations, together with a photograph of the present building. One should always state the reason or the necessity for the work to be carried out. Consent is only required if the character of the building is to be changed in any way. For instance, in the case of a thatched building, a change in roof shape or style or the insertion of a dormer window will obviously need consent. This includes altering the style of the ridge. A change from long straw to combed wheat reed and vice versa also requires listed building consent, as does changing from straw to water reed.

When applying for a historic building grant from a local authority, it is usual to include three estimates of the likely cost. However, it will be found that there are huge regional variations; not all authorities accept applications for historic building grants. As well as the roof, other parts of the fabric of the house may be eligible for assistance, including chimneys where they are to be repaired or reinstated with their original pots, and walls and parapet copings when original features are reintroduced. Windows and doors may also be eligible if those that have been inserted later are replaced with original timber types. All grants are discretionary, and they are never awarded retrospectively. If an application relates to a thatched roof then grants are given for a specified form of thatch, usually long straw or combed wheat reed rather than water reed. Minor repair costs, such as filling bird holes are not covered. If a house is considered to be in an affluent area, then sometimes grants are not given at all. Even when grants are offered, they may only be awarded for up to 25 per cent of the total cost of the work, with an upper ceiling limit. Grants are not intended to cover the total cost of the work involved but to encourage a high standard of repair and workmanship.

Some local authorities stipulate that the applicant must have resided in the property for a certain period before becoming eligible for a grant. Others insist that if the applicant moves house before a specified number of years after the award of a grant, usually five, then it must be repaid. Local authorities only pay the grant after the final invoice has been received and after the work has been inspected and deemed satisfactory by a council officer.

Grants are more likely to be available if the building lies within a conservation area and particularly if it is on the National Register of Buildings at Risk. A copy of this can be obtained from English Heritage, which in certain circumstances also offers grants, especially if the property has a Grade 1 or Grade 2* listing. English Heritage normally requires a detailed history of the previous type of thatch used on the building.

With regard to the cost of thatching a cottage, a fairly small one may possibly be done for £7,000 in wheat reed, or less in water reed. However, the average cost to rethatch a roof is between £10,000 and £20,000, depending upon the size. An average cottage requires about 4 tons of material. The construction of just a new ridge would cost in the region of £1,000–2,000, but an elaborate one adds considerably to the expense and a corn dolly adorning the top may cost £100 or more. Thatchers usually quote per foot or metre for ridging. It is normally recommended that the ridge be renewed about every twelve years. If a house has a thatched porch, this will also require fairly frequent attention, as it takes the full flood of rainwater cascading from the main roof and therefore endures harsh conditions.

In order to spread the cost, some owners put aside about £1,000 a year for future repairs and general thatch replacement. The type of thatch material, its availability and quality affect costs, as does the number of dormer windows, hips and roof valleys. The thatcher assesses these by measuring their total foot or metre runs. The distance the thatcher has to travel to reach the property and transportation of the material also affect the price. It may be best to obtain estimates from more than one thatcher and enquire whether VAT is included. If scaffolding has to be erected, then this will be an additional expense.

Assuming that a minimum thickness of 1 foot (30.5 cm) will be required, and working in thatchers' basic squares (100 square feet or 9.3 square metres) of surface area, a cottage may require twelve of these squares, approximately six on each side of the roof. Thatchers usually quote prices in these basic squares, as measured on the sloping roof surfaces. The price of constructing the eaves below the thatch and the barges is normally included. A quote from a thatcher using long straw may be £1,000 plus VAT per basic square. This means, in our example, the total cost for the rethatch of the cottage would be £12,000 plus VAT. If combed wheat reed was used instead of long straw, the cost would probably be dearer by about £100 a square. Sedge, if available, would be even more expensive. A Norfolk reed roof may cost £800 plus VAT per square but much depends upon its location, whilst imported water reeds would be cheaper. Twenty-five years ago, the price of Norfolk reed was nearly twice that of combed wheat reed, which again was more expensive than long straw. However, the situation is now very different.

Unfortunately, thatchers often encounter difficulty in obtaining sufficient supplies of home-grown thatch materials of suitable quality. Many favour using imported products such as Polish rye straw, much to the annoyance of conservationists, for which they would probably pay about £450 to £500 a ton, compared to English straw at around £600 or more a ton. They also purchase South African veld grass or Polish, Turkish, French and Hungarian water reeds, all at around £1.50 to £1.60 a bundle, which is again much cheaper than Norfolk reed and English combed wheat reed. Prices, of course, vary depending upon the quantities purchased and the load sizes delivered. However, from an owner's point of view, the initial price of material is important but also of even greater importance is the life of the thatch. It would prove even more costly to use a cheaper product if it eventually proved inferior and only lasted about ten years, compared to one that may last forty or more. Norfolk reed would have the longest life.

One can obtain a rough estimate of the area of a thatched roof by taking two measurements. The first is the vertical dimension of the thatch from wall to wall when measured over the top of the roof. The figure obtained is therefore the sum of the two slopes from eaves to apex, plus the thickness of the two eaves. The second measurement is the horizontal length of the thatch at the eaves level, including the thickness of the barges at the ends. The two measurements multiplied together give a good approximate idea of the main roof area and allow a rough estimate of the cost.

However, it is unlikely that a full rethatch will be necessary. In the case of combed wheat reed and long straw, it is more usual to fix a new top coat of thatch over the old, after it has been prepared back to a firm base, as explained in Chapter 3. This considerably reduces the expense of the work, as material costs will be reduced by about 30 per cent and labour costs will also be less. In the case of water reed, it is more likely that the whole of the old thatch will have to be removed and a new thatch put on. In some cases, an unexpected cost may be encountered if, for example, the battens or other timbers are found to be damaged and need renewing.

In certain instances, if there is only a small damaged area, the thatcher may be able to draw out some of the thatch and insert small bundles of new reed of the correct length. The new reed is securely fixed and a leggett dresses the old and new reed interfaces together, so that the repair assumes the same level and homogeneity on the main roof. The passage of time soon harmonizes the colours of the old roof and the patch. After removing old thatch from a roof, the thatcher has to dispose of the waste; they cannot burn it on site, as this would infringe most insurance policies. This removal cost is normally included in the estimate, as is the cleaning up of the site after the job is completed.

If a thatched roof fails to live up to expectations, it is possible to pursue a claim through a small claims court. This offers an informal hearing and no costs are awarded, so it is not usual to instruct a solicitor. This is therefore the most economical way but unfortunately it covers only disputes up to £5,000, which is well below the cost of rethatching a roof but may be all right for minor roof problems such as reridging. Much will depend upon whether there was any written or verbal agreement between the thatcher and the client regarding the longevity of the roof. Rather than pursuing the alternative of costly litigation it may be worthwhile to get a mediator appointed to resolve the dispute. For example, if the thatcher is a member of a recognized trade association then this body may be willing to help and appoint an independent conciliator.

As well as the maintenance cost, the owner of a thatched house will have the extra expense of insurance. Most major insurance companies will now insure thatched buildings but all charge special premiums because of the increased fire risk – although the extra risk is relatively small, as statistics reveal that only 1.5 per cent of thatched properties in Britain are likely to be involved in a roof fire during any one year. In fact, during the whole of the last century, only one person lost their life in a thatched house fire. Nevertheless, a £200,000 home will probably cost an extra £100 or more a year to insure, compared with a tiled or slated one – 50p extra per £1,000. Some insurance companies differentiate between a straw and a water reed roof because they consider the latter less vulnerable. This is probably because water reed is slightly less combustible and the roof is more tightly packed and therefore marginally safer as regards the rate of spread of fire. This is especially true when straw thatch is dry and air can penetrate below the surface, and even more so when there are bird holes in the roof.

If a fire does break out it is obvious that more damage will occur with straw and water reeds than with tiles and slates. This means that the potential liability of the insurance company for damage would be greater, as the fire would be likely to spread more rapidly. A burning thatched roof will often collapse into the house, causing considerable extra damage. If a cottage forms part of a row, then fire fighters may have to make a firebreak by pulling thatch away from a neighbouring roof, which is not on fire, in an attempt to stop it spreading.

It is worth 'shopping around' to obtain premium estimates before making a commitment to a particular company. An alternative way is to use a reputable insurance broker, who will do this preliminary groundwork. A broker will know which insurance companies look most favourably on thatched properties. Some companies specialize in insuring thatched roof properties at reasonable rates, and these are listed in the Useful Addresses section at the end of the book. Incidentally, it is possible to obtain a discount of 10 per cent on a thatched roof insurance policy if you are a member of the Thatched Property Association, see Useful Addresses at the end of the book. Insurers who specialize in thatch assess when the roof was last thatched and its present condition, rather than using a postcode risk assessment. They also enquire whether the building is of timber-frame, cob, stone, brick, or lath and plaster construction.

The level of the premium will depend on the construction of the thatched property and also whether it is isolated or attached to a neighbouring house. Another factor will be whether any fire-proofing of the thatch has been carried out or sprinklers, smoke detectors, etc. installed. A further consideration will be whether the property is connected to a mains water supply, so that an ample amount will be available for fire-fighting. Mains water is always preferred to other sources, as it has a reasonable immediate pressure. It takes valuable time to arrange equipment to pump well water with sufficient pressure for fire-fighting, and the Fire and Rescue Service is limited in the quantities of water it can carry by wagon. The distance of the thatched property from the nearest fire station and the ease of access from the road will also be factors noted by the insurers.

Some roofs are completely covered with wire netting for protection but this may lead to higher fire insurance rates, because of the added difficulty in pulling the thatch away. An open fire or wood stove will also have a bearing on the premium, as will the soundness of electrical wiring. Another consideration will be whether the chimney is new and whether it has been lined and regularly swept. Finally, after the house is insured, the insurance company will often stipulate that the roof must be maintained in good condition. If a claim exceeds £1,000, which is extremely likely after a roof fire, most insurers will instruct an assessor to visit the property.

To conclude on an historical note, if a thatched house was not insured in the eighteenth century, and many occupants could not afford to do so, there was a good chance that in the event of a fire the firemen would not even attempt to put it out. The first insurance company, the Sun Fire Office, which was founded in 1710, issued plaques to its customers, with the symbol of a smiling sun emitting multiple rays. Customers attached these to the outside of their cottage walls to show that the buildings were insured and the firemen would then attend if a fire broke out, because they knew they would be sure of getting paid for their services! Incidentally, the Sun Fire Office was also one of the first insurance companies to form their own fire brigade.

7

Unusual Thatched Buildings and Curiosities

One of the most unusual thatched buildings stands in the centre of London, on Bankside, close to the Tate Modern and nearly opposite St Paul's Cathedral. It is the Globe Theatre, and is unique because it is the only thatched building allowed in central London, thatch having been banned for many centuries because of the fire risk. The present building represents a full-scale reconstruction of the old Globe Theatre, where actors first performed many of Shakespeare's plays. The original theatre was built with a thatched roof in 1598–9, with three tiers of galleries circling the rectangular projecting stage with an open space around, where the 'groundlings' stood in the cheapest area to watch the plays. The law banning thatch in London, which was passed in 1212, was widely abused and thatch was still in use during Shakespeare's time. In 1613, during a performance of Henry VIII, a spark from a cannon being used as a prop set the thatch ablaze and the playhouse burned to the ground. In 1614, it was rebuilt with a clay and tiled roof but the Puritans closed it down, with other London theatres, in 1642. It was demolished in 1644 and it was not until 1989 that traces of the foundations were discovered. Owing to the prolonged and strenuous efforts of the late American actor and director, Sam Wanamaker, in the late twentieth century, a recon-struction of the Globe was finally authorized, close to the original site. Building work commenced in 1992 and performances on stage were underway a few years later.

The new theatre was built using a basic green oak frame structure with oak laths and lime plaster walls. The seats were also made of timber. Green oak has a relatively low combustion rate when ignited and a fire-resistant board was incorporated within the walls. The thatch selected for the roof was Norfolk reed, with a sedge ridge. The material was impregnated with a fire retardant. Owing to the fire risk, a 1-inch (2.5 cm) thick fire protection board separated the thatch from the rafters, to give a three-hour barrier delay in the spread of a fire. This precaution was supplemented by a sparge drencher system placed in the ridge, which would automatically drench the thatch with water in the event of a fire. The Thatching Advisory Service was deeply involved and consulted throughout the design stage and the building project.

Another unusual thatched building may be found hidden away in a remote corner of the Royal Botanic Gardens at Kew. This is Queen Charlotte's Cottage, which is only open to the public on the first spring bank holiday. Surrounded by trees, it was used as a summerhouse by the wife of King George III to give tea parties and picnics. She and her husband loved the cottage and spent many happy hours there with their children. Queen Charlotte last visited it in 1818, not long before she died, and afterwards Queen Victoria used it for many years.

The Globe Theatre, London

Queen Charlotte's Cottage, Royal Botanic Gardens, Kew, Surrey

The two-storey cottage dates from 1772 and was designed in the rustic style favoured by the royal family and the wealthy at that time. It set the style for the later *cottage ornée*. It was constructed of brick and timber-framing; the upper storey was a later addition. The roof was rethatched in 1998 with Norfolk reed and the block ridge pattern of closely cut points is a faithful reproduction of the original, details of which were obtained from early records. There are two brick chimney-stacks in the central section of the ridge. When I last saw it the thatch appeared to be prone to bird damage, as a result of its peaceful location, surrounded by trees. As with the Globe Theatre, a heat-sensitive automatic sprinkler system was installed in the ridge in case of a fire. Many William Hogarth prints adorn the downstairs reception room and upstairs the walls and ceiling display an intricate trelliswork, interwoven with flowers painted by Queen Charlotte's daughter, Elizabeth. Incidentally, a further royal connection with thatch may be found in nearby Richmond Park, in the shape of the Thatched House Lodge, the residence for many years of Princess Alexandra, the granddaughter of George V, and her husband Angus Ogilvy.

A thatched manor house in the tiny village of Hammoon, near Sturminster Newton in Dorset, has a grand porch of classical

127

proportions at the front – most unusual for a house with a thatched roof. Made of local Purbeck limestone, it has a shaped gable with strapwork. As such gables with multi-curved sides became fashionable in the early seventeenth century and strapwork decoration with interlaced bands in the sixteenth, the porch was probably built in the Elizabethan or Jacobean period. Strangely, the banded Tuscan columns of the doorway fail to harmonize in scale with the porch itself, so it seems likely they were introduced later. The main part of the house is thought to be approximately a century older than the porch and dates therefore to the early sixteenth century. The manor house is L-shaped and built with stone ashlar and rubble. Many additions and alterations have been made since it was first built. The front south-east elevation was constructed with a beautiful two-storey bay, incorporating stone mullioned windows. A huge sycamore tree has towered beside the house for many years and unfortunately still casts a shadow on the thatched roof, making it prone to moss formation. In the second half of the twentieth century, the appreciable expanse of roof was thatched with combed wheat reed, with a plain ridge. A small dormer window peeps through it.

Dorset has one of the highest concentrations of thatched buildings in Britain. In the village of Puddletown, there is a thatched petrol station. It has a gabled roof, with a tufted ridge decorated with scallops and points. Two square brick chimneys rise over the top. It is very unusual for a commercial garage to be thatched, in view of the inflammability of the products stored and served on the forecourt.

Although thirty thatched churches still survive in England, several are no longer used for worship. Most of them are to be found in East Anglia, with a few in the West Country. However, a curious one may be found in the village of Roxton, in Bedfordshire. It was built as a barn and converted at the beginning of the nineteenth century, officially becoming a place of worship in 1808. It originally belonged to a local farmer, Charles Metcalf, who wanted a Congregational chapel in the village. During his lifetime, he even conducted the occasional service there. Later, two wings were added. The roof has always had a ridge decorated with scallops and points, and a rustic tree trunk verandah surrounds and supports the perimeter of the eaves. A separate conical-shaped thatched canopy shelters the front door.

The Congregational Church at Roxton, Bedfordshire

Another unique church, St George's, is hidden away in the tiny settlement of Langham in Dorset. It is difficult to find on any road atlas, but it lies towards the extreme edge of the Blackmore Vale, between Buckhorn Weston and Gillingham in the west of the county. It is interesting in that it was built in the twentieth century – it is most unusual for a thatched church to be built so late. It was constructed in 1921, in memory of those who lost their lives during the First World War. The Royal British Legion, also established in 1921, have since held many services there on Remembrance Sunday. E. Ponting designed the tiny church in a simple Arts and Crafts Gothic style for the local Manger family, one of whom lies buried beneath it. It stands in an isolated spot with trees close by. The hipped roof follows the curvature of the stone rubble walls and there is a small thatched porch guarding one entrance. Combed wheat reed was chosen as the thatch material.

A unique thatched castle, the only one in England, also stands in Dorset, about 4 miles (6.5 km) to the east of Dorchester, near Woodsford village. Called Woodsford Castle, it dates back to 1337, when Edward III granted William de Whitefield a licence to crenellate a manor house. The fortified manor house has been lived in throughout its history, which is most unusual for an ancient castle. The ownership changed many times, but only by inheritance until 1978, when the Landmark Trust acquired it. This organisation, based at Maidenhead, in Berkshire, provides an excellent service by saving unusual buildings thought to be at risk. It restores them and then lets them to the public as holiday homes. Woodsford Castle may be rented in this way by contacting the Landmark Trust (telephone: 01628 8259201). It can accommodate up to eight people.

When first constructed, with local Purbeck masonry, it was most unlikely that the castle would have been thatched, as this would have made it too vulnerable under siege. Its position near a ford over the River Frome was probably the chief reason for its original fortification. However, the fact that it was a very long, narrow building later allowed it to be thatched, as the correct pitch angle could be achieved. It was extensively restored in about 1850 and it then became a farmhouse. It stands three storeys high, which is most exceptional for a thatched building. It has battlements and loopholes and the massive thatched roof has an area in excess of 333 square yards (278 square metres). It once had five projecting towers but one only survives. The projecting round turret on the west wall contains a newel staircase, giving access to the former guardroom and antechamber. Originally only the first floor would have been used for living accommodation; the ground floor, consisting of a series of interconnected vaulted rooms, would have been used purely as service and storage rooms.

There is another thatched castle, but it is just a reconstruction of a Norman castle built by the Duke of Boulogne in the twelfth century. It is called Mountfitchet Castle and was constructed in 1984 on the site of the original motte near Stansted, Essex . It is open daily for visitors from 10 am to 5 pm, March to November. A replica thatched Norman village has been built near to it and all the buildings are enclosed in a wooden palisade. Both the castle and the village are built with timber and thatch, like the originals; even the well in the village has a small thatched canopy sheltering it, as do a dove and pigeon cote and various chicken houses. Scenes from everyday life in Norman Britain are depicted inside each thatched building. These include a church, a prison, a forge, a weaver's hut, a potter's hut, a brew house and a hawk house. There is an exhibition of a banquet on a long table in the castle and in the village a kitchen is displayed, together with a house that twenty people would have shared, often with their animals to help keep them warm.

Mountfitchet Castle, Stansted, Essex

Brew house at Norman village, Mountfitchet Castle

Hawk house at Norman village,
Mountfitchet Castle

131

The largest area of thatch in Britain covers a barn at Tisbury, in Wiltshire. Situated at Place Farm, it was formerly an abbey grange and lies close to another group of fifteenth-century buildings. It measures about 220 yards (200 metres) long and the total roof area covers 1,450 square yards (1,212 square metres). When it was rethatched in the early 1970s, five thatchers toiled for four months. They used about 270 tons of Norfolk reed, which involved carrying about 130,000 bundles and an innumerable number of iron hooks up to the roof.

Although not so long as the Tisbury barn, a terrace in Dorset claims the record for the longest stretch of thatch on domestic housing. The thatch measures 120 yards (110 metres) in length and extends over eleven cottages and a general store. The name is simply The Buildings, and it is situated on the outskirts of the hamlet of Manswood, on the Witchampton road. The cottages were built about 200 years ago with cob walls, and the original thatch material was long straw. A series of entry gaps, at intervals of every two cottages, links the front gardens with the rear. Small brick extensions with slated roofs have since been added at the rear. The post box set in a wall bears the initials VR, dating it back to Queen Victoria's reign; such boxes are now fairly rare.

In contrast, Godmanstone, also in Dorset, claims to have the smallest thatched public house in England. The fifteenth-century inn, called the Smith's Arms, was previously a blacksmith's forge and King Charles II once stopped there in 1665 to have his horse shod whilst out hunting. He is reputed to have asked for a drink but the blacksmith could not serve him because he had no licence, so there and then the King granted him one. The front of the one-storey inn measures just over 10 feet (3 metres) across, with a depth of about 45 feet (13.7 metres) and the eaves are only 4 feet (1.2 metres) from the ground. A combed wheat reed roof has sheltered the inn for many years, and the walls were constructed of cob, faced with local flints. The river that flows alongside the garden was once used by the landlord to keep his bottled beer cool.

The Smith's Arms at Godmanstone, Dorset – one of the smallest pubs in England

Whilst on the subject of tiny houses, in the United States of America, miniature English thatched cottages that are exact replicas of original ones are constructed in perfect detail, reduced in size by precise scales of ½, ¹/₂₄ or ¹/₄₈. One of the leading experts in this field is Glenda Cavanaugh of Blaine, Washington but several other craftsmen and hobbyists in America are also keen miniaturists of English architecture. The miniature thatched cottages are placed in realistic backgrounds, representing the tranquil scenery of the English countryside.

Returning to the subject of real buildings, Palmers' Old Brewery at West Bay Road, in Bridport, Dorset is the only thatched brewery in Britain and possibly in Europe. It dates to the eighteenth century and it has a record of continuous beer production ever since. The roof has four separate elevations of water reed over two parallel buildings, which are joined together along their length. The gabled pair thus forms an M-shape roof and the end gable walls have raised parapets enclosing the thatch. In addition, the brewery has one of the few surviving undershot water-wheels in Britain. The gigantic 18-foot (5.5 metre) metal wheel weighs over 5½ tons. Another brewery, St Peter's at South Elmham, near Bungay in Suffolk, is not thatched, but it does have a thatched bonded warehouse that was formerly a seventeenth-century timber-framed barn. The exposed underside of the reed thatch rests on huge oak timbers and the gabled roof provides an ideal insulated cover for storing beer and other drinks, as the warehouse remains at a fairly constant temperature throughout winter and summer. It is reported that a ghost stalks the grounds, in the form of a lady dressed in white; perhaps she comes to admire the beautiful block ridge with its points, which tops the building.

There are hundreds of thatched pubs scattered around the country but one of the more unusual is the Master Thatcher at Taunton, in Somerset. It is not only different because it is a new building but also because of the large area of its thatch. Six thatchers took ten weeks to cover the roof of the 110-foot (33.5 metre) long building, with 9,000 bundles of water reed. Another unusual pub, the Drum Inn, may be found in the village of Cockington, near Torquay, in Devon. It also has a huge thatched roof but it is unique because the acclaimed architect Sir Edward Lutyens (1869–1944) designed it. He was normally associated with much grander commissions, such as the Viceroy's House in New Delhi, the Cenotaph in Whitehall, Liverpool Cathedral, neo-classical country houses and even on a smaller scale, Queen Mary's dolls house.

The building of the Drum Inn commenced in 1934 and it opened its doors to the public in 1936. It was built with special bricks, specified by Lutyens, and the upper wall elevations were lime plastered and then lime washed. Two wings project from each end of the main building and the magnificent thatch sweeps continuously out over them from the main roof area. The roof was originally thatched with local combed wheat reed and two tall chimney-stacks tower over the inn.

Also at Cockington is an unusual cottage, known as the Gamekeeper's Cottage. Hidden by woodland, it was built with random stone rubble in 1517, most probably as a farmhouse. During the nineteenth century, the local gamekeeper lived there and reared pheasants in the surrounding woods for the pheasant shoots, which in those days were very profitable to the landowner. The last gamekeeper, George Giles, occupied the cottage in about 1920. Unfortunately, vandals burned it down in 1990, leaving an empty shell. The local Torbay Council decided to rebuild it and an accurate reconstruction arose from the ashes. The thatched roof is hipped and one side of the cottage has an upper section curiously constructed of slatted rustic timbers, where pheasants would have hung. The opposite side of the cottage has a single chimney-stack rising through the thatch.

The Gamekeeper's Cottage, Cockington, Devon

It was unusual to thatch toll-houses because of the risk of arson by rioters protesting against paying the tolls. The system of turnpike roads and toll-houses introduced in the eighteenth century served two purposes. One was to pay for the maintenance of the roads but they also made travel safer. One of the toll-keeper's duties was to inform travellers of robbers known to be operating in the area and also to alert the relevant authorities. The Snowdon Turnpike Cottage at Chard, Somerset was one of the few that were thatched. Built of flint in 1839 at the fork of Snowdon Hill, it had one storey and the walls were polygonal, as was usual with toll-houses. It was constructed with Gothic arches around the windows and doors. Vertical wooden pillars were built circling the cottage to support the wide, overhanging eaves of the combed wheat reed thatch.

Another even more elaborate thatched toll-house stands at Lyme Regis in Dorset; it is known as the Umbrella Cottage because of the shape of its roof, which is like an inverted bee-skep. It was built in the first quarter of the nineteenth century, again with a polygonal shape, in the *cottage ornée* style. An architect later gave it many extra picturesque and extravagant additions. Details from different periods

The Umbrella Cottage,
Lyme Regis, Dorset

were incorporated into the small building, which had plastered walls. The eaves of the sleek thatch sweep down in an umbrella-like fashion onto free-standing timber posts. The two front pillars have owls carved on the capitals. A central chimney protrudes through the top of the roof. The cottage has traceried windows and also boasts a carved Flemish door, probably salvaged from another building.

A cottage that also possibly once served as a toll-house can be seen in the centre of Rayleigh, in Essex. It is unique in two ways: it is now Britain's smallest council house and has the honour of appearing on the town's coat of arms. Known as the Dutch Cottage, it is octagonal and has one small room upstairs and one downstairs. A single dormer window at the rear allows light into the top room. It was probably named the Dutch Cottage after Delft tiles, dating back to 1650, were discovered during renovation of the fireplace in the 1980s. The date 1621 is shown above the doorway. It is thatched with long straw and a central brick chimney-stack protrudes through the top. Despite its tiny size, a man, his wife, six children and a lodger lived there in Victorian times. Visits to the cottage, owned by Rochford District Council, may be arranged by telephoning the Rayleigh Information Centre on 01702 318150. The tenant kindly shows visitors around on Wednesday afternoons.

A cottage with an interesting literary connection can be found at Yealmpton, near Plymouth in Devon. It was once the home of the woman on whom the well-known nursery rhyme 'Old Mother Hubbard' was based. The verses describe her shopping expeditions to buy food and clothes for her very eccentric dog. The writer of the rhyme, Sarah Catherine Martin (1768–1826) was a frequent visitor to the local manor house where 'Old Mother Hubbard' worked as a housekeeper. It is said that the character of the housekeeper not only intrigued her but also inspired her to write the rhyme in 1805. The cottage, built of stone rubble in the early sixteenth century, not surprisingly now bears the name Old Mother Hubbard's. It was originally built as two cottages and the original 'Old Mother Hubbard' lived in one of them in the late eighteenth century, after she had retired. The cottage has had a variety of uses since those days and during the last few years has served as a restaurant. A water-reed thatch covers the building but no doubt it was formerly thatched with local Devon combed wheat reed. One end is gabled, whilst the other is hipped over an extension. A thatched finial of a dog with a bone makes a fine decorative top for another restaurant called Old Mother Hubbard's, situated near Newton Abbot, also in Devon.

A strange-looking summerhouse, called the Bear's Hut, may be found in Killerton Park, now owned by the National Trust. The park and gardens are situated about 2 miles (3 km) to the north of Broadclyst, in Devon. The Bear's Hut gained its name from the fact that it once housed a Canadian black bear for its aristocratic Victorian owner. The head gardener built the hut in the early nineteenth century. The walls are sturdy timber logs and the hipped roof is thatched in combed wheat reed, with a tuft pinnacle ridge. The interior separates into three rooms and these are as strange as the exterior. One room, with a cobbled floor, has basketwork on its walls and ceiling, whilst pine cones decorate the walls and the ceiling of the second room, which has a bay window. The floor of the third room, known as the Hermit's Chamber, consists of the knuckle bones of deer and deer skins cover the ceiling; the room also has a sixteenth-century Dutch stained glass window, obviously salvaged from another building.

Another Victorian thatched summerhouse may be seen on the north bank of the River Yare at Thorpe St Andrew, near Norwich. It is next to Gurney's Boatyard and it is unusual because it was moved section by section to higher ground in the 1990s, to save it from persistent flooding. It now stands about 450 yards (400 metres) from its original site, where it was built in 1861. It later became the home of a wherryman for many years and the accommodation consisted of a single room downstairs and a loft room reached by a ladder. The building was constructed of timber and was originally thatched; however, over the years the roof deteriorated and was replaced by corrugated iron. After it was moved to its new site, it was completely renovated and thatched with Norfolk reed. During the renovation process the timber walls were painted green, the colour most favoured for external decoration by the Victorians. The original arched doorway and windows were repaired and the single chimney-stack was rebuilt. In the eighteenth and nineteenth centuries, the leisured classes favoured thatched rustic summerhouses. Nowadays, many people often have new ones built in their gardens as decorative features. They come in many shapes and sizes, although most of the ones now being built are fairly small and often round or octagonal.

A garden summerhouse, Dorchester, Dorset

As well as summerhouses, thatched children's playhouses, gazebos, pseudo-lich-gates, arbours, garden parasols, and other curiosities such as bird tables and dovecotes are now being constructed by small companies and by some thatchers, who usually make then during the wetter winter months. Thatched inn-signs may also be seen, as well as thatched anglers' huts beside popular fishing rivers. Some wells are even thatched, such as the one at East Morden in Sussex, where rough timber poles support the canopy. It seems strange that a shelter is needed to keep well water dry!

An angler's hut on the River Test at Longstock, Hampshire

A rare sight is the Stembridge Tower Mill, a thatched windmill, which stands at High Ham, near Langport in Somerset. It is the last of its kind left in Britain. It was closed down as a working one, grinding floor, in 1910 but the National Trust took over its care in 1969. It has four full sails, once covered with canvas. An unusually shaped thatched canopy with a gable-end protects the top of the 28-foot (8.5 metre) high structure. Immediately below the large sails, small wooden-framed windows placed in a vertical line admit light into the various floors. The circular tower enclosing the machinery and supporting the sails was built with stone rubble on a raised earthen platform in 1820. This prevented people from

The thatched Stembridge Tower Windmill, High Lam, Langport, Somerset

getting too close to the revolving sails. The former miller's cottage lies close by and it is thought that it too was originally thatched. Several mills around the country were formerly thatched but the majority suffered deterioration and then winter gales caused further damage. The National Trust has saved another windmill, the Pitstone Mill, on the green at Ivinghoe in Buckinghamshire. It bears the date 1672 and is believed to be the oldest windmill in Britain. It has four full sails, extensively renovated, and a gable-shaped canopy sheltering the top.

In the early 1970s, plastic thatch was marketed as a substitute for the genuine article. It was claimed that the product had the appearance of Norfolk reed but many people thought it looked artificial unless it was viewed from afar. The manufacturer also claimed it had the advantage over real thatch of being fireproof, immune from bird attack, easy to apply and waterproof. The waterproof claim later proved to be untrue, as after some time, it often developed splits as climatic changes opened up the fixing joints. It was applied by securing it directly onto the battens, or over roofing felt. When applied in this way, it looked very thin and quite unlike the warm, deep layer of a real thatched roof. It obviously gave little insulation to the house and when it rained, the noise inside was similar to that under a corrugated iron roof. To overcome this problem, the plastic was sometimes fixed over an existing unkempt thatched roof to retain the insulation properties of the underlying thatch and improve the appearance. This presented yet another problem as it prevented the underlying layer from breathing and encouraged decomposition. The era of plastic thatch was short-lived but a few examples may still be seen around the country.

8

Thatched Buildings in the West Country

This chapter and those that follow give a review of a broad cross-section of villages and towns with thatched buildings. Villages which are especially highlighted contain collections of exceptionally charming or unusual thatched roofs. Some of the buildings are also of historical importance or are situated in villages or towns of particular interest. Most of these will therefore be worth visiting for reasons other than to see the thatched roofs.

Many of the old cottages described have undergone several changes of use during their long lives. The fact that they still survive indicates that they were substantially built despite the use of cheap local materials; the poorer ones have long disappeared.

DEVON

Devon has a host of cob and thatched cottages. The outside walls of most are attractively whitewashed and they form a sight well known to most West Country holidaymakers. An excellent example of a large cob and thatched village is Cheriton Fitzpaine, near Crediton. It is set in rolling hills and many of the cottages are gathered around the fifteenth-century church. The latter is well worth a visit to see its three separate black and white roof sections. The long thatched building near the churchyard was the village school. Cheriton Fitzpaine also has some quaint old almshouses that have an exceptionally large number of chimneys.

Another very good example of a cob and thatched village is nearby

Thorverton. This village is also fairly large and set in hilly country. A stream runs through it, with a pleasant bridge crossing over it. The smart thatched roofs of the cottages complete a picturesque scene, together with the pillared butcher's shop, which was built in the eighteenth century. Morchard Bishop, to the west, boasts one of the longest rows of thatched cottages in England.

A less beautiful but still interesting large cob and thatched village is Newton Poppleford, a few miles north-west of Sidmouth, in the Otter valley. It has a variety of thatched buildings, including an old toll-house at the top of the long main street. Nearby, thatched guest-houses and cottages mingle. An antique and curio shop is thatched, as is the Exeter Inn, which has an unusually shaped roof. About a mile to the east of Newton Poppleford is Bowd. The local inn here has a beautiful long stretch of thatch and the ridge has been immaculately ornamented.

Otterton, which lies to the south on the River Otter, also has many cob and thatched dwellings. There are also several red sandstone houses. Some of the properties were built over 300 years ago. The mixture of the various types makes the village most attractive. Woodbury, to the west of both Otterton and Newton Poppleford, is also very pretty, with many thatched cob cottages. A beautiful view of the surrounding countryside can be obtained from Woodbury Common and also from Woodbury Castle, an Iron Age hillfort just outside the village.

Colaton Raleigh, near Newton Poppleford, has many good examples of cob and thatched cottages. As the name of the village suggests, it once had a connection with Sir Walter Raleigh. It was here that he was reputed to have introduced and planted the first potatoes in England, and his father was once the owner of the manor house. East Budleigh, close by, also has many thatched cottages, a brook, a series of footbridges and also a very close association with Raleigh. The church here was attended by his parents and inside can be seen the family pew and coat-of-arms. The house where Sir Walter was born in the middle of the sixteenth century, lies in a valley just a mile (1.5 km) outside the village on the west side. Called Hayes Barton, it is fairly large and thatched. The roof has a block ridge and three end gables, as it was built in an E-shape which together with the H-shape, was favoured in Elizabethan times when the popularity of houses built around courtyards declined. Hayes Barton has several chimneys intruding through the thatched roof and the main door has a pillared porch.

Bicton Gardens, just a mile (1.5 km) north of East Budleigh, are beautiful Italian-style gardens designed by André Le Nôtre, who also laid out the gardens at Versailles. There are many unique collections of trees, together with an American garden and a countryside museum. A miniature railway runs through the gardens.

Branscombe, a little further east on the other side of Sidmouth, has many cob and thatched cottages, especially in the upper part of the village, many of which are very old. The village has several streams and the setting is magnificent, as it is built on steep wooded slopes that fall away, through a chalk cliff valley, to the sea. The National Trust owns much of the surrounding land, including a thatched smithy, an old-fashioned bakery and some of the thatched cottages. The church is both very old and interesting. It is a small cruciform church, originally dedicated to St Winefrida, who died in the seventh century. The foundations are Saxon, but were built upon by the Normans. The thatched house directly opposite was originally a priest's house, and dates back to the thirteenth century. The other old thatched whitewashed cottages near the church, are typical of the general type found in Devon. The eaves above the upper windows are slightly raised in gentle curves, to maximise the available light in the upstairs rooms. Some of the cottages have thatched porches to complement the roofs.

Sidford is situated a couple of miles (3 km) north of Sidmouth and is therefore fairly close to Branscombe. The Blue Ball Inn is thatched and the roof is fitted, rather unusually, with rainwater guttering. No doubt this protects the inn's customers from water drips from the eaves during and immediately after rainstorms. The inn has a wooden upstairs front section, with doors set in the middle that could be opened to take in deliveries of stock. There are many rows of thatched cottages to be seen in the village and also several larger thatched houses, which are often fitted with thatched porches.

Fairly close to Sidford and Branscombe but to the north-east, is the village of Colyford, which has many terraces of thatched cottages. There are also several larger houses adorned with neat raised ridges on their roofs. Many of the bottom ridge edges have been cut with scallops and points but the occasional house has unusually long points mixed with the scallop and crescent shapes. There are also thatched farms, thatched guest-houses and a thatched restaurant in Colyford.

A few miles north-west of Colyford is Honiton, which gave its name to the famous Honiton lace, which was made in the surrounding area up to the end of the nineteenth century. The main part of this small market town consists of a long Georgian street, with many antique shops. However, there are a few thatched cottages on the west side of the town. Some of these were built in the sixteenth century, probably at the same time as the nearby chapel of the St Margaret's Almshouses. These are of interest because they were previously used as a leper hospital. Just outside Honiton, at Wilmington on the Axminster road, can be found a beautiful thatched house, now the Home Farm Hotel, which stands in several acres of its own grounds. It was constructed in the sixteenth century and inside are several original beamed ceilings.

About 4 miles (6.5 km) north-west of Honiton lies the village of Broadhembury. An important archaeological site, Hembury Hillfort, is located just outside the village. It dates back to around 4000 BC and during the Iron Age a huge earthwork was built there. Broadhembury has some lovely trees and a stream by the churchyard, and nearly all the houses and cottages are beautifully thatched. They are arranged in two terraces, which lead down to a small hump-backed bridge and represent one of the best collections of quality thatching in Devon. Most of the cob walls are coloured white and date back to the seventeenth century. The village also has an interesting fifteenth-century priest's house, called Church Gate, near the church. The roof is divided into two sections, one half thatched and the other slated, although it is unlikely that either material was used on the original roof. Augustus Toplady, who wrote the hymn 'Rock of Ages' became vicar of the church in 1758. During his career, he had many disputes with the Methodist preacher, Charles Wesley. The village pub is thought to have been the church house.

About 3 miles (4.8 km) south-west of Broadhembury can be found the village of Talaton. This has many pleasant thatched cottages and a thatched school-house. Gittisham, a few miles away, to the south-west of Honiton, also has many thatched roofs. Although it is in a hollow, there is a wonderful view of the surrounding countryside from the top of the nearby hill.

Another good example of quality group thatching can be seen in the pretty little village of North Bovey on Dartmoor. There are many excellent thatched roofs in this tiny village, which also has a pleasant village green, an ancient cross, a fifteenth-century church and an old village water pump. There are also some fine oak trees by the green.

About 3 miles (4.8 km) away is the village of Lustleigh, which has always been esteemed for the quality of its thatching. It would be difficult to find better examples of a group of thatched granite-walled cottages anywhere in the West Country. Surface granite from the moors is widely used in the region, in contrast to the cob walls common in most parts of Devon. However, there are also some modern houses in the village. One of the best views on Dartmoor can be obtained from a hill just to the west of the village, over Lustleigh Cleave, which covers an expanse of magnificent granite rocks, river and wooded slopes. One of the rocks at Lustleigh Cleave is known as the Nutcracker Rock. It is said that at one time it was possible to push the rock a little way with a gentle touch to crack a nut and the rock would then roll back to its original position!

Widecombe in the Moor lies a little south-west of Lustleigh, and also has a lot of stone and thatch. There is also a lovely church with a granite tower. However, Widecombe is perhaps best known for its association with the song 'Widecombe Fair', which tells the story of Uncle Tom Cobleigh and Tom Pearse's grey mare. The village has a magnificent skyline view of boulders and rocks. Buckland in the Moor, a short distance south, has an attractive moor and woodland setting that makes a perfect background for its collection of fine thatched cottages, built on undulating ground.

Nearby on Dartmoor is Poundsgate, which has several thatched farms and also a thatched post office, and Holne, just a little to the south, has several very attractive thatched dwellings. A thatched rectory stands about a mile (1.8 km) down the lane from the church. This was the birthplace of Charles Kingsley, who became well known not only as a preacher of Christian Socialism but also as a famous writer of novels. A very old inn can be found near the church and the main cottages. Nearby are the magnificent Hembury Woods, owned by the National Trust.

On the northern edge of Dartmoor, the village of Throwleigh has many thatched cottages with walls of granite. It also has an old farmhouse called The Barton which, although long and low, has huge stone mullioned windows. An old thatched priest's house stands near the church and the ancient cross.

Close by lies the small village of Sticklepath, which also has many thatched cottages as well as an interesting nineteenth-century foundry, now owned by the National Trust. The adjoining village of South Zeal

Buckland in the Moor, Dartmoor

also has several thatched cottages. It was once a copper mining village. There is a very old and unusual inn in the village, which was formerly a manor house. South Tawton, adjoining the villages of Sticklepath and South Zeal, has several thatched cottages grouped by the granite-constructed church. The thatched church house has an arched stairway as a peculiar feature.

The pretty village of Drewsteignton, also on the north of Dartmoor, consists of a pleasant arrangement of a hilltop church and many thatched cob cottages, all gathered around the square. A couple of miles (3 km) outside the village is an ancient burial chamber known as Spinster's Rock. This was erected from four gigantic stones, three of them supporting the fourth. The arrangement forms the only remaining *cromlech* in Devon.

Also on the northern side of Dartmoor, but nearer to Exeter, is the village of Dunsford, which has many cob and thatched cottages and also a medieval church. From the top of the church tower there is a magnificent view not only of the thatched roofs but also of the surrounding countryside. Steps Bridge, a well-known beauty spot, lies just to the south of the village where the River Teign flows and where there is a spectacular gorge.

145

Moretonhampstead is a short distance to the south-west and has a thatched granite almshouse built in 1637. The long building has low granite mullioned casement windows and a Tudor-style stone drip-mound runs along the top. A short way to the east is Dunchideock. This charming place has an old post office with a thatched roof and verandah. Wooden pillars support the overhanging thatched roof. The village is rather strung out and a most unusual tall tower called Lawrence Castle overlooks it. It was built in the eighteenth century as a memorial to General Lawrence who served with the British Army in India.

Broadclyst is 4 miles (6.5 km) to the north-east of Exeter. The village is particularly pretty with many thatched white cob cottages to be seen. There are also several historic houses in the area, which incidentally is the centre of Devon's cider industry. The National Trust owns the mill, which stands by the River Clyst. Clyst Heyes, also near Exeter, over-looks the River Culme. There is a beautiful large thatched house on the riverbank and it is of unusual architectural interest. The building was started just before the end of the fifteenth century but took about another half-century to complete. It has a mixture of early Tudor and Elizabethan architecture and the thatched roof has been well preserved and renovated many times.

Silverton, about 6 miles (9.5 km) to the north of Exeter, is notewor-thy for a different reason. The collection of thatched cob cottages in the village was built at different periods, from the sixteenth to the nineteenth centuries. A little to the north of Silverton, by the side of the River Exe, is Bickleigh. The many thatched, whitewashed cottages make a photogenic picture by the river bridge and beneath the wooded hills overlooking the village. Bickleigh Castle, near the village, dates back to the twelfth century, but it was reconstructed in the seventeenth century. It has a thatched Jacobean wing. There is also a Norman chapel by the river and a rather grand gatehouse guards it.

South of Exeter lies Mamhead about 3 miles (4.8 km) north of Dawlish. It is worth a brief mention because of the lovely thatched gatehouse lodges at the entrance to its park. A few miles away, south of Teignmouth and nestling in a deep valley, is the village of Stokeinteignhead. There are many beautiful thatched cottages in the picturesque village and the church is worth visiting. It dates back to the fourteenth century and contains a 500-year-old rood screen and a mosaic-paved sanctuary.

Cockington, near Torquay

Further south, at Cockington, is an exceptionally well known and lovely thatched village. It can be visited via an unusual 2-mile (3 km) ride by carriage from the seafront at Torquay; alternatively, it can be reached on foot via the water meadows. The thatched roofs in this delightful place form a big attraction to tourists. Perhaps the best-known building is the thatched forge, which has three rough timber pillars supporting the overhanging roof. A replica of this forge is often seen on horse brasses. It dates back to at least the fourteenth century but ended its trade as a blacksmith's shop in 1971. Up to that time, the farrier made miniature horseshoes, which proved very popular souvenirs. Visitors also used to tuck little messages under the thatch, until the practice was stopped as being hazardous to the structure.

Traditionally, the blacksmith always lived in the nearby thatched Rose Cottage, which dates back to at least the sixteenth century. It has had a variety of uses since, including a handloom weaver's premises, a post office and village store. The weavers moved in 1939 to Weaver's Cottage, near the forge. Another interesting building in the village is the fifteenth-century Court Cottage, which was built as a long house, in

Thatched forge, Cockington

which both the farmer and his animals lived under the same roof. It has served many other purposes since, including a courthouse, a village school and later a shop.

Cockington Court, near the village, is a sixteenth-century manor house with a Georgian frontage. Part of the house has now been converted into a restaurant. There is a thatched lodge with overhanging upper-storey rooms, supported by timber, at the entrance to the drive to the house. Fire destroyed the original lodge and the present one was built on the same site in 1710. It has Gothic windows with straight heads rather than arches. A village cricket square completes a typical English scene in the grounds of Cockington Court. The Drum Inn in the village was described on pages 133–4, as has the Gamekeeper's Cottage near the lake.

Another delightful thatched inn can be found at Dartington, near Totnes. Called the Cott Inn, it has one very long stretch of thatch which sweeps smoothly and low at the end of the building. It was originally thatched with marsh water reed obtained from Dorset. It was established during the early part of the fourteenth century and has low timbered ceilings. It is also well worth visiting Dartington Hall and its lovely grounds, which are extensive. This used to be a medieval estate, but it was converted in 1925 into an arts, education and later rural industries centre. The gardens and parts of the hall are open to visitors.

The village of Dittisham, near Dartmouth, has some very pretty thatched cottages along the road leading to the ferry. It is also well known for its plum orchards. It has a peaceful setting with good riverside views. One of the oldest buildings is the 500-year-old Smugglers Cottage, which overlooks the River Dart. It was built with sturdy stone walls and is now thatched with Austrian water reed, instead of the original combed wheat reed. The church at Dittisham is very old and parts of it date back to Saxon times.

At Slapton, a few miles south of Dittisham on the coast, a most unusual long causeway road separates the sea and pebble beach from the large freshwater lake at Slapton Ley, a nature reserve for many bird and fish species. It once provided a source of water reeds that were used locally for thatching purposes. Although a few reeds are still cut, they are no longer used for thatching; discharge of nitrogen enriched water into the Ley has made the reeds grow too tall and soft. The long pebble beach at Slapton was used by the Americans as a training ground before the D-Day invasion. A memorial that stands on the beach was presented by the United States Army to the local villagers, who were evacuated to allow the training to take place. The occasional thatched house can be seen at Slapton, along with other roof types.

A short distance to the south is the village of Stokenham. This has many thatched terraced cottages, again mixed with other roof types. The Coachman's Arms separates the rooftop mixture in the main street. Several miles to the west, at the tip of Bigbury Bay, lies Hope Cove, including the hamlets of Inner Hope and Outer Hope. The former has a few cottages with quaint old patched thatched roofs. Most have small cobbled fronts, well decked with flower tubs in the summer.

Close to Hope is the village of Thurlestone, which has many thatched cottages with pretty gardens. The village also has an exceptionally good golf course and beach. The grounds of the Old Rectory at Thurlestone are often open to the public during the summer.

Along the coastline towards Plymouth, at the mouth of the River Avon, you will find Bantham. The Old Boathouse, which guards the narrow channel entrance, overlooking a quay and a small beach, has a picturesque thatched roof. The main Bantham beach is found over the headland, and is used for surfing. The area is popular with ramblers; scenic cliffs form a lovely background.

Ringmore is another lovely village just to the west of Bantham with many thatched cottages. Some are unusual, having tall crooked chimneys. Some of the cottages have slate roofs, a mixture of materials that make a pleasing picture. A little further west, towards Plymouth, is Holbeton, which also has many attractive thatched roof houses, some with raised ridges with points, others with flush ridges. The fourteenth-century church overlooks the village and it is worth a visit to see the unusual carvings and figures.

On the extreme opposite side of the county, in the north of Devon, are the villages of Croyde and Georgeham, just north-west of Barnstaple. Both have several quaint thatched cottages and in Croyde you will also find the Thatched Barn Inn, on Hobbs Hill. Near the villages are a bird sanctuary and nature reserve; also fairly close are the huge sand dunes and long beaches of Braunton Burrows and Saunton Sands.

Near Ilfracombe is Lee. Many visitors take a boat service there that operates from Illfracombe. Lee has quite a famous thatched cottage, called the Old Maids of Lee. It is open to the public and contains a fine collection of old dresses. Further attractions of the hamlet are the splendid trees and fuchsias.

Further to the west along the coast, near the car-free village of Clovelly, can be found the hamlets of Buck's Mills and Horns Cross. The former offers an attractive collection of thatched cottages with a view over the predominantly rocky and shingle beach below. The coastal roads in the vicinity pass through pleasantly wooded country. Horns Cross has an attractive thatched inn, a long building with a continuous stretch of thatch and a small separate thatched roof for the entrance porch. It is called the Hoops Inn, and an old-fashioned open coach forms an interesting feature in the garden. Another hotel, the Woodford Bridge Hotel, can be found at Milton Damerel, 15 miles (24 km) south of Horns Cross. It is a thatched fifteenth-century coaching inn and the River Torridge flows through its gardens.

The site of Chittlehampton, to the south-east of Barnstaple, dates back to Saxon times, and the village, built in the early part of the sixteenth century, claims to be one of the most attractive in Devon. The church stands on one side of the large village square and the remaining sides consist of thatched cob cottages. Many pilgrimages to the church were made in the Middle Ages, to visit the shrine there, dedicated to a Celtic martyr.

About 12 miles (19 km) to the south is the large village of Winkleigh, which also has many thatched cob buildings; several surround the village church. In the square, the Winkleigh Hotel overlooks the King's Arms, which has a thatched roof, part of which sweeps down to the top of the ground floor level. 3 or 4 miles (5–6 km) west of Winkleigh is Iddesleigh, which has an unusual charm because of the high density of thatched roofs that meet the eye in all directions. There appear to be rows of thatched cottages everywhere, most with white or brown walls. There is also an old thatched inn in the village.

Also of interest is the small town of Hatherleigh, south-west of Iddesleigh. It boasts a main street consisting of thatched cottages, with peculiar bulging walls and unusual chimneys. There are three rivers nearby that are popular for angling and there are also stretches of moorland.

North-east of Winkleigh is the little town of Chulmleigh, whose Barnstaple Inn has a thatched roof. It was built over 300 years ago and Charles I is reputed to have stayed there. About 6 miles (9.5 km) to the east of Chulmleigh can be found the village of East Worlington, which has a beautiful thatched rectory and nearby a thatched tithe barn, which is used as the village hall. Witheridge lies a further couple of miles to the east and has an attractive arrangement of several thatched houses and a church gathered around a square.

About two miles (3 km) south-east of Winkleigh is Bondleigh, which has some eye-catching cottages. These can be seen on the way to Sampford Courtenay, about 3 miles (4.8 km) south, towards Okehampton. Sampford Courtenay gained a place in history when a rebellion took place at the church house in 1549 against the introduction of the new English Prayer Book by Edward VI. Many of the villagers were hanged when the rebellion was quelled. In addition to its historical interest, the village justifies a visit to see its many thatched cob cottages, all tastefully decorated and enhanced below with well-kept gardens.

Going north again, on the northern coast of Exmoor at Lynmouth, there is a beautiful historic row of thatched cottages along the harbour. The thatched Rising Sun Hotel also overlooks the harbour and forms part of the terrace; the main roof has an attractive ridge with points and a separate thatched porch guards an entrance to the hotel. The terrace has a perfect setting by the sea and the village has a towering ravine as a background. There was a terrible flood disaster here in 1952, when the swollen river swept boulders through the village. Over 7 inches (178 mm) of rain fell in a few hours and the situation was worsened by high tides. It caused the death of thirty people. The River Lyn has been flood-protected since the tragedy and the destroyed homes have been rebuilt.

In the heart of Exmoor rests Brendon, which has many thatched, whitewashed cottages. A bridge constructed in medieval times can also be seen at the village. It was originally built to allow packhorses to cross the East Lyn River. On the southern side of Exmoor, Molland offers the thatched London Inn for hospitality. The interior of the nearby church was tastefully restored in Georgian times, and it is fitted with several tall box pews.

About 4 miles (6.5 km) south-west of Molland is Bishop's Nympton, whose long, sloping main street has many attractive thatched cottages. The church has a magnificent tower built in the fifteenth century.

Finally, in the far west of Devon, you will find Lifton, which has a few thatched roofs. It is interesting that marsh water reeds were used here, rather than the more usual combed Devon wheat reed.

CORNWALL

The number of thatched buildings found in Cornwall is very small compared to Devon, although thatch was once widespread. However, there are several attractive ones still to be found, some steeped in history. Most of the cottage walls in Cornwall are built from the local stone or cob and most are to be found in the southern parts of the county.

Veryan, south-east of Truro by the Roseland peninsula, contains several thatched buildings of different types. The most famous are the Round Houses, which have hemispherical roofs. There are five of these, two at each end of the village and one in the centre. They were

One of the round houses at Veryan

built between 1805 and 1811 and each cost £42. Most are painted white and each bears a cross on the top, fitted on the apexes and supported by metal caps. There is no obvious ridge on one of the houses, but the others all have a small ridge. The roofs of the pair at the top end of the village differ slightly. The pair at the other end of the village have thatched porches. There is a thatched restaurant near this latter pair and opposite is a house, also thatched. There is a mixture of long-straw and reed thatching to be seen in the village. The church at Veryan has a small but pretty garden lake by its side. Towards the Round Houses at the top end of the village is another restaurant, the Toby Jug, where both accommodation and cream teas are usually available. This restaurant itself is not thatched but a thatched house overlooks it.

St Mawes is fairly nearby, also in Roseland. It claims to be the warmest place in England, and has a beautiful sheltered position. It has some well-kept and delightful thatched houses overlooking the water's edge. Some are quite large, detached and set in their own grounds. One can get a closer look at their thatch along the hilly road on the other side of the bay leading to St Mawes Castle. A few of the houses have thatched porches bordering the pavement. The walls of one are completely but attractively covered with ivy, well trimmed so that it does not intrude onto the thatched roof.

The castle at St Mawes, built by Henry VIII as a military fortress, is well preserved. Across the water, Pendennis Castle can also be seen and the two castles guard the entrance to the Fal Estuary. There is a regular ferry service from St Mawes to Falmouth. During the journey across the bay, both castles can be seen, as well as the thatched houses along the seafront of St Mawes.

It is also possible to take a boat trip to visit the old thatched Smuggler's

Cottage at Tolverne to the north of St Mawes. It is very pretty and rests at the water's edge of King Harry's Reach. This is an extension of the Carrick Roads, across the waters of which a car ferry service operates. The roof of the Smuggler's Cottage at Toverne has a raised ridge, cut with points along its bottom edge. It has a thatched porch and also a pretty thatched canopy covering the well in the garden. The cottage has served as a restaurant offering excellent Cornish teas. Its beautiful water-side position has also been featured on television.

The Carrick Roads are a very wide and deep stretch of water but they can easily be crossed by car ferry to visit the village of Feock. This has a very pleasant position, as it is bordered not only by the Carrick Roads but also by Restronguet Creek. The village church is interesting, as the tower and belfry are separate from the main church. Although this appears somewhat unusual, it is found in other parts of Cornwall. There are two thatched cottages opposite the tower and belfry.

At nearby Come-to-Good, there is an old Quaker meeting-house in a secluded lane by the green amid trees. It was built with cob in 1710 and has a steep open-timbered thatched roof. The house was originally very small, 20 × 27 feet (6 × 8 metres) but it has since been extended. A catslide thatched roof was first added to cover an attached stable and a thatched porch was later built in 1967. There are about 400 such Quaker meeting-houses in England, but the one at Come-to-Good is believed to be the oldest. The building has shuttered casement windows.

Gweek dominates the end reach of the Helford tidal stretch of water south-west of Falmouth. An unusually shaped thatched roof can be seen on an octagonal house standing at the corner of the main street. Gweek also has a seal sanctuary, and the many quiet creeks in the vicinity are ideal for bird spotters; herons can be seen. Just 5 miles (8 km) to the east can be found Helford, which is reputed to be one of the prettiest villages in England. It has a large number of palms and beau-tiful flower-beds, as well as many white thatched cottages built on each side of a very narrow creek. There are also a few houses with slates on their roofs, which make a contrast with the thatch. Steep hills rise on either side of the village to complete the scenic picture. To the west of Gweek lies Helston, once one of the four stannary or coinage towns, where all smelted tin was brought to be tested for quality and taxed. There are a few thatched cottages there including the pretty Whitstone Cottage, built with stone and cob.

Further south, at the Lizard, the coastal village of Coverack was formerly a smuggling stronghold. Many of the houses have thatched roofs, as the village faces east and is sheltered from the prevailing west winds. It is interesting to note that thatch is rarely encountered in Cornwall in villages facing west and thus exposed to severe weather. It is therefore never necessary to use weighted ropes to hold the roofs down, as is done in certain coastal areas of Ireland and the Isle of Man. Towards the north of the Lizard, at St Anthony, can be found Penhaligon's Cottage built of local sandstone and with a thatched roof.

Cadgwith Cove also enjoys a sheltered position and many thatched stone cottages are found there. The roofs all appear to be at different levels, owing to the hilly nature of the streets. The thatch in the village is reed. The cove at Cadgwith is tiny but one of the most picturesque in the county. Incidentally, this fishing village is an excellent place to buy lobsters and crabs. Just south of the village a magnificent cliff-top chasm, called the Devil's Frying Pan, can be seen. It was formed when a sea cave collapsed. The approach to Cadgwith is down a very steep and narrow lane, at the top of which is Ruan Minor, which also has a few thatched houses. The church there has an ivy-covered tower, which was added in the fifteenth century to enlarge the original very small church. Cadgwith Cove and Ruan Minor are both close to the Lizard Point, where the famous lighthouse can be visited. Very near to Cadgwith Cove and the lighthouse is another minute inlet called Church Cove. There are some pretty thatched cottages in its immediate vicinity and also some farms, to remind one that there is agriculture in this apparently bleak area of the Lizard. There is a serpentine rock souvenir shop at Church Cove.

On the northern side of Cornwall is the old village of Crantock, south of the River Gannel. The famous surfing resort of Newquay is just 4 miles (6.4 km) away. Crantock was renowned for its smugglers, many of whom were reputed to have frequented the 400-year-old local inn, the Old Albion and to have stored their booty there. The inn has a thatched roof and a block ridge with undercut edge points. The ridge also has the fairly common ornamentation of horizontal liggers and cross-rods. In the churchyard near the inn, are the old village stocks. The last man placed in them was reputed to be a smuggler's son, in 1817. Trebellan, about 2 miles (3 km) south of Crantock, also claims a tradition of smuggling. The Smuggler's Den is a thatched farmhouse restaurant. The quaint building encloses a small courtyard on three sides, so the roof is in three main sections. A chimney-stack stands at each gable end.

Further east along the northern coast is the popular but small seaside resort of Bude and just a couple of miles away towards the Devon border is the little town of Stratton. This hillside town has some quaint old thatched properties along its narrow streets. A manor house that later became the Tree Inn once had an occupant who led the royalists to victory at nearby Stamford Hill in 1643. The pretty village of Poughill, adjoining Stamford Hill, contains several thatched cottages and delightful gardens. The church is interesting because it has two large medieval wall paintings. The present church dates back to the end of the fourteenth century.

Marhamchurch is also very close to Bude. It is a delightful place, with many thatched cottages surrounding its large square.

Somerset

There is a host of thatched buildings in Somerset, the walls of many of which are constructed of the local yellow Ham stone, quarried from Ham Hill and cut into suitably sized building blocks. Red sandstone from the Quantocks, is also often used. There are, in addition, cottages built of cob. In the neighbourhood of Minehead, on the northern coast, there are several groups of beautiful thatched cottages in the various villages and hamlets. In the higher town area of Minehead itself are some delightful red and yellow cottages with thatched roofs, many of which line the steep steps leading to the large Church of St Michael. The steps are narrow and surfaced with tiles and cobblestones. The cottage chimneys are tall and they stand at the side of the cottages, intruding a little into the street. There are many strange-shaped cottages in the area and the view looking back over the winding way to the top of the hill is very picturesque.

Selworthy, situated about 4 miles (6.5 km) west of Minehead, is famed for its beautiful sheltered setting and most of the houses in the village were originally thatched with combed wheat reed. A particularly lovely group of seven old cottages can be found by the little green, near a stream and surrounded by trees. They have latticed windows

An unusual roof level at Selworthy

and thatched gable porches. Large chimney-stacks stand and bulge to ground level at the sides of the cottages, which is common in this region. They were often used in association with bread ovens inside the cottages. The white-painted church at Selworthy gives a magnificent uninterrupted view over Exmoor. Another building of interest is a fourteenth-century tithe barn at the rectory.

A couple of miles (3 km) to the south-east of Selworthy is Tivington. There is a fifteenth-century restored thatched chapel in the village, adjoined by a cottage that was originally a priest's house and which shares the same roof. Allerford, 1½ miles (2.5 km) to the west of Selworthy, has some pretty red stone thatched cottages, with exterior bread oven chimneys. The house that served as the village school is also thatched. The cottages are gathered near an old two-arched packhorse bridge and a beautiful walnut tree. There are more such trees at Bossington, about a mile (1.5 km) away. The cottages here are also mainly thatched and their upper windows are tiny. Lynch, which separates Allerford from Bossington, has a quaint group of thatched cottages standing near the old mill and close to the manor house and a chapel built in the sixteenth century.

The little hamlet of Horner, about 1 mile (1.5 km) south of Allerford, has an attractive group of thatched cottages, overlooked by beautiful woodland. A small packhorse bridge spans the stream at the bottom of the wooded cleft. The village of Luccombe is a mile (1.5 km) away and also has several thatched cottages near the churchyard. Most are white and some again show evidence of bread ovens.

Porlock rests between Exmoor and the sea. It is a large village and an excellent location for touring and horse-riding. It also has a good collection of thatched cottages near the church, the walls of most of which are either stone or cob. The row of thatched cottages at Porlock Weir have chimneys protruding from their sides. In this design, typical of many south-western counties, the chimneys have to be exceptionally tall to clear the top of the thatch safely. The spire on the parish church at Porlock is unusual in that it is made of wood covered with shingle. The streets of Porlock are very twisty and there is a rather notorious steep hill to test the motorist. The quaint Ship Inn in the High Street once had the poet Southey as a customer, while there, he composed a sonnet on Porlock.

The Royal Oak Inn at Winsford, on Exmoor

The village of Winsford borders the River Exe to the south of Porlock and Minehead. Several attractive thatched cottages are to be seen in the centre of the village. The twelfth-century Royal Oak Inn, a former farmhouse and dairy, also has a thatched roof which sweeps with a good overhang to protect the upper-storey window, which is built out from the front main wall. Near the inn is an old packhorse bridge and fishing is available in the locality. Winsford's position in the Exmoor National Park ensures a beautiful rugged moorland view.

The town of Dunster, about 3 miles (4.8 km) south-east of Minehead, boasts an interesting collection of medieval buildings, including a castle, an old mill and a tithe barn. The castle, built during the eleventh century on the top of a hill, has been continuously inhabited since that time. An intriguing folly, known as Conygar Tower, dominates the other end of the High Street. It was built during the eighteenth century on the top of a tall mound. There is also a pretty group of thatched cottages near the old packhorse bridge. There are many unusually shaped buildings, but perhaps the most peculiar is the one on the southern corner of the High Street, which has overhanging storeys and tiled roof. It was formerly a priory guest-house. There is also an old yarn market in Dunster and nearby an ancient inn.

A little to the east of Dunster on the coast can be found the village of East Quantoxhead. There are several thatched cottages in the village and a pleasant church and pond. The beach can easily be reached on foot from the village.

A further 8 miles (13 km) to the east lies the charming village of Stogursey. The main street has a mixture of several types of dwelling, including Georgian houses and also some neat thatched cottages. The church is very ancient, the Normans having built on Anglo-Saxon foundations. The remains of a priory building that stood near the church now constitute part of a reconstructed dovecot on the neighbouring farm. A short distance away are the ruins of a Norman castle.

The village of Crowcombe, nestling at the base of the Quantocks a few miles to the south of East Quantoxhead, has many good examples of thatched cottages. It also has a red sandstone church and a fine example of a church house that dates back to 1515. A thirteenth- or fourteenth-century stone market cross can also be found in the centre of the village.

In the Mendips, to the north of Wookey Hole, is the old mining centre of Priddy. An annual sheep fair has been held there in August for many

Sheep hurdle stack, Priddy

centuries. A thatched shelter protects the old traditional hurdles that are always stored on the village green. It was believed locally that the continuous presence of the shelter ensured that the village would continue to hold the fair. A plaque on it states, 'These hurdles are a symbolic reconstruction of the original collection store to form pens for the sheep fair which moved from Wells to Priddy in 1384, at the outbreak of the Black Death. The Fair is now held annually on the nearest Wednesday to the original date of the 21 August.' The local Mendip Society and the Mendip Hills Service renewed the 130 ash hurdles in 1997.

Mells, about 4 miles (6.4) south-east of Radstock, can claim to be

An ornamental garden well, Mells

one of the loveliest villages in Somerset. It contains several stone-walled thatched cottages, mingling among small greens, a stream and trees. Many of the cottages are built of yellow stone, which makes an attractive contrast to the grey of some of the others. Most are two-storeyed, owing to the higher load-carrying capacity of a stone wall compared to a cob one. There is also an Elizabethan gabled manor house in the village, which was formerly occupied by a member of the Horner family. One of the family was thought to be the subject of the famous nursery rhyme 'Little Jack Horner'. The church at Mells contains a Horner Chapel and several mementoes of the Horner family.

Taunton, the county town, has on Hamilton Road an interesting long thatched building, surrounded by lawns, called St Margaret's, which was once a leper hospital. Thatch was probably used because it could easily be fumigated and also pulled away, if necessary, for destruction. In those days, it was thought that thatch could spread leprosy, so there must have been some difficulty in persuading someone to carry out the task. The building was later reconstructed as an almshouse and has more recently been used as offices. There are other old almshouses in Taunton.

Old Prospect Farmhouse, Mells

Walton, about 3 miles (4.8 km) south-west of Glastonbury, has a thatched rectory, built in the fifteenth century. Another 3 miles (4 km) to the south-west is the windmill described on pages 138–9 dominating the scene at High Ham. A thatched late medieval priest's house stands at Muchelney, south of High Ham. It is now owned by the National Trust. It was built in the fifteenth century with stone obtained from the local quarries and has been little altered since that time, other than the later construction of an upper floor dividing the great hall. The building is low and has beautiful stone-mullioned windows. Several chimney-pots on the roof break through the line of the thatched ridge, which is simply ornamented with cross-rods and liggers. Many of the houses in the village also have mullioned windows and it is thought that these were originally salvaged from the ruins of the old abbey.

The village of Pitney, about 3 miles (4.8 km) away to the north-east has many thatched stone-walled cottages around the church, the small town of Martock to the south also has many old thatched houses constructed of stone. There are several other old buildings in the town and some date back to the fourteenth century.

At Ilminster, a fine row of typical West Country whitewashed thatched cottages can be found fairly near the colonnaded market house in the square. The white cottages make a refreshing contrast to the many yellow Ham stone buildings in the immediate vicinity. The village of Stocklinch, a couple of miles (3 km) away, contains some more warm, mellow Ham stone buildings. Many are pretty cottages topped with thatched roofs. An old church stands among them and there is also, rather unusually, a second church in the village. An old thatched farmhouse can be found approximately a mile (1.5 km) from Stocklinch at Ilford Bridges. It is of interest because it is thought that Judge Jeffreys, the famous hanging judge, once used it as a temporary court.

About 4 miles (6.5 km) from Ilminster and about the same distance from Crewkerne is the beautiful village of Hinton St George, centred around a wide main street. The thatched old four-gabled Priory Cottage can be found there, together with many Tudor, Jacobean, Georgian and a few Victorian buildings. Many of the houses are constructed of Ham stone. Priory Cottage is opposite the medieval cross in the main street. An unusual ceremony takes place in the village each year, on the last Thursday of October. The clocks have then normally changed and it becomes dark early enough for the 'Punky' celebration to be held. This is a warm-up for Hallowe'en and the children of the village have a procession through the streets, traditionally with lanterns made of turnips and mangolds. The ceremony is unique to Hinton St George.

Yeovil has a magnificent beauty spot known as Nine Springs, at the foot of Henford Hill. The name originates from nine separate springs that feed a lake surrounded by beautiful trees, shrubs and many small paths. A delightful rustic thatched cottage once overlooked the scene. In addition to the main hipped thatched roof, it had a separate stretch of thatch covering a timbered verandah. The walls were also made of timber. Sadly, it was allowed to decay and no longer exists. However, a smaller version was made and stands as a folly at Aldon Lodge, in the grounds of a nearby house.

About 6 miles to the west of Yeovil, in the village of Stoke Sub Hamdon, a new fifty-property thatched estate has been built, using local Ham stone, and North Coker, on the southern outskirts of Yeovil, boasts an imposing thatched manor house, Hymerford House. The property dates back to the fifteenth century and Gothic stone mullioned windows harmonize with its rendered stone built walls; guttering collects the rainwater discharged from its large thatched roof.

Just to the north of Yeovil, Mudford has a former blacksmith's premises, now called Church Cottage. During its restoration, it gained a new roof, after the pantiles were stripped away and replaced with a thatch of Austrian marsh reed. The former smithy had originally been thatched but certainly not with imported reed. Castle Cary, also to the north of Yeovil, harbours a very ancient thatched inn, the George Hotel, which dates to 1452. Stones salvaged from a Norman castle were used to build it; the foundations of the destroyed castle still survive nearby. The inglenook fireplace in the inn has a supporting timber prop taken from an elm tree, which reputedly grew in AD 900. The thatched roof has a verge of stone slates at the eaves over rainwater guttering. The strange beehive structure opposite the inn by the market hall served as the village lock-up in 1779.

9

Thatched Buildings in East Anglia

The counties of East Anglia contain a large number of thatched buildings. When they were built, the huge growths of Norfolk reed and sedge ensured a ready supply of materials. The introduction of pantiles, manufactured from the local clay, offered an additional choice in the eighteenth century. The walls of the buildings were also built from locally available products. Many of the thatched cottage walls were constructed of brick and flint. The bricks were originally made from the local clay and the flints obtained from the chalk deposits in the region. The clay bricks or lumps were unfired, as it was not until the seventeenth century that the modern type of fired brick became widely available in England. Many houses were also built of timber, owing to the vast expanses of woodlands in the area, which yielded an unlimited supply.

A large number of houses were constructed in the timber-framed style. It is of interest that the introduction of timber-framed houses in Elizabethan times was to allow the weight of the roof to be more easily carried and transmitted to the ground. This is not so important with a lighter thatched roof as with a heavy tiled one. However, the use of a timber frame allowed the walls to be in-filled between the timber boxes with a variety of materials such as wattle and daub. Flint and chalk mixtures were also used as the in-filling in East Anglia. In the late seventeenth century, it became more common to use bricks as the in-filling in many regions of England, but it was found unnecessary to bond them together because the timber-frame construction carried the main load. The bricks were often arranged in a herring-bone pattern to obtain watertight joints.

NORFOLK

Norwich forms a good centre for the Norfolk Broads, and Salhouse Broad lies to the north-east of the city. The area provides many acres of reed swamps that yield material suitable for thatching, although the total acreage has declined considerably during the last few decades. The picturesque village of Salhouse overlooks the lovely waters of the Broad and its All Saints Church has a thatched roof and an arcade which dates back to the fourteenth century. The church also boasts a small sanctus bell attached to the rood screen. It is thought that only one other such bell exists. It is interesting to recall that, during the Middle Ages, thatch was first introduced as a temporary roof-covering for churches. Today there are still many churches scattered throughout the countryside with thatched roofs, the majority in East Anglia. In addition to the church, there are some beautiful Norfolk reed thatched cottages to be seen at Salhouse. Several of the roofs are finished with delightful and richly ornamented ridges.

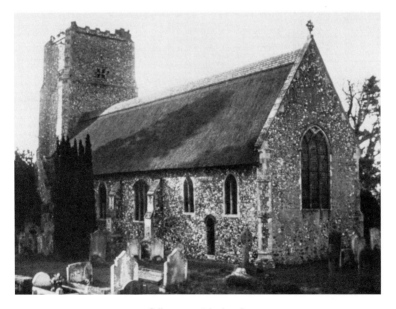

Salhouse parish church

Horning, the popular Broadland yachting and angling centre, is very close to Salhouse. Ye Olde Ferry Inn, a well-known and friendly visiting place near the Horning ferry, has a magnificent Norfolk reed roof. The thatching, in an unusual two-stepped layer, was done by fixing a wide apron of thatch below the block ridge. It finishes about halfway down the roof and the edge is cut in line with the bottoms of the dormer windows, which have small aprons below them. The ridge of the roof has scallops and points and this form of ornamentation is an exceptionally common feature in East Anglia. A further stretch of thatch, in the shape of a sectioned cone, shelters some circular bay windows abutting from the wall of the inn, under a gable end of the thatch. There are several other interesting and charming thatched buildings in Horning. Typical of these is the thatched barn that stands at Horning Hall, about 1½ miles (2.5 km) to the east of the church. This thatched building was formerly used as the chapel for St James's Hospital, which no longer exists.

The neat little village of Woodbastwick sits between Salhouse and Horning. It contains some delightful thatched houses, although there are some pantile roofed properties as well. It also has a thatched shelter on the green and a small thatched church. Another village in the area is

A thatched shelter at Woodbastwick

Coltishall, by the River Bure just to the north-west of Salhouse. Attractive scenery surrounds it, including some lovely pine trees. The Church of St John the Baptist has a continuous thatched roof, sweeping over both chancel and nave. It is rather unusual in that it contains some windows that date from Saxon times. Just outside the village is another church in a ruined state.

Another quaint thatched church can be found in the tiny village of Hoveton St Peter, which lies about 3 miles (4.8 km) to the east of Coltishall. The church, like the village, is rather small; it is approximately 40 feet (12 metres) long and about 18 feet (5.5 metres) wide. The church at Irstead, a further 3 miles (4.8 km) to the east, also has a thatched roof and the exposed underside of the thatch can be seen from inside..

Potter Heigham is a popular yachting centre on the banks of the River Thurne. The Church of St Nicholas in the old village has a thatched roof over the nave and chancel. It also has a round Norman tower. In addition, the village has a rather unique three-arched bridge that dates back to the thirteenth century. Horsey Mere, just to the north-east, is very brackish because only a large sand-dune separates it from the North Sea. Many unusual birds and other wildlife can be found here as a result of the salinity. The little Church of All Saints at Horsey has a thatched roof that again covers both nave and chancel. It also has a Saxon round tower that was topped in the fifteenth century with an unusual octagonal belfry. In contrast, the church at nearby West Somerton has a thatched roof only over the nave. This church commands a good view of the sand dunes and the sea.

Rollesby Broad is about 3 miles (4.8 km) south-east of Potter Heigham. The village of Rollesby has some lovely old thatched cottages, which date back to the sixteenth century. Many equally fine thatched roofs can also be seen in Stokesby, another 3 or 4 miles (5–6 km) to the south. There are also pantiled roofs alongside the thatch. The church has a thatched roof that again covers both nave and chancel, whilst the fourteenth-century church at the nearby village of Beighton only has a thatched nave.

Further to the north, on the coast at Paston, there is another thatched church surrounded by woodland; this is the Church of St Margaret and it dates from the fourteenth century. The nave roof is thatched with Norfolk reed and inside the exposed timbers and beams can be seen. There are some fourteenth-century wall paintings, including a large St Christopher. One of the finest examples in Norfolk of a thatched tithe barn, built in 1581, is also situated in the village. It is approximately 162 feet (49 metres) long and the buttressed walls are constructed of flint, with brick dressings. A series of tie and hammer beams support the massive thatched roof. The North Norfolk Historic Buildings Trust bought the barn in 1996 and it has since been rethatched. It is interesting to note that Paston has never had an inn during its thousand-year history, a most unusual phenomenon.

The pretty village of Bacton nestles close to Paston, and its church has a partially thatched roof, similar to the one at Paston. The ruins of Bacton Abbey are also worth a visit, they are known locally as Bromholm Priory. Further east along the coast, Waxham has a great barn built around 1570 and it is the largest in Norfolk. The stone buttresses, supporting the flint and brick walls, were originally salvaged from a demolished priory building during the Reformation.

Ridlington, 2 or 3 miles (3–4 km) to the south of Bacton, has a lovely thatched barn made of brick, with Dutch gable ends; these are a reminder of East Anglia's former close contacts with the Netherlands. The barn stands opposite the church, which is also of interest because of the gigantic key required to open its antiquated door. Crostwight village is close by and the church here has a thatched roof over its chancel. Inside there is decorative work depicting a tree with the seven deadly sins.

At Erpingham, to the north of Norwich, is a farm that has a recently restored thatched Dutch barn, dating to the late seventeenth or early eighteenth century. The lower walls are built of flint and the upper sections of brick. It has central cart doors and ventilation slits; tie beams and collars support the thatched roof.

The barn at Hales Green, just off the Norwich to Beccles road, is one of the oldest brick barns in England, dating to 1480. It formerly belonged to the partially ruined Hales Hall, which was built by Henry VII's Attorney General. It has five large doorways and several ventilation slits. It was restored and rethatched in 1996 after several years spent under a corrugated iron roof. The nearby village of Hales has a small church with a thatched roof over both nave and chancel. It also has a Norman round tower and an unusually beautiful Norman doorway.

The lodge to Costessey Park, on the western perimeter of Norwich, was built in the late eighteenth century and was designed in the *cottage ornée* style. A beautiful conical thatch protects it and a chimney-pot protrudes through the apex of the roof. A little further south, about 6 miles (9.5 km) from Norwich, is the tiny village of Ketteringham, which has some lovely thatched and timbered cottages next to the church, which inside has many fine old brasses.

Much further south, is Bressingham, near the border with Suffolk. Its many beautiful thatched cottages, set in orchard scenery, make a delightful picture and there is also a thatched inn opposite the church. A further attraction to visitors is Bressingham Hall, which contains a remarkable collection of steam engines, tractors, fairground engines and a miniature railway. The large grounds and gardens are splendid.

There is another thatched church at Caston, a few miles to the south-west of Norwich. It has an interesting history of roof changes. In medieval times, it had a thatched roof but in the middle of the nineteenth century, the decision was taken to convert to Welsh slates. However, owing to problems with leaks, it reverted to thatch. Another thatched roof shelters the church at the nearby village of Rockland St Peter. Several old thatched cottages, together with some pantiled houses, border the green.

At Reedham, to the south-east of Norwich, the east perpendicular tower of the thatched Church of St John the Baptist is massive. A 70-foot (21 metre) high windmill makes an interesting landmark just 3 miles outside the village. The structure, one of the finest in East Anglia, is in working order and open to visitors.

There are several other thatched churches in the county. Sisland, about 3 miles (4.8 km) to the west of Hales has one, built in the eighteenth century, as does Seething, which nearly adjoins Sisland. The church at Stockton is quite small, as is that at Fritton, very close to the Suffolk border. The latter also boasts a very early Norman round tower. The thatched roof is divided into two separate sections, one covering the nave and the other the chancel. An ornamented ridge adorns both sections.

SUFFOLK

Herringfleet lies a couple of miles south-east of Fritton but is in Suffolk. It also has a thatched church with a Norman round tower. However, the tower is not of quite such an early date as the one at Fritton. An old thatched barn also survives at Herringfleet, with walls that are a mixture of pebbles and bricks. The building was once used as a refectory for the nearby Augustinian priory, which was founded in the thirteenth century. Traces of the site are still evident. The beautiful village of

Somerleyton is very close to Herringfleet, on its eastern side. The entire village was created in the *cottage ornée* style when Somerleyton Hall was reconstructed in 1844. There are many lovely thatched cottages in a delightful setting of village green and pump. Somerleyton Hall has magnificent grounds surrounding the main house. A maze, constructed from clipped yew trees, forms an intriguing feature of the garden.

At Barsham, near Beccles, the nave roof of the Church of the Most Holy Trinity is thatched and the church also has an early round tower. The rectory, which stands close to the church, is of interest because Nelson's mother was born there in 1725. The nearby village of Ringsfield also has a thatched church.

Some delightful thatched almshouses can be seen at Homersfield, about 7 miles (11 km) to the west. The almshouses are arranged in a horseshoe-shaped terrace and an ornamented raised ridge caps the wide and low sweeping expanse of thatch. A thatched canopy, supported on pillars, shelters a well in the garden.

Several miles to the east, on the coast near Lowestoft, is the village of Pakefield. The church on the cliff is somewhat exceptional because of its date and roof type. It was constructed after the Second World War and yet was still given a thatched roof. The original church had been destroyed during the war.

A much older but also exceptional church can be seen at Reydon, further south near Southwold. The roof appears to be completely tiled when viewed from one side, but a closer inspection of the other side reveals it is thatched; this dual-material roofing was carried out in 1880. Although thatch was fashionable at that time, the clergy appeared not to think so. They deemed it better for the church to be tiled on the front, where the road passed, with only the back roof thatched where it would be less noticeable.

In contrast to this reticence, a very long, proud stretch of thatch can be seen on the nave roof of the Church of St Peter at Theberton. It has a round tower and a Norman doorway, and was not unknown to smugglers during its past history. The church at Bramfield, which lies to the north-west of Theberton, is also cloaked with a richly ornamented thatched roof, decorated with a full-length apron of alternating long and short points, halfway down the thatch slope. A detached round tower makes a rare feature, standing a little distance from the main church; it has very thick walls and also some medieval bells.

There are many thatched villages and cottages in farmland settings in Suffolk. John Constable, the major English landscape painter of the nineteenth century, frequently used them in his work. The son of a prosperous miller, he spent much of his youth at Flatford Mill, which is now owned by the National Trust. It is located on the River Stour at the southern boundary of Suffolk, by the side of a wooden bridge with the famous Willy Lott's Cottage nearby. There is a thatched cottage at the foot of the bridge leading to the mill and Willy Lott's Cottage.

The pretty village of Higham is about 4 miles (6.5 km) away, to the north-west of Flatford Mill, hiding among lovely tree-lined slopes. An unusual thatched house adjoins old Higham Post Office. The top third of the roof is thatched and ornamented with scallops, liggers and cross-rods, but the bottom two thirds is tiled. A rare combination of thatch and tiles is therefore incorporated into the same roof slope.

Delightful countryside surrounds Whatfield, about 7 miles (11 km) to the north of Higham, and several very old thatched cottages are found there. About 3 miles (4.5 km) away to the west is the picturesque village of Chelsworth, whose many thatched cottages are made even

The charming village of Chelsworth

171

more attractive by the artistic timbers employed in their design. The River Brett runs by the village and adds further charm. Lindsey, about 3 miles (4.5 km) south of Chelsworth and Whatfield, contains several ancient thatched buildings. Especially noteworthy is the Chapel of St James, which is surrounded by a garden. The exact age of the building appears to be lost in antiquity but a thatched roof still protects it, as it has for innumerable centuries.

An outstandingly beautiful thatched village is Cavendish, a few miles south of Bury St Edmunds. The many attractive thatched timber and colour-washed cottages emphasise the popularity of this type of dwelling in the south of Suffolk. The cottages have been well restored and cared for, and the walls of many of them are coloured pink. The picturesque thatched roofs are finished with fine pointed block ridges. Many of the roofs are of the outshot type, in which one side extends below the level of the other side – a form of construction once fashionable in Suffolk. They gather round the very large village green, near the fourteenth-century St Mary's Church. The church is unusual because it has a jutting stair turret and the tower conceals a small room

Restored cottages at Cavendish

uncommonly fitted with a fireplace. The church also has a sixteenth-century brass lectern, which it is believed was donated by Elizabeth I.

The main street of Monks Eleigh, called simply The Street, follows the River Brett and on the opposite bank may be found a number of thatched and timbered cottages on Swingleton Green.

To the north-east of Bury St Edmunds, lies the village of Ixworth Thorpe, which has the very small thatched Church of All Saints. The Norman doorway is tiny, only 3 feet (90 cm) wide and just over 5 feet (1.5 metres) high. The building also has an unusual wooden bell turret and one of the bench ends inside the church depicts a thatcher with a comb. Another small Norman church with a thatched roof can be found in the village of Thornham Parva, a few miles to the east of Ixworth Thorpe. Inside is a beautiful retable, the paintings on which have been dated to the beginning of the fourteenth century.

There are many other thatched villages around Bury St Edmunds. Typical of these is Flempton, about 4 or 5 miles (7–8 km) to the north-west. It has a church, a green and close by it a quaint row of cottages with thatched roofs. Dalham, through which the River Kennet runs, has a great number of thatched cottages. Most of them have white painted

The saddling stalls, July Racecourse, Newmarket Heath

The weighing room, July Racecourse,
Newmarket Heath

Thatched house, Newmarket town

walls with trim gardens reached by little footbridges. The spot is also of interest because of Dalham Hall, once owned by the family of Cecil Rhodes, who played a prominent role in the history of South Africa. Although fire destroyed most of the original hall, the new one built in its place can still claim to be the highest point of the county.

Newmarket is the main centre for flat horse-racing in England and the headquarters of the Jockey Club, with its racehorse museum. Studs and training establishments abound in the area, and the July Racecourse has three thatched buildings: a very attractive long thatched roof, with a ridge ornamented with points shelters the open-fronted saddling stalls that overlook the parade-ring; the weighing room also has a pretty thatched roof with a finial of a jockey riding a racehorse on the centre of the ridge; and a small thatch covers a Tote betting building in the members' enclosure.

CAMBRIDGESHIRE

Cambridgeshire has a host of thatched dwellings, the highest density in the south, fairly near to the city of Cambridge. Many of the thatched roofs are of long straw but there are also reed roofs. St Benet's Church, in Cambridge, is the oldest building to be found in the county. It dates back approximately 1,000 years and has a Saxon tower. There are several historical items, including an old iron hook once used for pulling down burning thatch.

The nearby village of Fen Ditton offers a well-known vantage point, at Ditton Corner, for watching the Cambridge Eights races, held on the river during May, and the thatched cottages in the village are a familiar sight to its many sporting visitors. A little further east is Lode, balanced on the edge of the fens. It contains a picturesque group of thatched cottages and also a thatched village hall. Another feature of renown in the village is Anglesey Abbey, now administered by the National Trust and open to the public. It was founded in 1236, but was converted into a manor house at the end of the sixteenth century. The building has recently been modified and contains many art treasures. The gardens are both extensive and beautiful.

Further east is Great Wilbraham, which also has many thatched cottages. Several of them have hollyhocks and other attractive cottage-garden flowers to enhance the charm of their thatched roofs. The village of Kirtling lies further east still, and offers some fine examples of long barns with thatched roofs standing alongside the village pond. There was once a magnificent Tudor mansion there, where Queen Elizabeth I was lavishly entertained. It is now in ruins, but a new house stands on the site, which still retains the original gateway of the Tudor mansion. The house, which is moated, can be found near the Roman Catholic Church. The hamlet of Upend adjoins Kirtling and this is worth a visit to see its lovely thatched cottages.

Grantchester, about 2 miles (3 km) south of Cambridge, is well known to literary scholars through the poem of Rupert Brooke, who once lived there. The Red Lion Inn there has a thatched roof, and a good collection of thatched cottages can be found near the Church of St Andrew and St Mary. Further south from Cambridge, the village of Barrington reclines on a slope by the River Cam. This charming spot has a thatched inn, the Royal Oak, which is timbered. Several of the cottages in the vicinity are also thatched and, along with orchards, they border the very large village green. Foxton, just a mile (1.5 km) away, has many thatched cottages, several of which are timber-framed with plastered walls. They contrast with the modern brick which is also found in the village and the old flint church.

There are several interesting thatched buildings in Pampisford, about 5 miles (8 km) to the east of Foxton, including the late sixteenth-century Chequers Inn. Many thatched cottages also line the village street and it is made even more pleasant by the many beautiful trees that surround it. Another building of note in the village is the timber-fronted old post office, which stands opposite the inn. The remnants of an ancient defensive ditch, known as Brent Ditch, can also be found just outside the village.

Orchards surround Meldreth, about 3 miles (4.8 km) south-west of Foxton, and the village has several attractive thatched houses. The heads of two huge fire hooks adorn the inside walls of the church; these were once attached to long poles for pulling thatch away from burning roofs. The small village green still has a whipping post, old stocks and the base of an ancient cross.

The tiny village of Abington Pigotts is 4 miles (6.5 km) away to the west, and has many picturesque thatched and tiled cottages along the village street. The trees and orchards further enhance its beauty. Nearby, the great barn at Wimpole is thatched with water reed and the walls are built with timber on brick footings. Wimpole Hall is well worth a visit, as it is one of the finest mansions in the county. It was built around 1640 and added to in 1740 by the Earl of Hardwick, the Lord Chancellor.

Hinxton village lies to the east of Meldreth, near the Essex border. It boasts several pretty thatched dwellings, but there is also an unusual mixture of timber-framed and Victorian yellow brick cottages. The occasional timbered house has a jettied storey. The neighbouring parish of Ickleton also has many thatched cottages, some of which are again constructed of yellow brick. There are several other interesting old houses to be seen in the village. Rare medieval carvings decorate the coping of the churchyard wall, including a crocodile and a fox.

Great Chishill is further south, near the borders of Hertfordshire and Essex. An exceptionally picturesque group of thatched cottages faces the church there and an old water pump is still in evidence outside one of the cottages. Just a mile (1.5 km) from the village, an old windmill complete with sails can be found.

The large attractive village of Comberton about 4 miles (6.5 km) west of Cambridge has many old buildings, including a collection of quaint thatched cottages by the brook. About 3 miles (4.8 km)

The Fox and Hounds Inn at Elsworth. (A thatched bus-shelter beyond)

further west, Bourn has several thatched barns in its immediate vicinity. It also boasts one of the oldest windmills in England, dating back to 1636 and still in working order. The windmill is of the post-mill type, in which the sails, body and machinery all revolve around a central post to face the wind by moving a large beam at the rear.

Four miles (6.5 km) to the north of Bourn and about 8 miles (13 km) west of Cambridge, you will find Elsworth. Many pretty thatched cottages line the streets of this village, which also has a thatched bus-shelter. A stream winds its way among the cottages and under several rustic timber bridges. An Elizabethan house, formerly used as the Guildhall, and a manor house of the same period stand alongside the village green.

Eltisley lies a short distance to the south-west and contains many charming thatched cottages gathered around the large village green and church. It is recorded that a sister of Oliver Cromwell was married in the church in 1636. Croxton, 2 miles (3 km) west of Eltisley in Croxton Park, has several thatched cottages. Most are

A thatched cottage at Elsworth

weather-boarded and an attractive timbered house adjoins them. The nearby church and lake make a delightful backdrop for the thatched roofs.

Fairly close by, Great Gransden is a splendid village with many timber-framed thatched cottages, most of them with white or pink plastered walls. A few miles to the north can be found the Roman town of Godmanchester with an unusual collection of old thatched cottages constructed of brick and timber. Many examples of other types of timber-framed houses built in the sixteenth and seventeenth centuries are also to be seen in the town.

Brampton lies a short distance to the west of Godmanchester. There are many quaint old cottages in this village and a few have long-straw roofs. Other buildings of interest in Brampton include an old watermill, a 300-year-old inn and a farmhouse where Samuel Pepys, the diarist, resided. An unusual obelisk signpost stands on the village green.

Good examples of thatched roofs and brick and timber-framed cottages can be seen in Hemingford Grey, which is a short way to the east of Godmanchester. The village commands beautiful views from the banks of the River Ouse, and the church stands on the bend of the river. One of the timber-framed cottages dates from 1583. There is also a twelfth-century manor house in the village, which is surrounded on three sides by a moat. The river runs along the remaining side of the grounds of the house. Hemingford Abbots neighbours Hemingford Grey and contains many immaculately thatched dwellings. It also has a thatched inn, the Axe and Compass. An elegant ridge, with scallops and points, adorns the roof.

Fen Drayton is close to Hemingford Grey, and has a miscellany of thatched buildings, including some timber-framed ones. One property of historical note bears a motto written in Dutch over the door; it translates as 'Nothing without labour'. It is believed that the

A thatched inn-sign at Fen Drayton

Dutch engineer Vermuyden, who drained the fens and reclaimed thousands of acres of wasteland during the seventeenth century, once lived in the house. The Three Tuns Inn overlooks the village stream and it has a beautiful thatched roof, richly ornamented with scallops and points. An adjacent section of the inn is timber framed and tiled. The inn has an attractive sign, mounted on a post and protected by a small conical canopy of thatch. The inn probably dates to the fourteenth century and inside are some magnificent carved oak ceiling beams.

All Saints Church at Rampton, a few miles north of Cambridge, has one half of its roof thatched and the other half tiled. Yew trees surround the church, which has been a place of worship since the twelfth century. The thatched St Michael's Church, at nearby Longstanton, on the other hand, has not been used for regular worship since 1954, although two services a year are held. The Redundant Church Fund now cares for the thirteenth-century church; the thatched roof, like the one at Rampton has a block ridge with points. Unfortunately, thieves stole the church bells during a dark night in 1969. It remains a mystery how they were removed, lowered 70 feet (21 metres) to the ground and spirited away.

About 4 miles (6.5 km) north of the city of Cambridge is Landbeach, which contains some thatched and timber-framed houses. Several thatched barns are also to be found in the surrounding fields. Just a couple of miles away to the south is Milton, which still has a few old thatched cottages, despite the building of many modern houses in the locality. One of the more interesting thatched buildings is known as Queen Ann's Lodge; in former times it served as an inn. It has a collection of old medallions on its walls.

March sprawls in the northern part of Cambridgeshire. The town was well-known for its large railway marshalling yard; now it is much visited to see the Church of St Wendreda, which has a magnificent double hammer beam roof, one of the best examples to be seen in East Anglia. There are some noteworthy old thatched buildings in the town and the Ship Inn, with a thatched roof, dates to Georgian times.

Ramsey is 10 miles (16 km) away to the south-west. A few single-storey thatched dwellings, constructed of yellow brick, remain in the town. Most have tall brick chimneys and shuttered windows. Unusual features of the thatched houses are hatches in the gable walls that allow access to the attics under the roofs. When the houses were built, provision was made for entrance to be gained to the attics from the outside and not the interior. Other places of interest in Ramsey are the remnants of the fifteenth-century gatehouse, formerly part of Ramsey Abbey, which was founded in the tenth century. The National Trust now administers it and it is open to the public. Seven miles (11 km) to the north-west, close to Peterborough, is the large village of Yaxley. A thatched inn stands in the centre and there are also several delightful black-and-white thatched cottages nearby. South of Ramsey is Kings Ripton, where a new estate incorporating several thatched houses has recently been built.

In the east of the county, 2 miles (3 km) south-west of Soham, is Wicken, with its four village greens. Wicken Fen was used at one time for the production of sedge, a much-used local fenland thatch material. The National Trust has preserved the fen since 1899 and it is kept as near to its original state as possible. It is now a nature reserve and it represents the last stretch of natural undrained fenland in East Anglia. Sections of the fen are open to the public and these are of special delight to all those who enjoy walking, viewing the huge growths of sedge and studying bird life. There is a 2-mile (3 km) nature trail winding its way through the fen. A restored windmill reminds visitors of the original method used to drain the fens and reclaim land by pumping the water into the dykes. A thatched roof covers the Coach and Horses Inn in the village. Spinney Farmhouse just outside the village is of historic interest because one of Oliver Cromwell's sons once lived there.

Burwell Fen lies a little to the south of Wicken and the manor house in the village has several thatched stone barns. A windmill, in its original form, can also be viewed near the village. The churchyard at Burwell has a tombstone carved with a flaming heart. It marks the communal grave of eighty-two people, who died tragically by arson in 1727. They were enjoying a puppet show in one of the barns when a man deliberately set fire to the thatched roof after nailing the barn doors shut. He later confessed to the crime on his deathbed, saying he had done it to spite the puppeteer.

10

Thatched Buildings in the
South and South-east

DORSET

A host of thatched cottages and various other thatched buildings can be found in Dorset, and a few of the more unusual ones were featured in chapter 7. Most of the thatched roofs traditionally consisted of combed wheat reed, although some were also thatched with local marsh water reeds. Long-straw thatching can also be seen, particularly in the south-east of the county. Norfolk reed is less common but imported reeds have now become more widely used, as in many other English counties.

The county town of Dorchester forms a good centre for touring Dorset. A thatched building of note there is the Hangman's Cottage, which stands by the River Frome, running alongside the prison and overlooking the water meadows. This is where the executioner used to live. Other interesting thatched properties on the outskirts of Dorchester include the cottage at Higher Bockhampton where Thomas Hardy, the novelist, was born in 1840 and the former residence of William Barnes, the Dorset dialect poet, at Winterborne Came.

The interior of the Thomas Hardy cottage, in Thorncombe Wood, can be visited during the winter months only by appointment with the tenant; it has been a National Trust property since 1948. In the summer months no appointment is normally needed. The cottage garden, which contains many English flowers, is always open to the public, so the exterior of the cottage can be readily seen. Hardy's grandfather built the cottage in 1800 with cob walls, which were later

Thomas Hardy's cottage at Higher Bockhampton

faced with bricks. The churchyard at Stinsford, about 3 miles (4.8 km) away, is also worth a visit as Hardy's heart was buried there in 1928, although his ashes rest in Westminster Abbey.

The former residence of William Barnes at Winterborne Came consists of a beautiful thatched rectory, in a *cottage ornée* style, surrounded by a mixture of open parkland and woods. Near the rectory lies the tiny church, where William Barnes was rector for over twenty years during the second half of the nineteenth century. He was buried in the churchyard there. Barnes also preached in the now redundant church in the nearby tiny village of Whitcombe, which contains an exquisite group of thatched cottages. They were built with cob and stone rubble in the late seventeenth and early eighteenth centuries.

Stratton is just to the north-west of Dorchester and contains modern thatched homes, as well as old thatched cottages built with flint-coursed walls. It also has a thatched pub, the Saxon Arms. Stratton was one of the very last manors in Dorset to retain an open-field arable system, which explains the presence of several old farm buildings in the centre of the village.

Perhaps one of the most famous villages in Dorset is Tolpuddle, owing to its historical link with the trade union movement. It is situated about 7 miles (11 km) east of Dorchester. Here, in 1831, six farm labourers collectively attempted to get an increase in wages and swore an illegal oath to form a trade union, for which action they were later arrested and transported to Australia. They eventually became known as the Tolpuddle Martyrs. There are many thatched seventeenth-century properties in the village and also a thatched shelter

The Martyrs' Seat, Tolpuddle

with a memorial seat, near the old sycamore tree under which the Martyrs originally met. Many of the cottages are thatched with long straw. In 1934, the Trades Union Congress built six cottages in memory of the six Martyrs – George Loveless, James Loveless, Thomas Standfield, John Standfield, James Brine and James Hammett. John Standfield's cottage still stands in the village; it is partly thatched.

An exquisite collection of thatched cottages can be seen at Milton Abbas, about 5 miles (8 km) north of Tolpuddle. This is thought to be one of the finest examples in the United Kingdom of an integrally planned village. It was built in the eighteenth century and consists of a single wide street of nearly identical thatched cottages, all uniformly laid out and separated from one another mainly in pairs. Wide grass verges border each side of the street, which runs up the hill from an artificial lake at the bottom. It is a most splendid sight when first seen and one gets the impression of being transported back in time. A thatched inn called the Hambro Arms, sits in the middle of the village, a long thatched building that contrasts with the uniform series of square cottages. The village rests in idyllic surroundings in a wooded valley and about a mile (1.5 km) away are historic Milton Abbey and the famous boys' public school.

The original village of Milton Abbas was located close to the Abbey church and it then had a large number of streets, inns and a brewery. When Joseph Damer, the first Earl of Dorchester, inherited the estates at Milton, however, he disliked the presence of the village so close to the mansion he proposed to build near the Abbey. He therefore ordered its complete destruction, and the present model village was constructed in its place, a mile away from the site of the old. The Damer mansion is today the public school. The thatched house situated near the Abbey and school is the only original village building that escaped the demolition order. Damer took twenty years to acquire all the properties he wanted and he had to open a sluice gate to flush out an uncooperative lawyer who opposed his plans and refused to move!

There are many lovely groups of thatched cottages to be seen in the hamlets and villages nestling in the Piddle Valley, west of Milton Abbas, many of which contain the word 'Piddle' in their names, such as Piddlehinton and Piddletrenthide. The former has an old thatched country inn called the Thimble. Puddletown was originally called Piddletown, but the name was changed as it was thought the new one sounded more seemly. In addition to these villages, other thatched buildings can be found in the hamlet of Plush, a little further north. A long stretch of thatch covers the sixteenth-century inn, the Brace of Pheasants. In keeping with the name, two perched birds sit on the top of the thatched roof, which at eaves level is attractively shaped around the upper storey windows. The inn was constructed by the integration and restoration of two cottages and a forge.

Alton Pancras is close by in the Piddle Valley and has a thatched village store and post office in the main street. The walls of the building are constructed of brick and flint, and the roof is gabled. About 1½ miles (2.5 km) to the north of Alton Pancras is Buckland Newton. Many attractive thatched cottages can be seen in the village, and the occasional house also has a thatched garage. To the south of Buckland Newton and about halfway between Cerne Abbas and Dorchester, is what is claimed to be the smallest public house in England with a thatched roof. It is the Smith's Arms at Godmanstone, which was described on page 132. There are other thatched cottages in Godmanstone, one house was once roofed with artificial plastic material, designed to give the house the superficial appearance of a thatched roof. It has since been rethatched.

The small village of Woodsford lies about 4 miles (6.5 km) to the

A bus-shelter, West Stafford

east of Dorchester and here there is the interesting thatched fortified house, called Woodsford Castle, which was also described on pages 129–30. West Stafford, about 3 miles (4.8 km) away to the south-west has several old thatched cottages. A thatch covers the local inn, the Wise Man. Barton Barn stands close by but other buildings now tightly encircle it. The thatched building was originally the main barn of the manor farm estate and was known as the Squire's Barn. The underside of the main roof, when seen from within, has a series of giant beams and crudely cut poles supporting the massive area of thatch. A hipped thatched porchway abuts the main body of the 400-year-old building. The barn has now been converted to residential use. A thatched bus-shelter can also be seen in West Stafford.

A thatched barn of a different type can be seen at Broadmayne, just to the south-east of Dorchester. This is a good example of an old tithe barn. Broadmayne also has several thatched cottages. A magnificent, very large tithe barn can also be seen at Abbotsbury. Unfortunately, about a half of it is derelict, although a substantial area of thatch remains on the rest. This section is now used as a smugglers' adventure centre for children and is open to the public between Easter and October. It dates from the fifteenth century and is approximately 173 feet (53 metres) long and 30 feet (9 metres) wide. Its size is a reminder of the old economic system when payment was made in kind or large volumes of produce, rather than cash.

Abbotsbury consists primarily of one long street, lined with thatched cottages mingling with a few slate-roofed ones. The walls of most are built of orange-tinged stones. Many of the roofs are thatched with the local Abbotsbury water reed. An unusual feature of the village is that the pavements are raised well above road level. In keeping with the long straggling nature of the village, a restored thatched medieval long house forms part of one of the long terraces. Along the street stand several thatched craft shops, a café, a restaurant and a small converted thatched barn. Some new thatched cottages in a small estate can also be seen on the eastern side of the village. In order to harmonize with the surroundings, they were built in the local vernacular style. Abbotsbury also boasts sub-tropical gardens, complete with peacocks and many rare plants. The famous Abbotsbury Swannery is also located near the tithe barn. It is the largest swannery in England, and has been in existence from at least the end of the fourteenth century.

The village of Littlebredy hides in a wooded valley 4 miles (6.5 km) north of Abbotsbury. There are many delightful cottages thatched with combed wheat reed, and a thatched roof covers the village hall, which also has a separate thatched lean-to roof over a small extension. The hall was at one time the school. Another thatched house occupies the area between the village hall and church.

A picturesque cottage, Littlebredy

Beautiful grounds adjoin the church and the public are welcome to walk through them. The church was considerably rebuilt in 1850 and has a spire. The stone used in its construction was imported from Caen in Normandy. Two original bells are still in the church, the oldest dating back to 1400.

Frampton, 5 miles (8 km) north-west of Dorchester, has a long street, which is made attractive by the miscellany of thatched cottages that line one side of it. There are no buildings on the other side of the street, which is a distinctive feature. In addition to the thatched cottages, there is also a thatched guest-house in the village.

There are still a few ancient thatched refectory barns surviving in England, where the monks of old used to dine. One good example can be seen at Toller Fratrum, about 3 miles (4.8 km) north-west of Frampton. The Knights of St John of Jerusalem, the Hospitallers, once used it. They were a religious military order that arose out of the Crusades and included knights, clergy and brothers. The well-preserved thatched refectory barn stands close to the manor house and a little medieval church. One or two thatched cottages are also to be seen in this rather remote village.

Further north-west still is the village of Rampisham. Its picturesque post office, opposite the inn, is topped with a thatched roof. The many thatched patches on the roof show its long history of repairs. A small separate canopy of thatch shelters the entrance. There are several thatched cottages and farm buildings in the immediate vicinity. Corscombe, a little further in the same direction, also has several thatched buildings, among which the Fox Inn is one of the most impeccable. It dates from about 1600. A continuous stretch of thatch covers the long building and two small thatched canopies protect the entrances. The interior is tastefully ornamented with a fine collection of country utensils, including many made of old brass and copper. There are also agricultural implements and prints depicting hunting scenes. Incidentally, the inn was featured in the film *Rogue Male*, starring Peter O'Toole.

In the extreme west of Dorset, a very beautiful but peculiar thatched roof can be seen on the Umbrella Cottage at Lyme Regis, described on page 135. Two other lovely thatched houses are prominent on the sea front, along the Marine Parade. One of these, with pink-washed walls, is a little unusual because rainwater guttering is fitted under the eaves. The houses were built in the first half of the nineteenth century and rich Victorians used them as holiday homes. Lyme Regis was once a favourite resort of Jane Austin. Mary Anning was also a well-known former resident, who collected many of the fossils that abound in the area; some of the largest and best are now exhibited in the Museum of Natural History in London. Incidentally in 1980, the town was temporarily transformed back to Victorian times, when *The French Lieutenant's Woman*, based on John Fowles's novel, was filmed there.

The seaside resort of Charmouth is close to Lyme Regis, and has many thatched buildings in the main street, including cottages, restaurants and a former hotel, now converted into flats and apartments. Some of the houses have bow windows. The former hotel stands at the top of the main street. Also of interest is the Queen Armes Hotel, which is not thatched but boasts many historical connections. Catherine of Aragon stayed in the building on her arrival in England in 1501 and in 1651 King Charles II stopped there during his flight from Worcester. The main street runs up a hillside and the overall picture is most charming. The beach at Charmouth, like that at Lyme Regis, is an excellent place to hunt fossils, and it forms part of the Heritage Coast.

Further east lies Burton Bradstock, close to the sea, the cliffs and Chesil Beach. This delightful spot contains many stone-built thatched cottages and an inn with a well-kept thatched roof. Chideock, just a few miles away, is a lovely picturesque village with a miscellany of thatched buildings. In addition to thatched cottages, the main street has a hotel, a seventeenth-century inn, a restaurant, guest-houses and a mixture of farms, all topped with thatched roofs.

Symondsbury, which nestles nearby, off the Bridport to Axminster road, is well known for its excellent thatched roofs, and several good examples of sandstone thatched cottages can be found there, as well as a large barn. It also has a 600-year-old thatched inn, called the Ilchester Arms. Just outside the village, at West Mead, on the way to Bridport, a new estate of thatched cottages has been constructed in the local architectural style.

There is another 600-year-old inn at Shave Cross, a little further north, in the Marshwood Vale. This inn, built with cob walls and a thatched roof, claims to have the oldest skittle-alley in Dorset. A thatched porch protects the doorway. The north-east road from Shave Cross leads to the pretty village of Stoke Abbott, near Beaminster. The main street is very narrow and almost all the buildings along it are thatched, including a terrace of cottages and a thatched inn with a small tiled extension abutting at right angles. There is a twelfth-century church.

A lovely sixteenth-century thatched inn called the Worlds End can be found further east near Almer, between Bere Regis and Wimborne. The long continuous thatched roof has an ornamental block ridge and a separate thatch covers a right-angled extension at the end. The odd name is due to the fact that four parishes meet at Almer. Inside, an array of old agricultural implements decorates the bars. A little to the north-west, on the other side of Blandford, is the pretty hamlet of Hammoon. This contains a good example of a sixteenth-century manor house, with a thatched roof, as described on pages 127–8.

A short distance to the west lies Sturminster Newton. This small market town has a mixture of thatched houses, including cob and timber-traced constructions. The White Hart Inn is thatched, as is a solicitor's office. In addition to the thatch the village offers much else of interest. William Barnes, the Dorset dialect poet, was born on a farm just outside the town and attended school near the church. Thomas Hardy also lived in the town for two years, while writing *The Return of the Native*. Another place of note is the fine medieval six-arched bridge that spans the River Stour and connects Sturminster to Newton. There is also a seventeenth-century water-mill that is still in working order and open to visitors. A thatched house stands opposite. The nearby village of Hazelbury Bryan has some new thatched cottages built in the local vernacular style.

Lulworth Cove is convenient to reach from both Weymouth and Swanage, and attracts many visitors. The pretty village of East Lulworth has many long-straw thatched cottages and houses. Some of the houses are constructed in a right-angled shape and the hipped thatch sweeps round to cover both roof sections. The thatched Castle Inn is situated in the village and nearby can be found the remains of Lulworth Castle, which was constructed in the sixteenth century but gutted by fire early in the twentieth century. The hamlet of Kimmeridge borders Lulworth and most of its cottages are built of stone and topped with thatched roofs. The Romans used bituminous shale, found in the cliffs at Kimmeridge, to make coins and jewellery. Today, an oil rig pumps crude oil from the underlying strata surrounding Kimmeridge. The famous ruins of Corfe Castle tower over the nearby village of Corfe, which has a mixture of stone and thatched dwellings. Some of the thatched roofs have lovely raised ridges.

Thatched temple in Japanese Garden, Compton Acres, Poole

WILTSHIRE

Many thatched villages and hamlets surround Salisbury. Typical of these is Steeple Langford, in the Wylye valley to the north-west. This contains several cottages constructed of brick and topped with thatched roofs. Houses built with flint are also to be seen, designed with a chequered pattern that is a fairly common feature in Wiltshire. There are several man-made lakes formed by flooding old gravel pits. Stockton is another Wylye valley village with many thatched cottages. It also has several other old buildings, including an Elizabethan flint farmhouse with a great barn. Some quaint seventeenth-century almshouses may also be seen in the village. To obtain an outstanding view of the Wylye valley, it is worth visiting Stapleford. This village has some charming thatched cottages to complement the scenic views.

Teffont Magna, to the west of Salisbury, has several pretty thatched cottages around the church, which has a portion of an Anglo-Saxon cross dating back to the ninth century. There are several small bridges crossing the stream in the village, which hides in the wooded valley of the Nadder. Most of the cottages by the stream have individual stone slab bridges to reach their doors.

To the east of Salisbury lies West Dean, overlooking the Hampshire border. Dean Hill rises 500 feet (152 metres) above the village and offers magnificent views of the surrounding countryside. A sprinkling of thatched roofs can be seen in the village, which has a pleasant green and river to complete the scene. Downton, to the south of Salisbury on the A338, also has many thatched cottages. A good collection can be seen along The Borough, which passes the long village green. Most are brick and among them is a very long stretch of thatch covering a whole terrace of cottages. Also of interest is the Moot, where an ancient ditch surrounds some stepped seating cut in the grass with a double horseshoe ring.

To the north of Salisbury is Durnford, in a valley by the River Avon, where several roofs thatched in long straw can be seen. Most of the thatched cottages have walls of flint and date to the seventeenth century. Netton is close to Durnford, and several good examples of thatched walls and boundary-markers can be seen in the hamlet and its immediate vicinity. Wilsford, which is also close to Durnford along the Avon valley, has many timber-framed cottages with thatched roofs. In addition, there are also houses constructed in the more familiar Wiltshire style of patterned stone and flint.

Superb views of the south, towards Dorset, can be gained from the village of Zeals, which contains many delightful thatched cottages. The village is to the west of Salisbury, near the borders of both Dorset and Somerset. At the other end of the county, similar views can be enjoyed at Liddington, just to the south-east of Swindon. The village has a large number of pretty thatched cottages and Liddington Castle offers wonderful views of three different counties: Oxfordshire and Berkshire as well as Wiltshire. In addition to the thatched cottages, Liddington also has a seventeenth-century manor house, which has an attractive pond created from a section of the original moat.

In contrast to these border villages, with views over several counties, Tilshead is set in the open spaces of Salisbury Plain. It contains many stone and flint thatched cottages, the walls of which are chiefly constructed in the chequered style. A few of the cottages boast ornamental pheasant finials on their roof ridges. Many ancient barrows and earthworks are found in this area of Salisbury Plain, to the north of Stonehenge. A very long excavation, called the Old Ditch, can be found near Tilshead. There is also the White Barrow, approximately 300 feet (91 metres) long, to the south of the village. These barrows were Neolithic burial places and the one at Tilshead is probably the longest in England.

South-west of Warminster stands the village of Horningsham, where a small thatched chapel called the Old Meeting House dates to the second half of the sixteenth century. It is interesting that it was originally built by Scottish workmen who had come down to Wiltshire to build Longleat House, which is close by. The Old Meeting House is perhaps the earliest Presbyterian chapel in England. The date 1566 is distinctly marked on the outer wall, just below the eaves and centrally above the large end windows. The roof has been kept in good condition and is capped with a neat raised ridge with points. At eaves level, the beautiful thatch sweeps in a smooth contour over the upper windows.

In the northern part of the county, an old malt-house with a thatched and partially tiled roof can be seen at Aldbourne, near Marlborough. The roof of the kiln area is fitted with tiles, no doubt for safety reasons. The village, although large, is one of the loveliest to be

Possibly the earliest Presbyterian chapel in England at Horningsham

found in Wiltshire. Several thatched cottages with colour-washed walls stand near the village green. Also nearby are an ancient stone cross, a pond and the church, which was built in the twelfth century. An unexpected sight can be seen inside the church in the form of two eighteenth-century fire engines. The village was quite famous once for straw and willow plaiting. It was also known for its bell-foundry, mainly making small bells for horses and farm animals.

Avebury, to the west of Marlborough, is renowned for its huge stone circle. Unlike those at Stonehenge, the stones at Avebury show no sign of having been worked. The circle was built at an earlier time than the one at Stonehenge, probably during the late Neolithic period, around 2000 BC. The village has many thatched cottages and a thatched great barn. There is also an Elizabethan manor house.

Pewsey and Bedwyn stand by the side of the canal and railway to the south of Marlborough. Both contain thatched properties and Pewsey has some shops that are thatched. It also has a rare example of a medieval cruck house with a thatched roof. The house is of half-timbered construction and is winged with cruck-ended gables. The thatch is long straw. Many thatched cottages, houses and farm buildings also lie between Pewsey and Bedwyn, several very close to the railway line. In the days of steam, they must have suffered an increased fire risk from the sparks emitted from passing trains. However, most appear to have survived, which illustrates that thatch is perhaps more difficult to ignite than one might expect. The thatch in this region is mainly long straw, although some reed is also evident.

Castle Combe, a few miles north-west of Chippenham, must be one of the most beautiful villages in England. It is located in a wooded valley and a little stream meanders under the arched bridge, and was used during the making of the film *Dr Dolittle*. Gathered nearby are an ancient market cross and a picturesque collection of cottages grouped around the church. The walls of the cottages are of Cotswold stone; some are roofed with thatch and others with stone tiles. The main hotel was originally a seventeenth-century manor house. The Roman Fosse Way passes by the western side of the village.

Lacock, 3 miles (4.8 km) south of Chippenham, rivals Castle Combe for the title of most beautiful village in England. All the houses are old and they span many centuries of architectural styles, from the medieval period to the eighteenth century. Some are of stone, others are timbered,

Thatched shop at Wilton

and several have thatched roofs. A fourteenth-century barn overlooks the hotel. Lacock Abbey belongs to the National Trust, as does the rest of the village. The abbey dates to the thirteenth century but was converted into a house during the sixteenth century.

Between Chippenham and Marlborough is Calne. Many people know the town because of its world-famous bacon industry. A little to the south-west of the town can be found the village of Sandy Lane. The nineteenth-century Church of St Mary the Virgin and St Nicholas here has a thatched roof over its timber-framed construction. A thatched porchway shelters the entrance. In addition to the church, there are many thatched cottages in this delightful spot. The unusually named Clyffe Pypard perches on a tree-covered ridge to the north-east of Calne and also boasts many thatched cottages.

AVON

The former county of Avon now incorporates parts of Somerset and Gloucestershire. A charming collection of thatched cottages and other buildings can be seen on the 400-acre (162 hectare) Blaise Castle Estate, a few miles north of Bristol. They include an early nineteenth-century dairy, which has been retained in its original thatched form. There is also a hamlet of nine thatched cottages in the *cottage ornée* style gathered around a village green and pump, also built during the early nineteenth century, when thatch was fashionable for planned, integrated model villages throughout England. Other buildings on the estate include a castle with four battlement towers, erected as a folly in the late eighteenth century, after which the estate was named. There is a corn mill on the estate and a folk museum, which has a typical old farmhouse kitchen, among other items.

Portishead, to the west of Bristol, overlooks the sea from a tree-covered hillside. One of its oldest buildings has a thatched roof and also the remnants of a moat around it. It is known as the Grange and can be found in the High Street; the manor bailiff once lived in it. A thatched former toll-house guards the road junction leading to Stanton Drew, from the Chew Magna road to the south of Bristol. It merits attention because of its unusual hexagonal shape. On the eastern outskirts of Stanton Drew, a series of ancient stone circles stand in a field. The three circles consist of massive upright stones which are thought to date from approximately the same period as those at Avebury. Also of interest at Stanton Drew is the medieval rectory with Gothic windows situated near the bridge over the River Chew.

Badminton House stands in the village of Badminton, 5 miles (8 km) east of Chipping Sodbury. The Palladian-style house has been the home of the Dukes of Beaufort since the seventeenth century, and it is open to the public on many days of the year. The park is internationally famous as the venue for the Badminton horse trials, which are often attended by the Queen. The hamlet of Little Badminton, which borders the edge of the park, has a fine collection of tiny old thatched cottages around the green. It is believed that many of these date back to at least the sixteenth century. An ancient turreted dovecot dominates the green and it has the same number of nesting holes as there are days in the year.

HAMPSHIRE

Combed wheat reed remains a popular thatch material in Hampshire, especially in the western regions, but long-straw roofs are frequently encountered; the local Hampshire marsh reed and some Norfolk reed are also used to a limited extent

There are many thatched villages around the town of Fordingbridge, in the extreme west of the county. The town itself boasts a thatched butcher's shop in the main street. Some of the communities to the north-west of the town formerly belonged to Wiltshire; typical of these is the charming village of Martin, where a lot of thatch and cob may be seen. About 3 miles (4.8 km) away to the east can be found the tiny village of Rockbourne. A stream meanders through the main street, which is bordered by several thatched cottages of brick and timber-framed construction. The manor house in the village is partly Elizabethan and has a fourteenth-century barn. The remains of an excavated Roman villa stand about ½ mile (800 metres) away. This consisted of a very large number of rooms, with baths and mosaic pavements. A few miles to the east, on the edge of the New Forest, can be found one of the forest region's most beautiful villages, Breamore, which has several thatched Tudor cottages positioned at the corner of the village green. Most are timber-framed with brick in-fillings and some of the roofs are thatched with reed, others with long straw. Thatched porches are also to be seen. Incidentally, one of the few

A thatched bus-shelter, Breamore

remaining Anglo-Saxon churches in Hampshire still stands in the village. The nearby Elizabethan manor house, Breamore House is also well worth a visit, as is the Countryside Museum.

Between Breamore and Fordingbridge, on the A338, may be found Upper and Lower Burgate. At Upper Burgate, next to Burgate Cross, a

A timbered cottage at Burgate

good group of thatched cottages can be seen along Fryern Court Road. Most are timber framed and thatched with combed wheat reed. At Lower Burgate are the thatched fourteenth-century Tudor Rose Inn and the Hourglass Restaurant, which has scallops on its block ridge. A separate thatched canopy at the front shelters the name of the restaurant and the main building is timber framed with brick in-filling in a herringbone style. There is a thatched antique shop a few steps away.

There is a holiday village just to the east of Fordingbridge at Godshill. This caravan park includes a thatched pizza eating house and a thatched gift shop. Other charming thatched cottages are scattered through the village. A little further east is Fritham, where a small thatched inn, called the Royal Oak, can offer hospitality. Approximately 1 mile (1.5 km) outside the village, an unusual collection of huge ancient yew trees may be seen at Sloden Enclosure.

South of Fordingbridge lies Ibsley. The thatched cottages in this village are ancient enough to have been mentioned in the Domesday Book. A bridge and several weirs provide an attractive setting, despite the busy A338 road. A popular stopping place is the Old Beams Inn, dating to the fourteenth century. The building is timber framed with brick in-filling and the thatched roof has a block ridge. A short

The Hourglass Restaurant, Burgate

Thatched pizza restaurant at Sandy Bay Estate, Godshill

The Old Beams Inn, Ibsley

distance along the road, beautiful thatched cottages such as the Old Smithy's and the Old Post Office still stand proudly displaying hood-moulds over their Gothic style windows.

A timber-framed cottage at Ibsley

Ringwood, nearby on the River Avon, has some pretty thatched cottages. Two thatched shops stand in the High Street, unusual in that they have wide wooden guttering under their eaves. A picturesque thatched licensed restaurant called the Old Cottage can be found just along the road in West Street. It was rethatched in 2002; the hipped roof passes over a series of eyebrow windows. Next door stands Monmouth House, where the Duke of Monmouth was held after his abortive rebellion of 1685 and from where he wrote unsuccessfully to his uncle, James II, begging for mercy. He was later taken to London and executed. Ringwood also has the beautifully thatched Fish Inn, near the bridge. Close by stands a thatched cottage called Little Thatch, with light pink washed brick walls and a thatched porch.

A thatched inn, the Sir John Barleycorn, welcomes visitors to the east of Ringwood at Cadnam in the New Forest. The property is covered with a long sweep of thatch and three individual thatched gabled porches shelter the entrances. Brook, near Cadnam, has a 600-year-old inn, the Green Dragon. The village also takes pride in its pretty thatched cottages bordering a small stream with a humpback bridge. One of the oldest inns in the New Forest can be found at Hinton Admiral, south of Ringwood. Called the Cat and Fiddle, it is over 600 years old and its unusual name may be based on that of the original owner, Caterine le Fidele. It is constructed with cob walls and roofed with thatch with a ridge of scallops and points. Another picturesque thatched inn, the Fleur de Lys stands a little further east in the New Forest at Pilley and claims to be even older, dating to the eleventh century. It has a thatched porch and a block ridge with points. Much smuggling took place at one time in its vicinity. Another thatched hostelry, the Candlesticks Inn dating to the fifteenth century, can be found on the B3347 road to Sopley, about ½ mile (800 metres) outside Ringwood.

Brockenhurst, nearby, makes a good centre for touring the New Forest, and also has some pretty thatched cottages. Its parish church was built on a mound on the top of a hill, once a fairly common practice in surrounding regions. The churchyard has a giant yew tree that is thought to be about a thousand years old and its branches span over 76 feet (21 metres).

Minstead, near Lyndhurst, has a beautiful secluded woodland setting. Sir Arthur Conan Doyle, the creator of Sherlock Holmes, lived in the village and is buried in the churchyard. The Rufus Stone stands nearby. It was erected in 1745 to mark the spot where William II, called Rufus because of his red hair, was killed by an arrow in a hunting accident. Furzey Gardens, just outside the village in School Lane, has a magnificent collection of shrubs, heather and flowers. A quaint long-straw thatched folk-cottage, built in 1560, stands in the gardens.

One of the most photographed villages in the New Forest must be Swan Green, surrounded on two sides by woodland and about ½ mile (800 metres) outside Lyndhurst. It contains a row of three beautiful thatched brick cottages and a detached one called Beehive Cottage. Some were originally constructed for the servants at a nearby mansion. They were built in the eighteenth century but have since been white colour-washed; their roofs are of combed wheat reed. A cricket pitch dominates the centre of the green and nearby stands the Swan, a pub where pony sales were once held. Commoners have farmed the forest for many centuries, after William the Conqueror first granted their privileged rights. Many ancient farmsteads still stand in the forest and Passford Farm, near Lymington, is a good example. The lovely farmhouse is timber framed and has an impressive thatched roof, with points along its block ridge.

There are many thatched villages in the region of Stockbridge and in particular along the banks of the River Test; one of England's best waters for trout fishing. At Longstock, just 1½ miles (2.5 km) north of Stockbridge, some picturesque thatched huts line the riverbank. The village itself consists of one long street of houses, many of which are thatched, with walls of a contrasting mixture of materials. Many are colour-washed but there are also timber-framed and red brick houses all in close proximity to one another. Leckford, about a mile (1.5 km) away contains some thatched timber-framed cottages, several of which have elegant raised ridges with points. Thatched timber-framed cottages can also be found in the charming village of Wherwell, about 3 miles (4.8 km) north of Leckford. It is difficult to dispute its claim to be the loveliest village in Hampshire. It has many old impeccably thatched timbered cottages, set in a wooded background. There is an excellent view of the Test valley from the west side of the village.

To the south of Stockbridge, along a branch of the River Test, is the small village of King's Somborne. An old thatched inn, the Crown, borders one side of the village green. The church, dominating the other side, has two rare fourteenth-century brasses depicting men wearing civilian cloaks and carrying short swords. They are exceptional because the figures are not dressed in priests' garments or armour, as would be expected. To the west of Stockbridge is Nether Wallop, where other typical examples of timber-framed thatched cottages may be seen here. There is also a mill in the village. About 2 miles (3 km) away is Broughton, which has many timbered houses and several old farmsteads which have their boundary walls capped with thatch.

A thatched wall can also be seen at Sutton Scotney, to the north of Winchester. It adjoins the garden entrance to the Sutton Manor Estate and it is thatched with marsh reed. At Crawley, fairly close by, thatched timber-framed cottages can be seen along the single main street, mingled with other houses built at different periods. The village of Easton, just to the east side of Winchester, has many thatched dwellings and also a church that dates from approximately the end of the twelfth century. The village can be visited on the way to Tichborne, which is a little further east and is a charming, unspoilt spot containing many thatched properties and sixteenth- and seventeenth-century houses.

Timber-framed cottages at Wherwell

A magnificent example of a thatched tithe barn can be seen at Hensting Lane, near Owslebury to the south-east of Winchester. Three tall, heavy buttresses support the end wall of the old building, which has a Sussex hip thatched roof over it. The main roof, covering the long sides, sweeps down low to about 6 feet (1.8 km) above ground level. In West Meon, further south-east, can be seen some beautiful thatched gabled cottages constructed with plastered and timbered walls. The River Meon flows by the village and it may be of interest to cricket lovers that Lord, after whom the famous cricket ground in London is named, was buried at West Meon.

THE ISLE OF WIGHT

Across the water from Hampshire, on the Isle of Wight, the main seaside town is Shanklin, which is skirted by the Old Village. This is a picturesque spot that contains many thatched cottages with roses and honeysuckle climbing their white-fronted walls. There is also a thatched restaurant on the main street. A beautiful wooded chine links the Old Village with Shanklin. Another village that attracts many visitors is Alverstone Mills, about 3 miles (4.8 km) from Sandown. There are several thatched stone cottages in the village and many offer teas during the summer. There is also an old water mill and boating is available on the stream. Another village full of thatched cottages and flower gardens is Newchurch, about 2 miles (3 km) further west.

The main road between Sandown and Newport passes through Arreton, about 3 miles (4.8 km) west of Newchurch. Arreton has an old thatched inn, the Hare and Hounds, and the farm attached to the manor house has a large old thatched barn. Godshill, to the south of Arreton, has many tidy tea gardens and quaint old thatched cottages which attract hosts of summer holiday visitors. Most of the cottages are thatched with long straw. An exceptionally photogenic group stands near the entrance to the churchyard. The church contains a very rare wall painting, known as 'The Lily Cross', dating from approximately 1450. Other items of interest in the village include a model village in the Old Rectory garden and an exhibition of shells. Four miles (6.5 km) to the north-west, the village of Gatcombe retains its unspoilt character. Stone-walled thatched cottages are to be seen there, nestling among the trees and near the stream. A magnificent Palladian-style house set in parkland overlooks the village.

Towards the western side of the island, Calbourne provides excellent picnicking areas in its immediate vicinity, north of the Brighstone forest. A quaint atmosphere prevails in Winkle Street in the village, which includes some low stone-walled thatched cottages, with flowers bedecking the walls. A little stream flows by to complete a much photographed scene. About 3 miles (4.8 km) to the south, is the village of Brighstone, a few miles inland from the waters of Chilton Chine, which has many tea gardens and old stone-walled thatched cottages. Hiding in a valley to the east is Shorwell, which also contains many picturesque old stone-walled thatched cottages, mainly gathered by the inn near the stream. There are some Elizabethan manor houses in the neighbourhood, which is rather unusual for such a relatively small village.

Freshwater Bay, on the more extreme west of the island, has a thatched church, built at the beginning of the twentieth century; it is therefore relatively modern for a thatched church. The land on which it was built had associations with Tennyson, the poet who lived in the village of Freshwater for many years.

SUSSEX

The Weald and Downland Open Air Museum at Singleton, spreads over an area of nearly 40 acres (16 hectares), approximately 5 miles (8 km) north of Chichester. It exhibits a collection of historic buildings from the south-east of England which have been saved from destruction and re-erected. They include a fifteenth-century wealden hall, a fourteenth-century farmhouse, an eighteenth-century granary and a nineteenth-century toll-cottage. Other exhibits include a sixteenth-century treadwheel and a reconstruction of a Saxon weaver's hut, which illustrates the early 'all roof and no wall' type of construction. The roof is thatched and the eaves reach ground level. The museum provides picnicking areas and nature trails through its wooded parkland. It also grows and harvests its own Maris Widgeon wheat for thatching purposes.

The Selsey peninsula lies to the south of Chichester. Despite its rather exposed position, thatched properties can be found. The small Thatched House Hotel, built on the sea front has its own garden, which leads to the sea. In a quiet lane near the town centre, there stands a large thatched house that has been the home of the astronomer Patrick Moore for many years. It is equipped with a weather-vane depicting a stargazer peering through a telescope. North of the peninsula, some picturesque thatched houses are sprinkled through the village of Sidlesham and also at Pagham, where the Church of St Thomas à Becket is found. This church was one of the earliest dedicated to the murdered Archbishop of Canterbury.

Just a few miles along the coast is Aldwick, close to Bognor Regis. The exclusive Aldwick Bay Estate here consists of a mixture of detached individually designed thatched houses with some conventionally roofed properties set among trees and shrubs. Many of the immaculately thatched reed roofs have varying layers and several display pheasants or cat finials on their ridges. Thatched walls and

Unusual roof levels, Aldwick Bay

garages can also be seen. An example of a Gothic-style church built in 1930 can also be found at Aldwick. It is the last stone church to be built in West Sussex.

Felpham adjoins Bognor Regis on its eastern side, but it has managed to retain its individual character. Several thatched cottages still enhance the village street. A rather famous thatched cottage stands in Blake's Road. As the name suggests, William Blake, the poet and painter lived there between 1800 and 1803. The house is built of flint, layered pebble stones and brick. The roof has a pointed block ridge and one section forms a catslide. The house stands close to the Fox Inn, where in 1803 Blake was arrested in the doorway for making allegedly seditious remarks to a soldier billeted there. Pear Tree Cottage stands a little way up the road from the Fox Inn. It is a quaint flint cottage with a thatched roof with an ornamented scalloped ridge. A little further east is the village of Rustington near the coastal resort of Littlehampton. Rustington boasts some old thatched properties and the nearby village of Poling has many thatched brick and flint cottages.

In the hamlet of Bignor, about 5 miles (8 km) north of Arundel, a fifteenth-century yeoman's house, roofed with long-straw thatch may be seen near the church. During its later history, the house became a shop, but it is now a private home. The walls supporting the thatched

William Blake's House, Felpham

A yeoman's house at Bignor

roof are timber framed. The wood is oak and the in-filling bricks, although there are also some flints. The walls are built on an unusually high stone foundation, which necessitated the building of steps to reach the front door. A thatched summerhouse stands in the garden. Nearby there is also a black and white timber-framed thatched house. At the other end of the village a small thatched barn stands opposite the farm and close by is another black and white timber-framed thatched house. One of the largest Roman villas built in Britain was discovered near Bignor and the site, covering several acres, draws many visitors. There are several small thatched huts to be seen covering the excavations. The site has fine examples of mosaics and a small museum, constructed from some of the original rooms, exhibits a miscellany of items found there.

Thatched timbered barn, Bignor

About 6 miles (9.5 km) to the east of Bignor is the village of Amberley. Many old thatched, timbered, brick and flint cottages line the narrow twisting lanes of this lovely village overlooking the River Arun. There are also the remains of a Norman castle that was once lived in by the Bishops of Selsey and later Chichester and a towered gatehouse, which was built during the fourteenth century. The church beside it has a peal of five bells, cast and hung in 1742. The peal is

Honeysuckle Cottage, Amberley

reputed to be the lightest in Sussex. A tennis court with a thatched umpire's seat may be seen from the end of the church graveyard. A little to the north, a historic thatched cottage can be found in the straggling village of Fittleworth. This is Brinkwells, where Elgar lived and composed several of his major musical works during the latter part of the First World War.

An intriguing thatched cottage stands at Henfield, to the north-west of Brighton. It is a sixteenth-century building known as the Cat House. Metal cats adorn the timbered-framed walls just below the eaves and the hipped roof is thatched with long straw. Local legend suggests that the metal cats were originally placed on the walls to remind the vicar that his cat had killed the owner's pet canary. The Cat House stands in the lane leading to the church. There are many other old interesting buildings and inns to be found in Henfield, some impeccably thatched.

The Thatched Cottage, located next to the church at Lindfield, on the outskirts of Haywards Heath, is a close-studded wealden house in an excellent state of preservation. It is believed that Henry VII once used the cottage as a shooting-lodge. Borde Hill Gardens lie about 2 miles (3km) to the north-west and are open to the public on certain days of the year. They contain many rare trees and shrubs, magnificent magnolias and camellias. The gardens at Heaselands, 1½ miles (2.5 km) west of Haywards Heath, are also open to the public on certain days. The undulating water gardens have waterfowl and an aviary.

Many picturesque old thatched cottages beautify the northern part of the village of Rodmell, to the south of Lewes. The village also boasts a very lovely church. On a historical note, Rodmell claims to be one of the areas in England where mulberry trees were first grown during the early seventeenth century. The leaves of the mulberry tree were used for feeding silkworms and Rodmell eventually developed a thriving silk industry.

The first house to be purchased by the National Trust stands at Alfriston, 4 miles (6.5 km) north-east of Seaford. The Clergy House was built in the middle of the fourteenth century for the parish priest. A thatched roof still protects this half-timbered and wattle-and-daub house, located beside the church.

Many old timbered houses remain in the village of Northiam, about 12 miles (19 km) to the north of Hastings. Silvenden Manor, has timber-framed walls and a thatched roof. The house is believed to date from the middle of the fifteenth century, although it has Tudor-style arches. Another manor house, Great Dixter, is not thatched but has one of the largest and grandest timber-framed halls to be found in England. Yet another historical timbered house, Brickwall, like Great Dixter, is opened to the public. Also at Northiam is an oak tree on the village green, named after Queen Elizabeth I. The Queen dined beneath its boughs in 1573.

11

Thatched Buildings in the Home Counties

The Home Counties contain many thatched buildings but their density decreases as one approaches London. The thatch is usually long-straw or water reed, including some imported material. Many walls of the older buildings are timbered, and plasterwork is much in evidence. The technique of pargeting the plaster came into favour – as a decoration on the exteriors of half-timbered houses – during the late sixteenth century and continued throughout the seventeenth. Its popularity fell in the middle of the eighteenth century.

ESSEX

The village of Chrishall in the north-west corner of Essex, contains several quaint seventeenth-century timbered cottages with thatched roofs. Also of interest in the village is the ancient earthwork mound, which is still surrounded by a moat. There is another collection of thatched timbered cottages at Langley, approximately 3 miles (4.8 km) to the south of Chrishall. They nestle near the church, which commands a magnificent view of the surrounding countryside. A large thatched barn dominates the approach road to the Norman church at Wendens Ambo, which is just a little to the east, near Saffron Walden. The expanse of thatch sweeps majestically over its three gables.

In Newport, 2 miles (3 km) south-west of Saffron Walden, some Victorian and older cottages surround the flint-built Church of St Mary the Virgin. They are roofed with an unusual combination of thatch and tile. Other buildings of interest in the village are the Crown House and the Monks Barn. The former has magnificent pargeting dating to 1692. This decorative technique, involving the incising of ornamental patterns into plasterwork, became very popular in the region. The Monks Barn, built in the fifteenth century, has dark red bricks laid in a herringbone pattern. The monks of St Martin-le-Grand once used the barn as their summer holiday home. A little further south-west is Manuden, which has two splendid thatched barns with timber and brick walls.

The small town of Thaxted is a few miles to the south-east of Saffron Walden. The name suggests that the town may be full of thatched buildings, but in fact, the opposite is true and there is only a handful of thatched roofs left in the town. However, the surrounding villages have a host of thatched properties. The three-storeyed Guildhall in Thaxted itself dates from the fifteenth century and each storey overhangs the one below, supported by timber posts. The ground floor, which opens on three sides, is of special interest because it houses long old pole hooks that were originally made for pulling burning

Thatched cottages at Birdbrook

212

The Cottage Museum at Great Bardfield

thatch away from roofs. The Church of St John the Baptist at Thaxted also rewards a visit, as it is judged to be one of the finest in Essex.

Birdbrook, to the north-east of Thaxted, near the Suffolk border, contains many fifteenth-century buildings, some timber-framed with jettied storeys and some thatched. One lucky owner of an old thatched cottage discovered a treasure trove under a flooring stone when he lifted it in 1977, consisting of about 100 gold sovereigns from the period 1825–45.

An unusual thatched building stands in the High Street of Great Bardfield 5 miles (8 km) to the east of Thaxted; it is the tiny sixteenth-century Cottage Museum that has been well renovated, with the thatched roof supported on open rafters. Despite its small size, it has a comparatively large chimney-stack. The museum exhibits many items associated with Essex's rural life, including a fine collection of corn dollies. Another feature of Great Bardfield is the brick tower windmill, which is readily visible from most directions. Wethersfield, about 3 miles (4.8 km) to the east contains many old houses but of special interest is the medieval thatched cottage which was formerly used as a chapel.

Felstead, well known for its public school, is about 7 miles (11 km) to the south. Oliver Cromwell's sons were just some of the many privileged boys who attended the school in the past. A thatched cottage called Quakers Mount stands by one of the several pleasant greens. The walls display a series of decorative moulded shapes depicting fishes, a wheatsheaf and a windmill; as I have said, this type of pargeting plasterwork is a typical feature of East Anglian architecture.

A few miles west of Thaxted, Henham and Ugley nestle close to one another. Both villages are charming and contain interesting groups of thatched cottages. The church at Henham overlooks an exceptionally elegant thatched cottage, while at Ugley a quaint group of thatched cottages borders the road to the west of the church.

High Roding, about 8 miles (13 km) south of Thaxted, boasts an unusual collection of gabled thatched cottages, many with plastered walls. Some appear to be only single-storeyed, owing to the sweep of the thatch passing the upper windows to the ground floor ceiling level. Most of the roofs terminate with tufted points. Some of the windows in the gable walls are sheltered with thatch moulded in the Sussex hip style, others have a gentle sweep cut over them in the eaves. A couple of miles (3 km) away is the tiny village of Aythorpe Roding. It contains some neat thatched buildings, including a timber-framed house constructed about 400 years ago, yet still in good condition. The village of Beauchamp Roding, a short way to the south, also has several thatched cottages and a fourteenth-century church, unusually built in a rather isolated position, in the middle of open fields.

Further south, at Chadwell St Mary, there are many new houses but a quaint fifteenth-century timber-framed house with a thatched roof still stands at the crossroads. Horndon-on-the-Hill, a little to the north, has a picturesque collection of thatched dwellings. There are many old buildings in the village, including a timbered inn dating to approximately the fifteenth century. Fobbing, about 3 miles (4.3 km) to the east, also boasts a 500-year-old inn. This village offers a contrast in roof styles, with thatched cottages mingling with tiled houses. Some of the cottages are in the wealden shape, where the building is constructed around a central hall and the roof sweeps continuously over the whole, including any overhanging storey.

Just a few miles away, in the Thames Estuary, is Canvey Island. The island was originally saved from the river by a Dutch engineer named

A thatched Dutch octagonal cottage
dated 1621, Canvey Island

Joos Croppenburgh, in 1622. He built a complete sea wall around it because it was subject to flooding by the spring tides. For his labours, he received one third of the island as a reward. Two thatched octagonal Dutch cottages, built in 1618 and 1621, remain there. One cottage was opened as a small museum in 1962. Octagonal thatched buildings can also be found in other parts of Essex. The tiny village of Little Bentley, in the north-east of the county near Colchester, has such a building. In this case, it is a thatched octagonal lodge, which can be found near the churchyard.

A second thatched Dutch octagonal cottage, Canvey Island

215

BERKSHIRE

The village of Pangbourne nestles along the banks of the River Thames at the junction where the Pang, a small trout stream meets the main river. It is still attractive, despite the encroachment of modern building development. Several seventeenth- and eighteenth-century houses, together with some lovely thatched cottages, survive in a pleasant riverside setting. The Pangbourne Nautical College sits on the top of the hill. There are good views of the countryside and river at the weir and river lock, but for really spectacular views of the countryside it is better to travel a little further north-west to Streatley. This Thames riverside village shelters in a deep gap that separates the Berkshire Downs from the Chiltern Hills and provides a good vantage point from the high ground at the back of the village. Some thatched properties are to be seen at Streatley, together with Georgian houses and a malthouse constructed in the nineteenth century. A bridge crosses the Thames at Streatley and leads to Goring, in Oxfordshire.

In the opposite direction, the road west from Streatley rises to the peaceful village of Aldworth, which has thatched cottages and a church that was once visited by Queen Elizabeth I. A yew tree stood in the churchyard for about 1,000 years and then not surprisingly suffered decay. Aldworth also has a canopied well that descends 372 feet (113 metres) below the surface, making this one of the deepest in England.

Sonning, also on the banks of the Thames but to the east of Reading, boasts many delightful timber-framed cottages topped with thatched roofs. An old mill also still survives in the village. The bridge that crosses the river to Oxfordshire, is one of the oldest spanning the Thames.

In the west of Berkshire, north of Hungerford, is the village of Leverton. A row of nearly identical thatched cottages, called Pepperpot Cottages, may be seen there. They were built at the beginning of the nineteenth century, along the lines of a planned integrated village. The thatched roofs contrast with the slate roofs over the porches of the cottages. The use of the two materials may have been a fashion compromise. At the time the cottages were built, thatch was fashionable despite the fact that slates were in plentiful supply throughout England.

Pepperpot Cottages, Leverton

A short distance to the north, Lambourn Downs provide excellent gallops for the training of racehorses. The limestone below the turf ensures a firm and well-drained surface to maintain the good going. The River Lambourn runs through the valley and many pretty thatched cottages are sprinkled along its length. The hamlet of Eastbury lies 2 miles (3 km) downstream from Lambourn. Several thatched timber-framed cottages border the river, reached by quaint little bridges. East Garston is a short distance downstream and has several thatched cottages along its twisting street. Welford, a little further south, also has many attractive thatched cottages.

The Berkshire Downs, to the north-east of Lambourn, are equally famous for the training of racehorses, and again many thatched cottages are scattered throughout the vicinity. The hamlet of Beedon, to the south of East Ilsley, also has a row of old thatched timber barns that are raised on brick plinths near the church, which has a huge four-teenth-century open timber roof over the nave.

SURREY

Claremont House, about ½ mile (800 metres) from Esher along the Oxshott road, is a Palladian-style house built in 1772 for Clive of India; 'Capability Brown' laid out its fine gardens. The house and grounds are open to the public on occasions. Claremont is also the name of a neighbouring estate which contains some beautiful detached thatched homes. This exclusive estate faces its own private golf course and also has the benefit of the nearby Oxshott Woods.

KENT

The number of thatched dwellings in Kent is very small in comparison to nearby Sussex. Tile-hung and pantile roofs are more familiar. At one time, Romney Marsh was a good source of cultivated water reeds for thatching. However, the reclamation of land and the development of the marsh for farming and other purposes have, over a period of time, destroyed the large areas of reed beds; only relatively small patches now survive.

At Bethersden, about 6 miles (9.5 km) south-west of Ashford, is a thatched timber-framed hall house, alone in the weald. It is a typical example of the type of hall house constructed in Kent during the late fourteenth and early fifteenth centuries.

Newington borders the western suburbs of Folkestone but still retains its pretty village character. A well-known building called Frogholt Cottage there has been the subject of many artists' paintings. The quaint thatched building has an overhanging storey which gives it considerable charm. To the west of Deal, in the centre of delightful parkland, lies Goodnestone. The old thatched post office there was formerly used as a rectory. Constructed in the Tudor Period, it is the oldest building in the village, with the exception of the thirteenth-century church. Just 2 miles (3 km) to the north is the village of Wingham, halfway between Canterbury and Sandwich. This charming spot has the thatched White Cottage Restaurant in the High Street, which dates from the sixteenth century. There is a park close by.

Barfreston, about 9 miles (14.5 km) to the south-west of Sandwich, has a village pond, a few farms and a group of thatched cottages. These hide in a small lane behind the tiny twelfth-century Church of St Nicholas. The church is unique for the quality of its carvings and mouldings. It is thought that the same masons who worked on Canterbury and Rochester Cathedrals were responsible for the exquisite work there. The stone used was imported from Caen, in Normandy. In addition to the expected religious figures and symbols, there are other carvings showing the more frivolous side of life, including a love scene, a drinking party, a falconer and a bear playing a harp.

In the north-west of the county is the village of Borden near the town of Sittingbourne. In the centre, near the church, is a large barn with a thatched roof.

No thatched churches survive in Kent but a formerly thatched Norman one, Our Lady of the Meadows, still stands at Dode, near Luddesdowne, south of Gravesend. It was built in 1367 but was in an advanced state of disrepair until it was restored in the early twentieth century by a local antiquarian. A Trust now maintains it. It presently has a plate glass roof and the Trust hope that one day it can be rethatched.

HERTFORDSHIRE

The majority of thatched buildings in Hertfordshire are to be found in the west of the county. A beautiful thatched roof covers the property belonging to the Ovaltine Dairy Farm, at Kings Langley. The thatch has a raised ridge with scallops and points. In contrast, squares have been skilfully cut under the chimney ridge area of the thatch. The roof completely surrounds the small upper windows of the building; ornamented thatched aprons lie below them.

The village of Aldbury lies on the edge of the Chiltern Hills a few miles inside Ashridge Park, to the north-west of Kings Langley. Many thatched cottages overlook the village green, which still retains its old whipping-post and stocks. A pond adds further charm to the scene. Other places of interest in the village include a seventeenth-century timbered manor house and some old thatched almshouses, which belong to the same period.

Further to the north, about 6 miles (9.5 km) north-east of Stevenage, may be found the village of Cottered. Here there is an extraordinarily long row of long-straw thatched houses. The walls are plastered and weather-boarded at their bases; these ground-level weatherboards help prevent the rain splashes, from the eaves of the thatch, spoiling the plasterwork. Dormer windows peep through the thatched roof, which at the end of the terrace sweeps down to ground-floor ceiling level. Two miles (3 km) further north is the remote village of Rushden, which contains a group of thatched cottages of exceptional quality and charm.

Charles Lamb once owned a small thatched cottage near the village of Westmill, about 8 miles (13 km) east of Stevenage. The cottage, called Button Snap, has been well preserved because of its literary connection. The thatched roof reaches down low and the small windows have a diamond pattern. The village also boasts a thatched museum which overlooks the inn, and displays items associated with the past life of the village. An ancient thatched barn can also be found nearby. Three miles (4.8 km) north-west of Stevenage, Great Wymondley contains several clusters of thatched cottages in varying states of repair. The village has many historical royal links; Cardinal Wolsey once entertained Henry VIII there.

In the extreme north of the county, 3 miles (4.8 km) south-west of Royston, is Therfield, which has many old thatched timbered cottages and also the carefully restored and thatched timber-framed Tuthill Manor. Parts of the latter building appear crooked, which gives it a quaint appearance. In addition to the main thatched roof, a small thatched canopy covers a bow window. Four miles south-east of Royston, you will find Barkway. Many seventeenth-century thatched cottages line the main street, and there is an old thatched antique shop. Most of the thatch in Barkway is water reed and the walls of the cottages are of pargeted plaster. The hamlet of Nuthampstead Bury nestles close by and contains several picturesque houses thatched with long straw and with mainly timbered walls.

Ashwell borders Cambridgeshire, about 6 miles (9.5 km) west of Royston; its spring pool feeds the River Rhee. There are many timber-framed buildings in the village, and a few of the old houses have jettied storeys. Some are roofed with thatch. A museum in the town displays agricultural implements connected with the past history of the village; including an array of straw-plaiting tools.

Brent Pelham, Stocking Pelham and Furneaux Pelham all cluster together to the south-east of Royston. They contain some beautiful thatched cottages with pargeted plaster walls. The Church of St Mary at Brent Pelham also attracts visitors to see the tomb of Piers Shonks, reputedly the last person to slay a dragon in England.

BUCKINGHAMSHIRE

Chequers, the official country house of the Prime Minster, is about 3 miles (4.8 km) outside the town of Princes Risborough and close to the villages of Monks Risborough and Ellesborough, south of Aylesbury, and all have thatched dwellings. There are many thatched and timbered cottages in the centre of Princes Risborough, some dating to the sixteenth century, and there is also an eighteenth-century manor house. Horsenden, which adjoins Princes Risborough, contains some lovely long-straw thatched houses, with ancient dovecots in their gardens. At nearby Monks Risborough, there are many fine examples of thatched and timbered buildings. It is thought that this village once belonged to the monks of Christ Church Canterbury, before the dissolution of the monasteries. The neighbouring village of Ellesborough also has thatched dwellings and a thatched pub, the ancient Rose and Crown Inn.

To the south-west of Aylesbury, at Long Crendon, can be seen many examples of thatched cottages constructed in the sixteenth and seventeenth centuries. The fifteenth-century timber-framed Court House, which King Henry VIII originally gave to Catherine of Aragon, is also there. The National Trust now owns the property. Two miles (3 km) to the north of the village is Chilton. Many old cottages warrant study here, including some with walls constructed of wattle and daub. There are some timbered cottages and many of the roofs are thatched. In addition, the village offers beautiful scenic views, as it is sited on high ground. Cuddington, about 3 miles (4.8 km) to the east, is slightly unusual in that it boasts two village greens, one of which contains the old village pump. There are many whitewashed thatched cottages in the vicinity and some contain wychert in their walls, a mixture of chalk and mud found exclusively in Buckinghamshire.

Winslow is located just off the main road linking Aylesbury with Buckingham in the north of the county. It is an attractive village with many long-straw thatched cottages, several with large overhanging gables. In addition, the village contains other old interesting buildings, including Winslow Hall, which contains many beautiful baroque wall-paintings and tapestries. There is also the Bell Inn, which claims that the notorious highwayman Dick Turpin was once a frequent visitor. The nearby village of Hoggeston is well endowed with thatched whitewashed cottages.

About 7 miles (11 km) south of Winslow lies the village of Weedon which harbours a host of thatched cottages and farmhouses and two thatched inns that overlook the small green. Many of the buildings have timber frames, in-filled with brick herringbone nogging. A mile north-west is Hardwick, where the lovely thatched St Mary's Cottage sits beside the church. A memorial may be found in the church to Sir Robert Lee, an ancestor of the former American Civil War general, Robert E. Lee.

To the north, near the town of Bletchley, can be found Newton Longville. This pleasant village features an Elizabethan manor house and many timbered cottages with thatched roofs. Further north, beyond Milton Keynes and near the border with Northamptonshire, is the village of Hanslope, which has many thatched cottages near its very tall towered church, which forms a well-known landmark for many miles over the surrounding countryside. Milton Keynes itself has not completely deserted the ancient craft of thatching. The Bovis development in the town is comprised of new thatched homes, with traditional black-and-white walls under thatch with block ridges of scallops and points.

12

Thatched Buildings in the South Midlands

OXFORDSHIRE

Oxfordshire contains a very large number of thatched dwellings, the majority thatched with long straw. There are many villages in the near vicinity of Oxford that display a profusion of thatched roofs. To the south-east, at Chalgrove, an unusual street of thatched cottages can be seen. A stream runs down each side of the road and the cottages are reached by a series of tiny bridges. Just outside the village, an obelisk marks the spot where a decisive battle was fought in 1643, during the Civil War.

To the south of Oxford, Radley has some houses that are of half-timbered construction and roofed with thatch. The village nestles along the banks of the River Thames and Nuneham Woods on the opposite side, stretch along the bank for about 2 miles (3 km). A rustic bridge leading to a wooded island in the middle of the river links these beautiful woods. There is a thatched cottage by the island and its lawn extends down to the banks of the river. The delightful scene of rustic bridge and thatched cottage makes a favourite subject for artists' brushes and pens.

Another pretty bridge and one of the oldest, spans the Thames to the north of Kingston Bagpuize. A quaint old thatched toll-house, with a rounded frontage lies near that village, south-west of Oxford. In the village, visitors also have the opportunity to see the gardens of Kingston House. These are open to the public on certain occasions during the year and display bulbs, flowering shrubs, roses and herbaceous borders.

There are many thatched villages around Didcot, to the south of Oxford, and Didcot itself has many charming thatched dwellings. A mile (1.5 km) south-east of the town can be found East Hagbourne, a picturesque village with many timber-framed cottages with thatched roofs. Bricks, arranged in herringbone fashion, form the wall in-filling on several cottages. Some of the neat gardens of the cottages are enclosed with walls constructed of cob and capped with thatch. The whole village was rebuilt in the seventeenth century after fire destroyed the old one, with the exception of the church. The smaller neighbouring village of West Hagbourne also offers a quaint collection of half-timbered thatched cottages set along the twisting roads and beside the village pond. Blewbury is 2 miles (3 km) to the south. The busy road passing through it has shattered its peace, but it still retains much of its original character, with many old houses and cottages with thatched roofs. Thatched walls may also be seen bordering the orchards and gardens in the village.

A little to the east, Aston Tirrold is set amid beautiful countryside. Both thatch and tiles cover the old cottages, which are mostly built of cob, although a few are half-timbered. Further south-east, near Sonning, may be found the delightful thatched Bottle and Glass Inn. The brick walls below the thatch have been coloured white to contrast with the interspaced black timbers. A pointed block ridge with a bird finial tops the roof. The rather odd name may date to the mid-eighteenth century when beer glasses were first introduced and used in pubs.

Harwell, to the west of Didcot, comprises a combination of the new and the very old. The Atomic Research Establishment symbolizes the modern world, while the many old buildings in the village remind us of the past. One of the few remaining thatched timber-framed cruck houses in England still survives here. The thatched roof spreads over the arched timbers that were fashioned in the fifteenth century. Other old buildings in Harwell include the church, parts of which date from the twelfth century, a fourteenth-century farm and some eighteenth-century almshouses. East Hendred, a little to the west of Harwell, contains some attractive thatched timber-framed houses and cob cottages.

Long Wittenham, to the north-east of Didcot, also has some beautifully thatched houses. Magnificent views of the surrounding countryside can be enjoyed at the nearby hamlet of Little Wittenham, while about a mile (1.5 km) to the north Clifton Hampden, sitting by the side of the River Thames, preserves some immaculately thatched homes and also the famous thatched Barley Mow Inn, dating from 1352, which stands just a few yards from the Victorian bridge that crosses the river. J.K. Jerome featured the inn as one of the settings for *Three Men in a Boat*. He once stayed in a room of this quaint lattice-windowed inn, but it is not known if he wrote the book there. A medieval cruck construction supports the thatched roof, which sweeps down low, and there is little headroom inside the inn. A small tiled gabled window is set in the thatch, beside another with a small thatched canopy. There is another elegant thatched hostelry at Clifton Hampden, the Plough Inn, which stands in the upper part of the village. A delightful sweep of thatch, topped with a small raised ridge, covers this old timbered building. The attractive nineteenth-century six-arched brick bridge spans the Thames nearby. It is reputed that the ghost of John Hampden, a cousin of Oliver Cromwell, who was killed by the Royalists in the Civil War, has been heard pacing the floor of one of the rooms in the inn; this room has since been named after him. A short distance downstream is the charming village of Dorchester and the tiny hamlet of Overy, which can be reached by crossing a bridge constructed in 1815. This hamlet has an exquisite setting and the many old thatched cottages enhance the scene, including one curiously named Mollymops. One timbered cottage has half of one roof slope thatched, with the other half tiled, an unusual occurrence.

Thomas Hardy based his tragic novel *Jude the Obscure* on the village of Letcombe Bassett, about 2 miles (3 km) to the south-west of Wantage; Hardy called it 'Cresscombe'. The village was famous for its watercress beds, watered by Letcombe Brook. Arabella's Cottage is a detached long-straw thatched building by the brook and it was here that Hardy's Arabella, Jude's future wife, lived. The neighbouring hamlet of Letcombe Regis also conceals some delightful old thatched houses, many of which are black-and-white timbered. One of these, the Old House displays an inscription on one of its walls, 'HKM 1698'. The thatch on the roof undulates over the house. The nearby Church of St Andrew contains several monuments to the Piggott family, the ancestors of the famous jockey Lester Piggott. Many racehorses are still trained in the area.

In the village of Sparsholt, 3 miles (4.8 km) to the west of Wantage, half-timbered cottages, roofed with thatch, can be seen. The village also has an unusually large church, parts of which date to the twelfth century. A further 3 miles (4.8 km) to the west, Woolstone hides in a dip on the Downs. This picture-book village has some lovely thatched dwellings.

About 6 miles (9.5 km) north-west of Oxford is Cassington. A collection of stone-walled thatched cottages gather around the green of this pretty village. Approaching the more rural Ot Moor area, to the north-east of Oxford, one finds the village of Stanton St John, which has several good examples of thatched farms and barns. John White, the founder of the State of Massachusetts was born in the village. Two miles (3 km) away, on the eastern edge of Ot Moor, the village of Studley has some lovely thatched timber-framed cottages and an Elizabethan house called Studley Priory.

Another village on the border of Ot Moor is Islip, which has several picturesque stone-walled thatched cottages. Edward the Confessor was born there in 1004. The ancient Monk's Cottage, with its thatched roof, stands by the Church of St Nicholas and a thatched canopy protects a large crucifix that stands nearby. Charlton-on-Ot-moor lies about 3 miles (4.8 km) from Islip and stone and thatched cottages line its streets. For many centuries, a May Day custom took place in the village, involving children carrying garlands of flowers and a floral rope from the school to the church. Beckley, to the south, has a main street of thatched cottages, with quaint crooked stone walls.

More stone-walled thatched dwellings cluster in the village of Great Tew, north-west of Oxford, near Chipping Norton. Set in park woodland, it is one of the loveliest villages to be found in Oxfordshire. Magnificent long-straw thatched roofs with scalloped ridges cover many of the seventeenth-century stone cottages; others have stone-slated roofs and mullioned windows. One of the thatched seventeenth-century cottages with mullioned windows boasts an impressive two-storeyed porch, added in the nineteenth century. The village stocks, also dating from the seventeenth century, still remain on the green.

The hamlet of Sarsden lies 3 miles (4.8 km) south-west of Chipping Norton. Some beautiful thatched homes with scalloped ridges stand in their own extensive grounds; again most date from the seventeenth century. Further south, the village of Taynton can be found by the

River Windrush. Most of the cottages there are kept in immaculate condition and some of them are thatched. Sir Christopher Wren visited the local quarries and some of the stone used for the building of St Paul's Cathedral came from this region.

In the extreme north of the county lies the village of Wroxton, 3 miles (4.8 km) north-west of Banbury. Most of the houses there are built with stone and many are also adorned with mullioned windows. The roofs consist of thatch or stone. Wroxton Abbey stands by the main road near the village. This gabled property was built during the early seventeenth century, on the site of an old priory. An embroidered quilt worked by Mary, Queen of Scots, is exhibited inside. The house also contains a bedroom in which George IV once slept. The village of Hanwell is a short distance away and this exquisite spot has not only thatched and stone-built cottages but also a fine Tudor castle.

The main road south of Banbury runs through the village of Adderbury. The magnificent church spire dominates the many thatched cottages and houses here. Many of these thatched properties were built during the seventeenth century.

GLOUCESTERSHIRE

The number of dwellings roofed with the local Cotswold slates in Gloucestershire exceeds the number with thatched roofs. However, the pitches of the slate roofs are very steep, just as one would expect with a thatched roof. This high pitch is required because the slates consist of split pieces of limestone, which can be porous if water is not shed quickly from their surfaces. A typical Cotswold slated roof has small slates at the ridge area, with larger ones at the eaves. In fact, there is a progressive increase in slate size from the top to the bottom of the roof. There is thus no smooth uniformity over the whole area, as is seen with a thatched roof.

Five miles (8 km) south-west of Cirencester, there are many attractive thatched cottages in the village of Tarlton, most of them built of stone. The countryside around Tarlton is pretty and several roads bordered by trees meet at the village. Also near Cirencester, but 3 miles (4.8 km) to the east, is Ampney St Peter. The houses here are constructed of Cotswold stone and most have thatched roofs. Tiny dormer windows peep through the thatch to give the houses a quaint appearance. The church in the village claims parts that date to the Saxons.

Bishop's Cleeve, about 3 miles (4.8 km) north of Cheltenham, has a timber-framed yeoman's house with a thatched roof. The small property has just one storey and a single chimney. About 6 miles (9.5 km) to the north-east of Cheltenham can be found the village of Gretton; this delightful spot has several old thatched cottages in the close vicinity of the Old Tower.

Further north, approximately 2 miles (3 km) to the east of Chipping Campden, the Cotswold village of Ebrington reclines on the hillside. It contains many thatched cottages set amid a lovely wooded area; again, most of the cottages are built with stone. Very close by, at Hidcote Bartrim, the National Trust administers Hidcote Manor Gardens, one of the most beautiful English formal gardens open to the public.

The small village of Ryton lies alongside the motorway in the north-west corner of the county. In its more peaceful days, the poet and critic Lascelles Abercrombie lived and worked in one of the small thatched cottages in the village.

WARWICKSHIRE

The western border regions of Warwickshire are particularly well endowed with timber-framed buildings. Houses built of sandstone are also encountered throughout the county, together with thatched roofs. There are a great number of thatched villages and hamlets in the vicinity of Stratford-upon-Avon and it is worth observing that the chimneys of the older buildings in the town itself are exceptionally tall. They were originally erected in this way so that sparks emitted from them could be carried away safely, instead of falling on their roofs, which were then thatched.

Many tourists visit the most famous thatched building in the county, Anne Hathaway's Cottage at Shottery, snuggling close to Stratford-upon-Avon on its western perimeter. Anne Hathaway was born in the thatched cottage and lived there until her marriage to William Shakespeare in 1582. The oldest part of the cottage was previously a fifteenth-century yeoman's farmhouse. An upper floor was added during the seventeenth century and the enlarged cottage then contained twelve bedrooms. For many years, the roof had a block ridge with points and was tastefully decorated with cross-rods to give an ornamented pattern. These blended with the latticed windows of the black and white timber-framed house. However, towards the end of the twentieth century, the ridge was replaced with a flush one to give a more traditional appearance. The Shakespeare Birthplace Trust now owns the cottage. Shottery also has many thatched timber-framed cottages, set in their own individual neat gardens.

Anne Hathaway's cottage at Shottery

About 3 miles (4.8 km) to the south-west can be found the pretty village of Welford-on-Avon. This has many thatched timber-framed houses dotted along the main street, sloping down to the river. A 70-foot (21 metre) high striped maypole stands on the village green, topped with a weather-vane in the shape of a fox. Three miles downstream, the Avon reaches the village of Barton, which has some excellent examples of thatched houses; the occasional one has an ornamental straw weathercock. A short distance further south-west, at Salford Priors, several thatched seventeenth-century timber-framed farm houses may be seen.

Five miles (8 km) to the south of Stratford-upon-Avon the village of Lower Quinton can be found. Some charming thatched timber-framed houses surround St Swithin's Church, which has an unusually large spire. Many people rate Ilmington, another 3 miles (4.8 km) to the south, the most beautiful village in Warwickshire. It boasts several stone thatched houses and cottages, a gabled manor house and a church that has many late additions, although it mainly dates from 1500. Hurdle makers have worked in the village for many centuries and this craft survives as well as that of the thatchers.

Another picturesque village lies 5 miles (8 km) to the east of Stratford-upon-Avon; this is Wellesbourne, comprising Wellesbourne Mountfield and Wellesbourne Hastings. The Stag's Head Inn has a thatched roof. In 1872, Joseph Arch, later to become an MP, called a meeting there to discuss the plight of local farm labourers. The attendance was so high that it had to overflow onto the green opposite. The historic meeting was the first step towards the formation of the National Agricultural Workers Union. The nearby hamlet of Butler's Marston, to the south-east, is also worth a visit to admire the lovely groups of thatched cottages.

Honington, a little further south has thatched cottages sprinkled along its sloping main street beside the green. The impressive Honington Hall dominates the village and is one of the finest mansions to survive from the Restoration period. Nearby Tredington still suffers visible evidence of the Civil War. The huge wooden door of the church bears battle marks and the remnants of some bullets still remain embedded in it. An attractive long-straw thatched property stands opposite the church that dates to Saxon times.

Edge Hill, another Civil War battlefield, towers 700 feet (213 metres) over the peaceful village of Radway in the south-east of the county. Trees surround this village of charming thatched cottages clustered around the green. An ancestor of George Washington, the first President of the United States of America, once owned the gabled Radway Grange in the village.

The village of Whichford, to the south-east, near the county border, has several thatched yeoman farmers' houses lining the village green. The stone houses have mullioned windows and some have stone roofs, which add variety to the adjoining thatched ones. Also of note in the village is Whichford House, near the church, which has a beautiful English country garden. Long Compton is only a couple of miles (3 km) away and is of interest because there is a thatched churchroom above the lich-gate.

Stoneleigh, a few miles south of Coventry, has a cruck-framed hall house; it is situated in Birmingham Road and the walls under the thatch consist of brick nogging set in timber panels.

HEREFORD AND WORCESTER

The counties of Herefordshire and Worcestershire have a large number of thatched dwellings and many of the old walls of the houses are half timbered, with in-fillings of wattle and daub. Examples of even earlier forms of house construction can be seen at the Avoncroft Museum of Buildings, 2 miles (3 km) outside Bromsgrove. This is an open-air museum with reconstructions of a variety of buildings, ranging from the Iron Age to modern times. An Iron Age hut, with low stone walls makes an interesting feature, with the conical thatched roof rising to a sharp pointed pinnacle. The top of the doorway reaches the same height as the eaves of the thatch. The eaves on each side of the doorway then sweep down to near ground level. The museum also has a thatched cruck-framed barn, with its timber-box walls in-filled with woven pales of split oak.

The A38 from the ancient cathedral city of Worcester passes through the village of Kempsey, where several very old thatched cottages may be found. Most of the roofs are thatched with long straw and a few display extraordinarily tall chimneys. In Upton Snodsbury, about 6 miles (9.5 km) east of Worcester, there are some excellent examples of timber-framed properties with long-straw thatched roofs.

At the foot of Bredon Hill, which rises to a height of 961 feet (293 metres), to the west of the market town of Evesham is Great Comberton. There you will find many thatched cottages and half-timbered farmhouses; also of interest in the village are the multi-holed dovecots, one of which is believed to be the largest in England. The adjoining village of Little Comberton also has a large dovecot at the manor house and the village contains many picturesque thatched timber-framed cottages, as does the nearby village of Bredon, beside the River Avon. It also contains the Fox and Hounds Inn, a beautiful thatched and timbered sixteenth-century inn. Other places of interest in this lovely village include a fourteenth-century tithe barn and the Norman cruciform Church of St Giles, with its fourteenth-century spire.

Also to the west of Evesham lies Cropthorne. This charming village has a long main street of many black-and-white half-timbered cottages with thatched roofs. There is also an old thatched post office and a seventeenth-century thatched timber-framed farmhouse; its many orchards further enhance the beauty of the spot. A row of timber-framed cottages was converted to form Holland House, the long thatched building seen in the village. Sir Edwin Lutyens, the early twentieth-century architect laid out its gardens.

The village street, Cropthorne

Three miles (4.8 km) south-east of Evesham lies Childswickham. Here thatched timber-framed houses can be found and also an ancient fourteenth-century cross at the roadside, near the church. The village of Sedgeberrow, to the south of Evesham, is also worth a visit as it contains another good collection of ancient timber-framed thatched cottages.

Offenham, about 2 miles (3 km) north of Evesham, is an attractive place with many thatched cottages and some old dovecots. A very tall maypole, topped with a cockerel, adds to the old-world atmosphere.

Further west at Eastnor, near Ledbury, are some excellent examples of timber-framed properties, with long-straw thatched roofs. Further west still is Bartestree, 3 miles (4.8 km) east of Hereford; long-straw thatched cottages are sprinkled throughout this village. Hampton Bishop, not far away, is worth a visit to enjoy its lovely thatched half-timbered cottages, with their neat gardens strung along the village street. The thatched Old Court Cottage was built in the sixteenth century and the nearby Norman church has a pyramid-shaped black-and-white timber-framed belfry with six bells.

Still going west on the other side of Hereford, is Mansell Gamage. This village boasts many black-and-white cottages, most topped with thatched roofs. Vowchurch, to the south-west of Mansell Gamage, also has some thatched cottages and the timber-framed post office has a thatched roof. A bridge spans the River Dore here, near the sixteenth-century Old Vicarage. The village has beautiful surroundings, as it is set in the tranquil Golden Valley.

BEDFORDSHIRE

There are a great number of thatched properties in Bedfordshire. At Ickwell Green, a most beautiful village to the south-east of Bedford, there is a collection of thatched houses completely surrounding the very large village green, which measures approximately ½ mile (800 metres) across. The houses are unusual in that they are low but still fitted with dormer windows. A large maypole stands in the centre of the green, together with an old smith's shop. The village of Old Warden is just 2 miles (3 km) away. In addition to its many pretty thatched cottages, the lodge guarding the road to Old Warden Park has a magnificent thatched roof. It is thatched with long straw and the ridge is richly adorned with scallops and points. A series of vertical rustic pillars support the roof. The shape is peculiar; the main roof section is curved but there are straight hip sections at the end, over-hanging the pillar supports. Another worthwhile place to visit is the Shuttleworth Collection, which is on the road linking Ickwell Green with Old Warden. The collection consists of aircraft and vintage cars gathered together at an aerodrome, which is open to the public. Clifton, 4 miles (6.5 km) south-east of Old Warden, also displays many good examples of thatched buildings.

In the extreme south-east of the county, the motorway passes the village of Caddington. Despite its proximity some thatched houses still surround the village green and the old village pump. The walls of the houses consist mainly of stone and plasterwork, with the thatched roofs descending low and neatly around the upper windows. There are also adjacent houses with tiled roofs.

The rather unusual building used as the Congregational Chapel at Roxton, 7 miles (11 km) north-east of Bedford, has been described on page 128. Roxton itself lies near the River Ouse, and many delightful thatched houses and barns may be seen by the banks of the river.

Ten miles (16 km) north of Bedford, Melchbourne has a complete street of thatched cottages that were erected in the eighteenth century. The village is also of note as it once formed a centre for the Knights Hospitallers. Nearer to Bedford at Clapham, a quaint thatched cottage overlooks a ford of the River Ouse. The Church of St Thomas of Canterbury has a rare and very large Anglo-Saxon observation tower. A short distance to the north-west, just outside the village of Stevington, a post windmill with sails may be seen, and a thatched cottage adjoins the approach to the mill. About another 3 miles (4.8 km) north-west, is a thatched inn at the riverside village of Odell. This spot has many stone-walled thatched cottages. The pretty neighbouring village of Sharnbrook also contains many thatched cottages. An attractive thatched terrace with ashlar walls stands just off the centre. The long stretch of thatch has an exceptionally high pitch. The roof sweeps below the level of the dormer windows, which are positioned extremely low, near the floor level of the upper rooms of the cottages. Harrold is also close to Odell and has many lovely thatched cottages near the octagonal Market House by the tiny village green.

A visit to the village of Stagsden, 5 miles (8 km) west of Bedford, is always worthwhile, to enjoy the Stagsden Bird Gardens. Well over a thousand birds, many of them extremely rare, are kept in this bird zoo and breeding establishment; it is open to the public throughout the year. The village is tiny but it contains several pretty thatched cottages. The road south from Bedford soon brings you to Elstow, which has many thatched houses and cottages. John Bunyan was born here and a miscellany of items relating to his life and work can be seen in Moot Hall, a medieval timbered building with an over-hanging upper storey. A little further south is Ampthill, where many old buildings with historical connections are preserved. Henry VIII and Catherine of Aragon were once frequent visitors and lived in a castle that no longer exists. Thatched cottages may be found in the town, including an attractive half-timbered group in Woburn Street which Lord Ossory built in the early nineteenth century for the workers on his estate. A neat row of thatched semi-detached cottages also stand on the Russell Estate, also built during the earlier part of the nineteenth century. The cottages appear nearly identical and the thatch sweeps over the windows in the gable walls in the form of a Sussex hip.

Several picturesque thatched cottages line the village green of Flitwick by the river about 2 miles (3 km) south of Ampthill. About 5 miles (8 km) to the west of the village can be found Woburn Abbey and the Wild Animal Kingdom, both of which are open to the public. Woburn Abbey is the stately residence of the Duke of Bedford and houses a magnificent collection of paintings and furniture; the Wild Animal Kingdom is set amid the surrounding parkland. The village of Woburn contains several attractive thatched cottages, some of which are constructed with contrasting red and white bricks. Other old build-ings may be found in the village, including several ancient inns. A magnificent thatched barn may be seen at the manor house of Milton Bryan, about a mile (1.5 km) away to the south. A little further south-west, Leighton Buzzard borders the River Ouse. It has many old buildings, including thatched cottages constructed of brick and timber.

NORTHAMPTONSHIRE

Thatched roofs are quite common in Northamptonshire, despite the competition of the locally manufactured Collyweston tiles, which are still made in the traditional way in the village of Collyweston, in the north-east of the county.

A village of historic interest in this north-eastern corner is Fotheringhay, where Mary, Queen of Scots, was beheaded in 1587. A row of thatched cottages can be seen very close to the site of the castle where the execution took place. Many of the older cottages in the village have exceptionally small doors. Further along the River Nene towards Kettering, beside a mill and ford, may be found Wadenhoe. This village contains a mixture of thatched and tiled roofs. It is set in beautiful countryside, with several farms and barns in close proximity.

A few miles to the west, the road north from Kettering runs through the village of Geddington. Most of the old cottages in the village are thatched as is the old post office. Other sites of note in the village are a medieval bridge spanning the River Ise and an ancient stone cross in the square. This was erected on the instructions of Edward I to denote one of the places where his wife's coffin rested during 1290, on its journey to Westminster Abbey. Just before reaching Geddington, the road from Kettering passes through Weekley, an attractive village which also has many thatched cottages.

Rockingham overlooks the River Welland, just north of Corby. Several old stone cottages with thatched roofs line the long main street of this hillside village. It is possible to obtain magnificent views of five counties by climbing to the top of the hill, and visiting Rockingham Castle. William the Conqueror built the estate and many early kings of England used it. Drastic rebuilding and alterations have been made since that time and the present building has components from nearly 900 years of English architectural styles.

The village of Gretton, 5 miles (8 km) to the north-east, resembles Rockingham in two ways: it stands on a hilltop from which outstanding views may be obtained, and it also contains several old thatched cottages. The house and gardens of Kirby Hall, which are open to the public, stand 2 miles (3 km) outside Gretton. The hall was built in 1570, but the architect Inigo Jones later inspired many alterations.

The road west from Kettering leads, after 3 miles (4.8 km), to the town of Rothwell. An intriguing thatched building stands on the outskirts of the town. A date on the door suggests it may have been constructed in 1660, and it is reached by a series of sharply rising stone steps.

There is another intriguing but smaller thatched property at the village of Flore, on the road west from Northampton. It is believed that ancestors of John Adams once lived there. Adams became President of the United States of America immediately after George Washington. As might be expected, the house is now called Adams' Cottage. It is interesting that the ancestors of George Washington also lived nearby in Northamptonshire, at the village of Sulgrave a few miles to the south. The small Elizabethan manor house, Sulgrave Manor, attracts many American visitors, as it is open to the public. Badby, to the west of Flore, is also on a hillside. It contains several picturesque thatched cottages set amid woods, parkland and lakes. Charles I hunted deer in the nearby Fawsley Park.

Another park with hunting connections can be seen near the village of Boughton, bordering the northern outskirts of Northampton. Boughton Park boasts falconry towers where hawks were once trained. The village also has some thatched stone cottages grouped around the green. The largest horsefair in the country was held at Boughton Green until 1916.

Wellingborough, to the north-east of Northampton, boasts a lovely thatched Tudor restaurant in Sheep Street, alongside other ancient buildings. There is also a thatched stone tithe barn originally built in the fifteenth century to store the tithes on behalf of Croyland Abbey. The barn stands behind the Hind Inn, where Cromwell stayed before the Battle of Naseby.

A few miles south of Northampton can be found Stoke Bruerne, near Towcester. The Boat Inn, is a delightful seventeenth-century thatched building, originally constructed from a row of thatched limestone cottages. The hostelry sits on the tow-path of the Grand Union Canal, beside a set of lock gates. The Waterways Museum stands on the opposite bank of the canal.

Some new stone and thatched houses have been built at nearby Silverstone and also to the west, at Middleton Cheney in Church View. Asby St Ledgers, between Rugby and Daventry, contains several twentieth-century cottages of stone and thatch mingled with the older ones. Many of the newer cottages possess windows that slide sideways, thus obviating the need for casement or vertical sash windows; a method especially suited to low roofed thatched cottages. New thatched homes have also been built at Barnwell St Andrew, to the south of Oundle in the north of the county. As with most new thatched developments, each individual home has been carefully designed to blend with the local vernacular style.

13

Thatched Buildings in the North Midlands and the Northern Counties

SHROPSHIRE

Shropshire has a lot of well-preserved half-timbered buildings. Many of these are black and white and thatched. The pretty village of Bucknell, in the extreme south-west corner of the county, near the borders of Wales and Herefordshire, contains a mixture of dwellings, some of stone and half-timbered construction and several with thatched roofs. Two miles (3 km) to the north is the hamlet of Bedstone, which has one or two thatched cottages, as well as a fifteenth-century timber-framed manor house. Another 4 miles (6.5 km) further north lies Clungunford, and hidden amongst its charming buildings is the Thatched Cottage, in Beckjay Lane. This timber-framed cottage dates to the fourteenth century and still retains some of the original wattle and daub between its timbers. The gable wall has a Welsh-style stepped chimney.

Further north, and 2 miles (3 km) south of Church Stretton can be found Little Stretton. All Saints Church has a thatched roof and small thatched gabled windows peep through it. Despite its Gothic windows, it is only about a century old; it was built in 1903, at the expense of Mrs Gibbon of the Manor House. At that time, it was unusual for thatch to be used for church roofs. The half-timbered building has whitewashed walls between its blackened timbers, which blend naturally into the surrounding countryside, where old cottages of similar colours abound. The neighbouring hamlet of Minton is worth a visit to gain an impression of how a small Anglo-Saxon settlement may once have looked. Cottages, farmhouses and manor house cluster in a rough circle around a small green beside an Anglo-Saxon mound.

A thatched church at Little Stretton

The road north from Church Stretton reaches, after about 3 miles (4.8 km) the village of Leebotwood. This attractive village has several pretty black-and-white timbered houses and also a thatched pub, the Pound Inn. An outside beam, dated 1650, gives a false clue to the age of this pleasant hostelry. In fact, the majority of the building dates from around 1480 and it served as a farmhouse until 1804, before its change of use. The inn has some fine Jacobean panelling. The thatched roof is of the winged type and is topped with a neat block ridge, ornamented with a cross-rod pattern. The points along the lower ridge edge are decorated.

Climbing the ridge known as Long Mynd will give a good idea of the villages in the neighbourhood of Church Stretton. It runs along the west side of the villages and commands fantastic views over the surrounding English countryside and the Welsh counties. It stretches, north to south, for about 10 miles (16 km) and is approximately 1,700 feet (518 metres) high.

Much further north, beyond Shrewsbury, is Loppington, about 5 miles (8 km) west of Wem, which has a thatched pub, the Blacksmith's Arms.

As the name suggests it was once a smithy but at the same time the village blacksmith served beer to his thirsty customers. It officially became a pub in 1984 after an extensive renovation, including a new thatched roof.

In the north-east of the county you will find Tibberton, about 5 miles (8 km) west of Newport. There are several Victorian cottages in the village but also several older dwellings with thatched roofs.

STAFFORDSHIRE

In the east of Staffordshire, at the village of Alrewas near Lichfield, the wide main street has many thatched houses constructed in the Tudor period, and most of the dwellings in the village are black and white. The locality was once famous for its basket makers, who used the osiers that grew along the banks of the River Trent. In addition to the river, the Trent and Mersey Canal flows through the village.

Further west, near the county town of Stafford is Walton, which has an old post office in the form of a fine thatched cottage. It also has an unusual church with a central spire and tower. The M6 motorway carves a path around the western suburbs of Stafford, and about a mile (1.5 km) to the west of it lies the small village of Seighford, which has retained many of its picturesque thatched cottages. About 8 miles (13 km) north of Stafford, the motorway also passes the village of Swynnerton. There are several thatched cottages here, together with an old smithy and an inn. A chestnut tree in the village is reputed to be the one that inspired Longfellow to write his poem 'Under the Spreading Chestnut Tree'.

A thatched farm cottage at Shallowford, 5 miles (8 km) north-east of Stafford, was burned down twice during the twentieth century. After each of these disasters it was rebuilt, refurbished and restored as carefully as possible to recapture its former self. This cottage, known as Izaak Walton's, is open to the public as a memorial museum. The anglers who visit it still revere Walton as the world's most famous angler, although he was born in 1593. He wrote *The Compleat Angler*, an acknowledged masterpiece in 1653, and secured himself a place in English literature, despite the fact that he only wrote one other book. He bequeathed the thatched cottage, then part of his farm to the town of Stafford, so that the rent money could be put to charitable purposes. The stipulations included the cost of apprenticing two poor boys, the provision of a marriage portion for a servant girl and finally the purchase of coal for those in need. The cottage is relatively small, with a black-and-white timbered exterior and the hipped thatched roof is of long straw.

Walton was baptized in the Church of St Mary in Stafford where he was born; his father kept an alehouse in the town. This church has a fairly unusual octagonal tower. Stafford itself is sprinkled with many ancient buildings, among which is a tiny picturesque timbered building with a thatched roof that adjoins the seventeenth-century Noel Almshouses in Mill Street.

The village of Ellastone lies further north-east between Stoke-on-Trent and Derby. Many people visit it because of its connections with *Adam Bede*, the novel written by George Eliot in 1859. Ellastone was Adam Bede's Hayslope, and some of the thatched houses identified in the book may still be found in the locality.

DERBYSHIRE

In the past, flax was often used as a thatch material in Derbyshire and up to the beginning of the twentieth century the verges of many thatched roofs were coated with mortar to strengthen them. The walls of the houses in the northern parts of the county were mainly constructed of stone, but many in the south were later built with bricks. Only a relatively small number of thatched properties remain in the county.

Two miles (3 km) north of the centre of Chesterfield lies the suburb of Old Whittington. A small stone house with a thatched roof, called Revolution House, can be found here. It was once an inn and was then called the Cock and Pynot. In 1688, William Cavendish, the fourth Earl of Devonshire and his associates used it as a meeting-place to plot the downfall of James II and put William of Orange on the throne. The thatched house is now a museum displaying a fine collection of seventeenth-century furniture.

Further south-west, two miles south-east of Ashbourne, near the border with Staffordshire, is Osmaston, one of the prettiest villages to be found in the county. The many lovely thatched brick cottages are set in a delightful park with a pleasant lake. The local Walker family originally built them for their estate workers.

To the south, about 10 miles (16 km) east of Burton upon Trent is Calke, well-known for its abbey and its large park. The Harpur family and their relations the Crewes lived in Calke Abbey from the end of the seventeenth century. This delightfully eccentric and reclusive family left most of the interior of the abbey completely untouched for over a century, before the National Trust took it over in 1986. One member of the family committed an unacceptable social blunder in the late eighteenth century by marrying a maid. Some seventeenth-century painted brick and thatched cottages with eyebrow dormer windows overlook the lake on the Calke Estate and are worth seeing.

NOTTINGHAMSHIRE

Thatch is now fairly rare in Nottinghamshire; much more common are the local slates and stones. However, Barton in Fabis, on the southern outskirts of Nottingham, still manages to keep some of its individual charm, with thatched cottages and thatched farms. The nearby suburb of Clifton, even closer to the city centre, has also retained some of its original rural charm. Thatched cottages line a village green that boasts an eighteenth-century gabled dovecot.

LEICESTERSHIRE

Leicestershire still has a fair sprinkling of thatched roofs, owing to its long agricultural history. Many of the old houses are timber framed, with walls in-filled with stones or clay. About 10 miles (16 km) south of Leicester, the M1 motorway runs alongside the large village of Lutterworth; here there are several good examples of timber-framed cottages with thatched roofs, one of which dates to the seventeenth century. The village is also of note because John Wycliffe, the religious reformer of the fourteenth century lived there when translating the Bible into English.

About 5 miles (8 km) north-west of Leicester lies Newtown Linford. Because of its proximity to the city, there are many new houses in the locality; but the village remains one of the loveliest to be found in the county. Several half-timbered cottages with thatched roofs line the sides of the road and several old timber-framed cruck houses still survive. These picturesque houses are furnished with thatched roofs topped with ornamented ridges. A large number of small points, similar to the teeth of a saw, have been cut along some of the bottom ridge edges. Bradgate Park, a wooded and rocky heath land, borders Newtown Linford. The park is now a nature reserve but still contains the ruins of Bradgate Hall, where Lady Jane Grey lived during the sixteenth century. On the day of her execution, after being Queen of England for only a few days, the oak trees near Bradgate Hall were severely lopped. Some still survive.

Hathern, further to the north-west, near the border with Nottinghamshire, has several old thatched cottages. On an historical note, the inventor of the Heathcote lace-making machine once lived in a thatched cottage here. At the time of its introduction, the machine revolutionized the art of lace making.

About 3 miles (4.8 km) from the northern suburbs of Leicester lies Queniborough, which has a Norman church with an exceptionally tall steeple. The village also boasts many exquisite old thatched cottages, the majority being built with the local ironstone.

There are several thatched villages in the vicinity of the town of Oakham, in Rutland. Again many of the thatched cottages were built with locally available materials – in this particular area, ironstone or limestone. At the beautiful village of Ayston, to the south of Oakham, there are many cottages constructed with the familiar light brown ironstone and topped with thatched roofs. They mingle with other cottages roofed with Collyweston slates.

At Exton, to the north-east of the town, there are many limestone cottages, many of which have thatched roofs. The village is set amid delightful scenery and by the broad acres of Exton Park. The church of St Peter and St Paul stands in the park and rewards a visit. It guards one of the finest collections of monumental sculpture to be found in England; most date from the sixteenth to the eighteenth centuries. The nearby village of Cottesmore offers several delightful stone houses with long-straw thatched roofs. The local quarries again yielded the stone from which they were built. Cottesmore became famous as a leading centre of fox-hunting in England; packs of foxhounds have been continuously kennelled here since 1788, although they were first established in Exton in 1732.

Edith Weston, 5 miles (8 km) south-east of Oakham, contains many thatched cottages built with local stone, all grouped around the village green. The village is named after Queen Edith, the wife of Edward the Confessor, who once owned it. At Lyddington, further south, the buildings are arranged entirely along a single street. Many of the cottages carry stones marked with dates embedded in their walls and these reveal that some were built when Elizabeth I was on the throne. Again, most were constructed with ironstone, although a few are of limestone. A long-straw thatched roof still covers a seventeenth-century farmhouse there but many of the cottages that were formerly thatched have since been roofed with less costly slates or pantiles.

About 6 miles (9.5 km) west of Lyddington, is Hallaton, on whose village green can be found an unusual buttercross in the form of a large conical stone with a small stone sphere on top, indicating that a market was once held there. Several seventeenth- to nineteenth-century thatched cottages surround the green, together with a thatched inn, the Bewicke Arms, which has a separate thatched porch sheltering its entrance. A game known as 'bottle-kicking' has been held on Easter Monday for many centuries between the village team and one from neighbouring Medbourne, 3 miles (4.8 km) away. The bottle consists of a small iron-bound beer cask and the two teams struggle for many hours to get it within their own village boundary. Traditionally, the vicar starts the contest by throwing pieces of hare pie over the two teams, and the contest ends with the beer keg drained by the winning team. The bizarre folk custom is known locally as the Hare Pie Scramble.

In the far west of the county is Market Bosworth, an old town with several very attractive thatched cottages. It also has historical associations, namely the Battle of Bosworth in 1485, which terminated the War of the Roses and took place a few miles to the south of the town.

Lubenham, just outside Market Harborough, has a historical connection with another civil war, the seventeenth-century one. Charles I stayed in the village on several occasions during the conflict. The little village still retains a few thatched dwellings.

LINCOLNSHIRE

Somersby, 6 miles (9.5 km) north-east of Horncastle, to the east of Lincoln, was the birthplace of Alfred, Lord Tennyson; he was born in a cottage that his father later extended for use as a rectory. A good example of a single-storey thatched dwelling stands just outside the tiny village. Although it was constructed in the seventeenth century as a single-parlour farmhouse, it is typical of the long houses built by the Anglo-Saxons, who shared their living quarters with their livestock. Dalderby, a couple of miles (3 km) south of Horncastle, has a lovely farmhouse with a thatched roof which is more conventional and larger than the rather unusual one near Somersby. A few thatched roofs can also be found scattered through the village of Thimbleby, 2 miles (3 km) west of Horncastle. A rare example of a seventeenth-century mud-and-stud cottage still survives in the village, and the church gives the impression it is rather large for the size of the village.

Crowland, in the south of the county, and just north of Peterborough, offers a sprinkling of thatched roofs, including a thatched tea-house with an unusual finial depicting a cup and saucer. Also of interest in the village is the fascinating stone triangular bridge formed from three circular sections meeting at an apex. It was built in the thirteenth century when the present streets were waterways. The bridge was left high and dry in the centre of village after the land was

Cup and saucer finial on café roof, Crowland

drained several centuries later and it now serves no practical purpose other than as an unusual scenic feature. Also worth a visit are the ruins of a Benedictine abbey less than a mile outside the village.

The small town of Alford, in the east of the county, boasts a brick-walled thatched manor house built in the seventeenth century. It claims to be the largest manor house in England but it is now a folk museum. Another well-known thatched building is the White Horse Hotel, which was originally a sixteenth-century posting-house; also of interest is the old windmill that still stands on the eastern side of the town. The north-east road from Alford leads, after a couple of miles (3 km), to the village of Markby, which has a very old thatched church that has been restored.

At the seaside resort of Skegness to the south-east you will find Church Farm Museum, a former eighteenth-century farmhouse. It displays a collection of agricultural and domestic bygones, as well as a thatched mud-and-stud cottage brought from the village of Withern and re-erected in 1982. Another restored thatched mud-and-stud cottage may be seen at the Billinghay Cottage and Craft Museum, near Sleaford. The limewashed cottage dates to the seventeenth century.

In the north of the county lies the village of West Rasen, about 3 miles (4.8 km) to the west of the town of Market Rasen. An old thatched post office and general store may be seen here. West Rasen also has a packhorse bridge that was built during the fourteenth century. South Willingham, south-east of Market Rasen, boasts a few lovely thatched cottages which add considerable charm to the village.

In the south of the county is the town of Spalding by the River Welland. Delightful fields of bulbs and flowers, reminiscent of Holland, surround the town and attract many visitors in springtime. Spalding itself boasts many fascinating old buildings; the White Horse Inn has an attractive thatched roof. The village of Fleet, to the east of Spalding, in the direction of the Wash, has a rather unusual four-teenth-century church, with a separate tower and spire; a thatched lich-gate guards the path to it.

CHESHIRE

A wood of Scots pine belonging to the National Trust overlooks the charming village of Burton, 7 miles (11 km) north-west of the ancient

Mill House, Raby

city of Chester. Many thatched white-walled and half-timbered cottages remain in the village. Charles Kingsley wrote about the lovely spot in his poem 'Sands of Dee'. The neighbouring hamlet of Ness is also well known, as the birthplace of Nelson's Lady Hamilton.

Three miles (4.8 km) to the north is the hamlet of Raby. Here you will find an early seventeenth-century thatched inn, the Wheatsheaf, a half-timbered building with dormer windows; its thatched roof has been well maintained and is ornamented. Nearby is a local beauty spot, Raby Mere. A thatched timbered mill house, with an ornamented block ridge, overlooks the quiet stretch of water at this delightful spot, which is popular at weekends for boating and picnics. The mill house was built during the same period as the inn at Raby. Many old thatched cottages still remain in the Bidston region of Birkenhead, to the north of Raby. Also of note is Bidston Hill, which has been conserved as an open heath for the public to enjoy. An old windmill makes a prominent and familiar landmark nearby.

Several half-timbered thatched cottages, mainly black and white and therefore called 'magpie houses', can be found in the tiny village of Peckforton, approximately 10 miles (16 km) south-east of Chester. A strangely ornamented stone beehive may be spotted in one of the gardens. It is carved in the shape of an elephant, with a castle on its back. Another intriguing building, to the north of the village, is a nineteenth-century castle designed by Salvin, set on a hill. More thatched cottages may be seen at Norbury, to the south of Peckforton.

At Little Leigh near Northwich, towards the north of the county, a delightful thatched timber-framed building with red bricks snuggles close to a farm. It has been a pub, the Holly Bush, for many years and a holly bush, after which it is named, still shelters it. Its smart block ridge displays a series of points.

South of Knutsford, at the small village of Lower Peover, there are many cottages constructed of timber and roofed with thatch. An old watermill is preserved close by, together with an unusual church with large overhanging eaves and black-and-white gables. An ancient inn neighbours the church. About 8 miles (13 km) to the north, the town of Hale, near Altrincham, now forms a part of Greater Manchester, but despite the encroachment of modern town buildings, several old properties still survive. One such is Hope Cottage, in Bank Hall Lane. This timber-framed cottage was built in the sixteenth century and during its long history it was once used for a short time as a mission. It has a lovely thatched roof, with a block ridge and neat points cut along its bottom edge. The ridge and points are immaculately ornamented with diamond-shaped patterns. Styal, a short distance to the south-east, also has several timber-framed thatched cottages, some with truncated crucks in their gable walls. One is aptly named Tudor Cottage.

The beautiful village of Barthomley, east of Nantwich also has some black-and-white timbered houses and cottages.

LANCASHIRE AND MERSEYSIDE

In the past, timber-framed thatched cottages were fairly common in the southern and western regions of Lancashire, and one, built in 1665, still survives at Hale, in Merseyside. This lovely village also has in its old churchyard the grave of John Middleton, a 9-foot (2.7 metre) giant who once defeated the best wrestler to be found in the court of James I. West Kirby, also in Merseyside still has some old thatched stone cottages.

Lancashire also caters for those who prefer to live in more modern thatched cottages. One of the earliest modern developments took place in the 1970s, when a thatched group of homes was built at Cleveleys, on the coast near Blackpool. The luxurious houses, with deep thatch aprons and block ridges harmonize with the more traditional cottages already dotted along the Fylde coastline. Another group of up-market thatched houses was built in the 1980s at Chorley, further south. Several thatched houses were also built in the 1980s on an estate at Abbots Mede, Formby, to the south-west of Chorley.

Many tourists visit Guy's Thatched Hamlet at St Michael's Road, Bilsborrow, near Garstang, north of Preston. A village cricket green with a thatched pavilion and a bowling green with a thatched club-house provide just two of the many attractions for lovers of thatch. A large thatched restaurant provides refreshments, as does Owd Nell's Thatched Country Tavern. Visitors are also welcomed to stay overnight at the thatched Guy's Lodgings and many do so especially to attend the Murphy's Irish Stout Oyster Festival, which is held on a regular basis.

YORKSHIRE

Very few thatched roofs remain in Yorkshire. This is mainly due to the great popularity of pantiles after they were first introduced from Europe at the beginning of the eighteenth century. Some do still survive in North Yorkshire, however. A few centuries ago heather was used as a thatch material in this region. For example, at East Witton, south of Richmond, cottages thatched with heather once surrounded the large village green. The houses were sometimes used in an emergency as a defensive stockade against the marauding Scots, who were a constant threat to many northern villages. The gaps between the houses were blocked up during raids. East Witton was completely rebuilt at the beginning of the nineteenth century. It still retained its basic original layout but without thatch. Heather survived as a covering for houses and barns in the Dales until about the middle of the twentieth century. At this time, a few could still be viewed in a ruinous state near Bowes, on the Pennine Way.

In Thornton Dale, between Scarborough and Pickering, an unusual ornamented thatched cottage remains close to the parish church. It has one chimney at one gable end and another one set in the middle of the roof slope; the latter position is unusual, as it would impede the rapid flow of rainwater from the thatch. Further north, on the coast near Whitby, the town of Captain Cook, is Runswick. Despite its apparently exposed position, it is sheltered from the northerly winds by the tall cliffs at the extremity of the bay. This sheltered situation has made it a popular holiday resort. In the past it also made it a practical proposition to roof some of the houses with thatch; a few still survive, along with the common red pantile roofs.

Thatched dwellings may be found in some of the villages surrounding the North York Moors. The Farndale area to the north-east has some very old cottages with thatched roofs. The valley is a well-known beauty spot and nature reserve; thousands of wild daffodils grow in the confines of this protected moorland locality. The nearby village of Hutton-le-Hole still retains the occasional ancient thatched cottage, but most of the stone houses constructed in the seventeenth century are now red roofed. This delightful moorland spot has a stream running through the centre and small white bridges span the sparkling water. The Ryedale Folk Museum, near the local inn, displays a miscellany of items connected with the rural life of the region. It also has a typical North Yorkshire cottage, built in the second half of the eighteenth century, which was moved from the village of Harome in 1972 and reconstructed at the museum. Harome itself still has a few old thatched cottages.

The village of Pockley, near Helmsley, also has a sprinkling of thatched roofs. There is also a converted thatched long house. Rievaulx, 3 miles (4.8 km) north-west of Helmsley attracts visitors to view its magnificent ruined twelfth-century Cistercian abbey. The village has just one stone thatched cottage. Harold Wilson the late former Prime Minister took the title of Lord Wilson of Rievaulx when he became a life peer in 1983.

Warter, east of York, in the East Riding has a row of nineteenth-century thatched cottages with whitewashed brick walls and some pseudo-timbers overlooking the triangular green with its war memorial. Thatched gabled dormer windows protrude from the roof along the terrace and thatched porches shelter the front doors. The cottages are the oldest properties in the village, which also retains its original cast-iron street lights. Interestingly, thatch was the universal East Riding roofing material until the mid-eighteenth century.

For lovers of thatch and horse-racing, a visit to the racecourse on the Knavesmire, just outside York, offers the prospect of a rewarding day out. It is not only one of the most successful and best managed racecourses in the country but it also has a total of six thatched buildings. The stewards' box takes the form of a small water-reed thatched structure on vertical supports that raise it high to ensure a good view of the races. In addition, there are four other huts thatched with water reed on the racecourse and also one thatched with long straw, at the far end of the paddock.

NORTHUMBERLAND

In the extreme north-east of England, at Etal near the Scottish border, an unusual street with thatched cottages can be seen leading down to a ford across the River Till. A particular feature is that at one end of the street there is an eighteenth-century manor house, while at the other there remain the ruins of a castle that James IV of Scotland destroyed in 1496. The village also contains a lovely inn with a thatched roof. Most of the buildings have whitewashed stone walls. It is very rare to find thatched roofs in a village so far to the north in England. However, Etal has retained its old thatched roofs, in a mixture with others of slates and pantiles. It is perhaps noteworthy that thatch was the traditional roofing material in the locality during the eighteenth century. Sandstone slabs were generally used in Northumberland.

Heather was also favoured for thatching, particularly on hill farms and villages, where it became locally known as black thatch. It would also have been used in some old market towns, such as Rothbury, near Alnwick; heather cut from the surrounding moorland would have roofed its traditional grey-stone houses in the eighteenth century. Some examples of heather thatching could still be seen at Broomley, near Stocksfield in the middle of the twentieth century. In Northumberland, unlike the more southerly counties that used heather, the plant was pulled up by the roots and then nailed to the closely fitted rafters of the roof. A coating of wet peat was then applied, followed by a further layer of heather with its roots upwards, sparred into the undercoat. Further peat was then laid on top until the finished layered thickness was about a foot in depth, making a good waterproof roof.

THE ISLE OF MAN

The Isle of Man, about 30 miles (48 km) off the west coast of northern England, boasts the world's oldest continuous parliament, the Tynwald, its own Manx language, its own currency, own stamps and a famous tailless cat. Its heraldic device of three running legs, joined at the centre, has been in use since at least the fourteenth century. It warrants a special mention regarding its thatch, as broom was once used on the cottages, which were constructed of stone or mud and clay. Other materials used in the past were bent, ling, rushes and turfs, all of which were available locally on the island. Later straw was used and the roof was bound horizontally with twisted straw ropes across its surface. The ropes held the thatch firmly down by tying them to pegs driven into the gable walls. Sometimes, heavy stones were secured to the ends of vertical ropes to weight them.

A few old Manx dwellings still remain on the island. Cregneish, on a peninsular at the extreme south-western tip of the island is a delightful village with old thatched cottages. Owing to its lofty position, it also offers stupendous views. The Manx Village Folk Museum maintains a number of thatched stone cottages and workshops, which depict many facets of the Manx way of life in the nineteenth century. The items exhibited include many associated with agriculture, weaving and furniture manufacture, as well as those of an upland crofting community. The thatched roofs of the museum buildings have been preserved and renovated in the roped style. The cottage of Harry Kelly, who died in 1934, makes an excellent example of the squat, simple but sturdy abode of a crofter and fisherman. The open-air museum is open to visitors from Easter to October.

14

Thatched Buildings in Wales,
Scotland and Ireland

WALES

Little thatch remains in Wales, although it was once used over a wide area, although not much in North Wales. The thatch mainly consisted of reed or straw, frequently laid over a support of wattle. The roofs were often coated with whitewash to reduce the fire hazard and this practice continued until the early twentieth century on some of the surviving cottages. Long straw was especially favoured throughout the Vale of Glamorgan and in parts of the Vale of Clwyd in the north. In West Wales, a technique known as 'thrust' thatching became the favoured local style. This involved the pushing or 'thrusting' tightly bound bundles of straw into an under-thatch, instead of the bundles being laid and fixed in courses. The thatch was also often raised into a cone shape around the gable chimney. Another feature was the use of twisted bands of rushes to decorate the ridge, eaves and gable.

Nowadays, slates cover most roofs in Wales, although Glamorgan in particular still maintains a number of thatched ones. The rural areas to the east in the mid-border counties also retain some thatch. The trend towards using solid roofing materials started even before the thinner Welsh slates became available in the late eighteenth and early nineteenth centuries. Stone slates were first used, especially in the north and south-east, to replace thatch. These later changed to Welsh slates when the latter became plentiful and cheap to produce and transport by rail in the nineteenth century. Many surviving old farmhouses and cottages give clues that they were previously thatched by

253

the steep pitches of their roofs and the high chimneys, which were originally installed to safeguard the thatch from falling sparks. Corrugated iron roofs, laid on decaying thatch, can still occasionally be seen in Ceredigion, Carmarthenshire and Pembrokeshire. The walls of seventeenth-century properties that survive in these counties were built with stone or more occasionally cob, with rounded corners on the houses. Scarfed or jointed crucks often supported the thatched roofs. Entry to the houses was usually gained by a door in the centre of the cottage, away from the gable wall where the chimney was sited.

In contrast, in Glamorgan, the entrance was often in the gable wall, alongside the protruding chimney-stack. Diana Cottage in the village of Merthyr Mawr, is a good example of this type. This delightful village, on the banks of the River Ogmore about 2 miles (3 km) south-west of Bridgend in Mid-Glamorgan, is well known for its thatched white-washed cottages. The majority have eyebrow thatched windows. Most are of stone and several are quite large, with two gable-end chimneys. Woodlands and meadows border the village, which lies close to Merthyr Mawr Warren, Britain's largest sand dune system. The ruins of Candleston Castle, once a fifteenth-century fortified manor house, stand at the edge of the shifting sand dunes that caused the house to be abandoned in the nineteenth century. Incidentally, parts of the Hollywood film *Lawrence of Arabia*, starring Peter O'Toole, were filmed here.

The pretty hilltop village of Llangynwyd, north of Merthyr Mawr but still in Mid-Glamorgan, boasts the oldest thatched inn in Wales, which can offer 350 different brands of whisky to its thirsty customers. The Celtic poet Wil Hopcyn, who wrote the old Welsh legend 'The Maid of Cefn Ydfa' was born in the village; the legend describes his tragic love affair with local girl, Ann Thomas. An impressive church with a tall tower stands near the inn.

St Nicholas, in South Glamorgan, contains a few thatched houses and cottages. The Museum of Welsh Life at St Fagan's, also in South Glamorgan, 4 miles (6.5 km) west of Cardiff, preserves many more traditional Welsh vernacular buildings from the fifteenth to the early nineteenth centuries. They include medieval cottages, a seventeenth-century Gower farmhouse called Kennixton (painted red to ward off evil spirits), a thatched fifteenth-century almshouse and a thatched seventeenth-century barn. They were all moved from their original locations and re-erected on site in the grounds of St Fagan's Castle, an Elizabethan

Abernodwydd farmhouse, now at The Museum of Welsh Life, St Fagan's

mansion surrounded by the walls of the former medieval castle. A toll-house, a cock-fighting pit and woollen and corn mills may also be seen in the grounds. The museum is open to visitors all year round from 10 a.m. to 5 p.m., seven days a week and on most public holidays.

South of Cardiff on the outskirts of Penarth, visitors can also gain a glimpse of fourteenth-century Welsh village life at Cosmeston Lakes Country Park. Here a medieval village, with authentically recon-structed thatched buildings, may be seen. The village stands in over 200 acres (80 hectares) of woodlands, meadows and lakes. Villagers dressed in medieval costumes work on the land, amongst ancient breeds of livestock. The park is open all year round.

Few thatched houses remain in North Wales, although Prestatyn still has a few. Just outside the town lies Rhuddlan and in its old town area, a single whitewashed cottage with a thatched roof manages to survive, in a region dominated by slate. The solitary cottage adjoins the ruins of a castle, which the Parliamentarians destroyed in the seventeenth century after the Civil War. A few miles to the south-east of Prestatyn may be found the village of Llanerch-y-Mor, just outside

Mostyn. This village offers hospitality at the thatched Ye Olde Tavern Inn. This unusual hostelry was formed by the conversion of two buildings, an eleventh-century chapel and a farmhouse. The chapel section now serves as the restaurant area, whilst the former farmhouse has become the bar.

In the east of Wales along the border counties, another thatched pub can be found at Marton in Powys, about 4 miles (6.5 km) south of Welshpool. Again the building was a farmhouse that became a pub. The property, now called the Lowland Inn, dates to the early eighteenth century and the white-walled hostelry has a beautiful thatched roof, with an ornamented block ridge. The history of the building through the ages is displayed in a series of old prints which hang on the wall inside the inn.

Those who seek a more peaceful spiritual atmosphere may prefer to visit the thatched stone-built Quaker meeting house, built in 1717 at Llandegley, near Llandrindod Wells, also in Powys. The building, called the Pales has a small thatched entry wing extending at right angles from the main section. The thatch has a cross-rod ornamented ridge. The meeting house remains open to visitors every day of the year and it enjoys wonderful views over the surrounding countryside.

In Gwent, thatch has greatly diminished but a good example of the craft may still be seen in Llanwern. The Thatched Cottage still stands in the village and this spacious two-storeyed house has sturdy walls built in a random array of limestone. In this area, in the seventeenth century, even small cottages were constructed to last unlike those in many English agricultural areas such as Dorset, where they were often built as temporary hovels to be deserted when employment arose and a farm labourer moved to a neighbouring area.

In Snowdonia, most roofs today are covered with slates but several were once thatched with reed or straw, again laid over a wattle support. The Isle of Anglesey, off the coast, also once contained thatched cottages but now just one survives at Swtan, at Church Bay. This cottage has been completely restored and is now used as a folk museum, open to the public at weekends from April to September. The white painted cottage has its thatch horizontally roped in the traditional style adopted for roofs exposed to south-westerly gales, as also seen in the Isle of Man and Scotland. The single-storeyed cottage has square chimneys at the gable ends.

SCOTLAND

A few thatched cottages still remain in Scotland but in the past thatch was a common roofing material, especially among the crofting communities. In the Highlands, temporary rough homes called shielings were used in the eighteenth century to shelter those tending cattle on high or remote ground during the summer grazing season. The shielings looked like Indian wigwams. They were conical, with just a single doorway, and were covered with wattle or thatch. Trees grew only sparsely in the Highlands and Western Isles because of the severe weather conditions and the Isles in particular were almost treeless. Thatch was therefore to be favoured as a roofing material, because less timber was needed to support its weight than with heavier roofing materials. The roof timbers used in the Isles were obtained from the fairly ample supply of flotsam that drifted onto the shore from the many shipwrecks that occurred along the rugged, storm-swept coastline. The larger timbers were frequently shaped into a cruck form to support the roof and the thatch was laid on top of an undercoat of brushwood and turf. The turf was placed on the brushwood in tightly packed squares and provided a good waterproof cover beneath the top thatch layer, which often consisted of heather. Sometimes turf alone was used.

This practice was not confined to the Highlands; in the Lowlands many of the rural peasantry still lived in cruck-framed turf houses, with a smoke-hole in the divot roof, until the late eighteenth century. These miserable dwellings comprised just a single room and the walls were built with granite boulders gathered from the moorland or along the shoreline. Sometimes, alternating layers of stone and turf or peat were used for the wall construction. Even as late as the 1860s, a third of country dwellers still raised families of eight or more in single-roomed houses. The thatch sheltering them consisted of turf or sometimes heather, ferns or broom.

Farmhouses in the eighteenth century were often built in the long house style, with living quarters, stable and byre sheltering under a common thatched roof. At Culloden, 5 miles (8 km) east of Inverness, one of the best preserved crofting farmhouses in Scotland may be found. It is named Old Leanach and the Battle of Culloden, which saw the defeat of Bonnie Prince Charlie's Highlanders, raged around it on 16 April, 1746. The farmhouse survived the battle and has since been renovated. There is now a visitor centre and museum on site. The

National Trust for Scotland is restoring the battlefields to the state they were in on the fateful day that saw the end of the Jacobite uprising.

In the Hebrides, crofters lived in single-storeyed houses with thatched gable roofs and the early ones, called black houses, were long, low, windowless buildings with no chimneys and a single central doorway. The smoke from the peat fires lit on the central hearth slowly diffused out through the heather thatch; there was no other outlet. The name black house aptly describes the bleak existence that the inhabitants must have led, with the inside of their home mostly in darkness unless the door was opened. In order to withstand the gales and harsh weather conditions, the thick walls were built with large rocks. Two rough parallel walls were first constructed, each about 2 feet (60 cm) thick, with a 2- foot cavity between them. This space was then filled with earth, peat, sand or gravel, making a total wall thickness of about 6 feet (1.8 metres). The thatched roof was designed so that rainwater from the eaves cascaded onto the earthen middle section (see fig. 74), before it eventually drained away. The water caused the inner core material to compact, making it draught proof and preventing the Atlantic gales from penetrating the dry stone walls, which contained no mortar. The eaves terminated over the middle of the walls, leaving a 2 foot (60 cm) broad stone ledge exposed. This enabled the

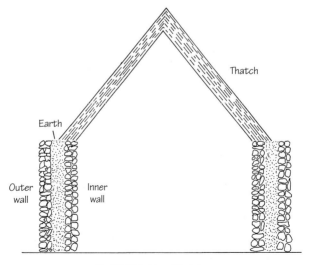

Fig. 74 Hebridean black house

turf or heather thatch to be held down with ropes, weighted with rocks placed along the top ledge of the outer walls. Despite this precaution, severe gales still caused havoc with the thatch and it often had to be replaced each year. However, nothing was ever wasted, the old thatch was put to good use as a fertilizer for potato beds.

Black houses were still being built towards the end of the nineteenth century in the Hebrides, but showed some improvements over the earlier ones. Small windows were inserted and chimneys were built at each gable end. The white houses that later succeeded them were similar except for their white-painted walls. These were only about 2 feet (60 cm) thick, as they no longer consisted of dry stone but of conventional mortar sealed masonry, making them draught free. One of this type can still be seen at Vallay Strand in North Uist. However, the thatch was still laid and held down by ropes weighted with stones suspended over the eaves. Ropes used in Scotland to secure heather thatch were called *siomans*. Netting later replaced them. Slates were also used as roofing material on some white houses.

On the Isle of Skye, rushes were widely used for thatching, as well as heather, and the roof was held down with ropes made from heather. The thatched roofs were often hipped rather than gabled and they were lashed down with the ropes fixed both vertically and longitudinally, either by pegs driven into the walls or anchored with stones. In contrast to the Hebrides, the black houses on Skye had overhanging eaves that shed rainwater clear of the outer walls. At the Skye Museum of Island Life at Kilmuir, a group of seven thatched cottages have been reconstructed to show the lifestyle of the islanders a century or so ago. It was a hard life of self-reliance; they made their own clothes, and seats, and kitchen utensils were sometimes fashioned from whale bones obtained from carcasses washed up on the shore. Of course they also distilled their own whisky. At the Croft Museum at Colbost, near Dunvegan on Skye, a nineteenth-century black house can be visited with a replica whisky still inside. Both museums are open to the public between April and October.

At Arnol, 11 miles (17.5 km) north-west of Stornoway, on the Isle of Lewis, a traditional thatched black house with a visitor centre and an interpretative display provides an insight into island life. The Lewis thatched house is fully furnished, a kettle hangs over a central hearth with an open peat fire but no chimney, and a spinning wheel stands in the corner. The interior gives an impression of the smoky reality of a crofter's life. Crofters suffered even greater hardships in the early nine-teenth century when many Highland families were forced to emigrate after being evicted from their crofts. As well as the black house, an attached barn, byre and stack-yard can also be seen and for comparison there is a furnished croft house constructed in the 1920s. The centre remains open all year except Sundays.

At Gearrannan, near Carloway, 13 miles (21 km) west of Stornoway, a whole group of thatched black houses are gathered together at the Gearrannan Black House Village. The Gearrannan Trust, a local char-itable trust founded in 1989, restored them, keeping their exteriors completely unspoilt to preserve the traditional look of a crofting village. However, the interiors were equipped with modern facilities so that they were suitable for letting, and on-site a museum, café and gift shop are available to visitors. Magnificent scenery surrounds the village.

For those who would like to experience living in a thatched black house, several are available for holidays in the Western Isles. For example, on South Uist, at Howmore, there is a thatched black house with a newly renovated byre. The Gatliff Hebrides Hostels Trust runs it and the property can sleep up to seventeen. The same trust also has two restored thatched black houses on the Isle of Berneray, just off the coast of North Uist, for letting and these overlook a beautiful sandy

Thatching a cottage at South Uist

beach. At Clachan Sands, also on North Uist, another traditional fully modernized thatched cottage is available for letting.

On the Isle of Harris, a thatched black house at Bowglass may be rented and at Scarastavore on the west coast, the Borvemor Cottage is also available for letting. A full list of thatched black houses available for holiday lets may be obtained from the Western Isles Tourist Board at 26 Cromwell Street, Stornoway, Isle of Lewis, HS1 2DD (Telephone: 01851 703088).

In southern Scotland, in addition to heather and broom, wild rushes and reeds were pulled for thatching and some were later cultivated for the purpose. This led to conventional thatching techniques being adopted, which involved laying tightly packed bundles in courses. In the late eighteenth century, particularly in the Kilmarnock area of Ayrshire, the use of straw for thatching came into vogue. After the thatching was completed, a mixture of lime mortar and chopped straw was spread in a thin layer over the thatch surface with a trowel. This proved to be better at protecting the roof against gales than ropes used before. Plain rather than block ridges were much favoured.

The most famous thatched building in Ayrshire must be Robert Burns's Cottage set in the Burns National Heritage Park at Alloway, 2 miles (3 km) south of Ayr. A notice attached to the cottage states:

BURNS COTTAGE
Robert Burns the Ayrshire poet
was born in this cottage
on the 25th Jan. A.D. 1759
and died 21st July A.D. 1796 age 37½ years.

The beautifully thatched cottage now has a modern sprinkler system set along its ridge as a fire precaution. Robert Burns was the first of seven children born to William and Agnes Burns, in the simple two-roomed cottage. He once described Scotland as 'the Land o' Cakes', meaning the simple oatcakes that kept many poor people alive; now Scotland's famous bard's birthday is celebrated annually at Burns suppers throughout the world, the main dish being haggis.

Another thatched property associated with Burns stands at Tarbolton, about 7 miles (11 km) north-east of Ayr. This is the Bachelor's Club, a seventeenth-century thatched house where Robert Burns and some friends founded a debating society in 1780. In an upstairs room, Burns was initiated into Freemasonry. The National Trust for Scotland now cares for the building and it is open to the public during the afternoons from April to September. It also remains open during October but only on weekend afternoons.

The National Trust for Scotland also cares for another property with a Burns association, Souter Johnnie's thatched cottage to the south-west of Ayr at Kirkoswald, 4 miles (6.5 km) west of Maybole. In one of his longer poems, the famous 'Tam O'Shanter', Robert Burns based his character Souter Johnnie on a shoemaker (a 'souter'), who once lived and worked in the thatched cottage. Stone figures depicting various other characters from the poem now stand in a restored house in the garden. Souter Johnnie's Cottage is open to the public during the same times as the Bachelor's Club.

A few miles south-east of Perth may be found the historic medieval village of Falkland, in Fife. The thatched Moncrief House, dating from 1610, faces the gatehouse of Falkland Palace. A carving on the wall states 'al praise to God and thankis to the most excellent monarche', a reference to James VI of Scotland, who succeeded to the throne after the forced abdication of his mother Mary, Queen of Scots. He also became the first Stuart King of England and Ireland in 1603. Falkland village gained its fame from Falkland Palace, the country residence and hunting lodge of eight Stuart monarchs, including Mary, Queen of Scots. The front of the palace has fluted columns and circular panels, making it one of the greatest examples of Renaissance architecture in Scotland. In 1952, the National Trust for Scotland took responsibility for the building and gardens, both of which are open to the public.

A link with the distant past has been created at the Scottish Crannog Centre, Croft-na-Caber, Kenmore, Loch Tay, north-west of Perth. It takes the form of an ancient Celtic lake or bog dwelling. Many such buildings were constructed from 500 BC and in some regions this practice continued until the sixteenth century. A huge conical roof, made from 4½ tons of thatch, supported by timber, shelter an authentic replica crannog, built on a series of wooden posts driven into the mud of Loch Tay. A log pier over the water leads to the house, whose thatched roof towers 25 feet (7.5 metres) high. In the past, about twenty people and animals would have shared such a building. Crannogs as well as providing accommodation, also served a defensive purpose. The Crannog Centre welcomes visitors from April to November.

At Denholm, in the Borders, a thatched cottage stands near the attractive village green. John Leyden, the son of a shepherd who became an esteemed surgeon, minister and judge, was born in the cottage in 1775. He also became a friend of the novelist Sir Walter Scott. The Victorians later erected an imposing monument to his memory on the village green, as a tribute to his much admired virtues and self-reliance.

IRELAND

Many thatched cottages still remain in Ireland and in the past thatch was very widely distributed over the whole country. A sound roof assumed great importance because of the incessant rain. As in Britain, the precise thatch material largely depended on its local availability; turf, heather, flax, water reed and straw from barley, oats and rye were all used in different areas. However, barley had only a limited use, and only on the humblest dwellings. Combed wheat reed was not used in Ireland, although it is now sometimes imported, along with Turkish reed and South African veld grass.

In the thatching process, the roof timbers of most rural cottages were first covered with a tightly packed layer of turf or sod and the thatch was then sparred directly into it. This solid type of thatch became known as a

Thatched dovecot at Clandeboye, Bangor, Co. Down

scraw roof. Interestingly, the underlying sod layer provided, probably inadvertently, a fire barrier beneath the thatch. About 100 listed scraw-roofed buildings still survive in Northern Ireland. However, County Down adopted the English fashion, involving the laying and fixing of straw bundles in the traditional style. The thatchers then plastered the finished roof with clay or mud along the ridge, eaves and barges. Thatch was also laid traditionally in parts of the east and south-east of the Republic of Ireland. Along the Atlantic coast, as in exposed parts of Britain, the thatch was anchored down with ropes weighted with stones or pegged to the cottage walls. The ropes holding heather thatch down were called *súgáns* in Ireland, similar to the *siomans* of Scotland.

Donegal, in the extreme north-west, had several options for thatch material. In the mountainous regions heather was much used, as it was in other Irish counties with a similar terrain, and it proved fairly long-lasting. Flax was also occasionally used in Donegal, as well as in Londonderry, Antrim and Fermanagh. The longest-lasting material of all was rye straw, which was specially cultivated for thatching purposes in Donegal and was widely used elsewhere. In the south-western counties of Clare, Cork, Kerry, Limerick and also Tipperary and Waterford, water reed gained favour owing to its local availability and durability. In contrast, towards the east in Kildare, Louth, Meath, Westmeath and Laois, oat straw was prominent. Good examples of thatching may still be seen in Louth at Carlingford, the famed oyster town of Ireland dating back to medieval times.

Most thatched rural cottages were just one storey and inside each room opened into the next one, rather than by passage entry. As in rural areas of England up to the end of the nineteenth century, floors often consisted of rammed earth or clay. Front doors opened directly into a room, although some of the larger ones had lobby entrances. In County Wexford, in the extreme south-east, a few lobby-entry farmhouses were built with hipped thatched roofs. These had either two or one and a half storeys, depending upon the load-bearing ability of the wall material. Slates started to replace thatch in some regions in the nineteenth century, and this continued into the twentieth century. However, changes took place much more slowly in country districts, and when thatch was replaced on the humbler dwellings, corrugated iron or asbestos was more likely to be used than slates.

In the distant past, as in Scotland, the Irish built thatched round houses called crannogs in lakes and bogs. They were constructed on artificial islands made with logs, peat, rushes or brushwood. The earlier crannogs date from the late Bronze Age and a replica one made with clay-and-wattle can be seen at Craggaunowen in County Clare, with its thatched roof fashioned from rushes. A narrow footbridge leads to it. The Irish National Heritage Park at Ferrycarrig, Wexford also has a replica conical thatched crannog within a defensive wooden stockade, making it an island fort. This one simulates life in the twelfth century and it includes homesteads, burial modes and other rituals. Villagers dressed in ancient costume enact various simple domestic tasks.

Northern Ireland

Northern Ireland boasts many folk museums that display either preserved or reconstructed traditional thatched cottages. The Ulster-American Folk Park at Castletown, 3 miles (4.8 km) north of Omagh in County Tyrone, relates the story of the many emigrants who went to North America. They exchanged a harsh life spent in humble thatched cottages, before being evicted from them, to one lived in log cabins on the other side of the Atlantic. The ownership of land became an integral part of the Irish problem for hundreds of years and relations between landowners and tenants impacted upon many major events in Irish history. Much of Ireland's population, until the mid-nineteenth century, lived in simple thatched sod houses. The poor farm labourers or cottiers who inhabited them had no land of their own, except for a small potato garden. Many were also forced to pay exorbitant rents to absentee English landlords.

The outdoor museum at Castletown not only displays original buildings but also has staff dressed in clothes of the period. One old

Thatched cottages, Ulster Folk and Transport Museum, near Belfast

thatched whitewashed cottage in particular attracts attention because it was the ancestral home of Andrew William Mellon, a well-known American banker, public official and philanthropist, who died in 1937. Another cottage on display is a reconstruction of the childhood home of Archbishop John Hughes, who became the founder of New York's St Patrick's cathedral.

The Ulster Folk and Transport Museum at Cultra, 10 miles (16 km) north-east of Belfast in County Down, also warrants a visit to see the many different types of cottages and farmhouses that were once common in Ireland. They include many thatched ones, as well as the Duncrun cottier's house from the Magilligan area of County Londonderry; the house was lived in until the middle of the twentieth century. It is thatched with marram grass or 'bent', which grows well in the sand dunes of the region. Its local availability made it the cheapest product to use but it had to be roped down to ensure stability against gales.

Also in County Down, at Crawfordsburn, about 10 miles (16 km) outside Belfast and near Cultra, may be found the Old Inn.

Underside of thatched roof, Ulster Folk and Transport Museum, near Belfast

A coaching inn built in 1614, it is reputed to be Ireland's oldest. It still retains the appearance of a typical seventeenth-century English coaching inn, with its immaculate thatched roof, half doors and leaded light windows. Many of these traditional features have disappeared long ago from most old coaching inns in England. Further links with England are the thatched farmhouses found in County Down that were built for English farmers between 1660 and 1720.

Another folk museum at Mullaghbawn, on the B30 between Crossmaglen and Camlough in County Armagh takes the form of a small traditional thatched farmhouse furnished in period style. It is open to the public by appointment only. Another small museum in

Armagh stands at Louggall, 6 miles (9.5 km) west of Portadown and consists of a traditionally thatched mud-walled farmyard cottage. It is called the Diamond or Dan Winter's House; Dan Winter made the decision with others in the cottage to form the Orange Order after the Battle of the Diamond in 1795. Maps and relics of the battle are displayed inside and it is open to visitors every day of the week. Another interesting thatched eighteenth-century property, called Bloomvale House, is located in Plantation Road, at Craigavon in Armagh. It is now the Ballydougan Pottery and for many generations local people have carried out various crafts under its thatched roof.

The National Trust cares for an impressive and elegant thatched eighteenth-century mansion, called Derrymore House, on the A25 at Bessbrooke, 4 miles (6.5 km) west of Newry in Armagh. It was the home of Isaac Corry, who became General in Chief of the Irish Volunteers and later Chancellor of the Irish Parliament. It is open for visitors at varying times during the summer months. The National Trust has also taken over responsibility for Florence Court, in County Fermanagh, one of Ulster's most important eighteenth-century houses, built by the Earls of Enniskillen. For lovers of thatch, the Heather House in the grounds will be of interest. It was originally built as a summerhouse with a heather thatch but it fell into disrepair and was demolished in the 1940s. Fortunately, it has since been reconstructed from a Victorian photograph. Exploratory excavations of the former site revealed the original post holes and also that the floor had been made of pebbles. Incidentally, Enniskillen stands by lovely Lough Erne and a little south along the opposite bank may be found Bellanaleck, which has a famous thatched restaurant with an extension containing a little Museum of Irish Lace.

Another interesting thatched building of a different type is Hezlett House, at Sea Road in Castlerock, between Derry and the Giant's Causeway. It is one of the few surviving seventeenth-century houses in Ireland and a cruck-truss supports its thatched roof. The National Trust again cares for it and the house, a former rectory, is open to visitors at varying times between March and September.

In County Antrim, the interior of a restored eighteenth-century farmhouse is exposed to its flax straw thatched roof. It stands at Dreen, near Cullybackey off the B96, and it was the ancestral home of Chester Alan Arthur, the twenty-first President of the United States of

America, from 1881 to 1885. His father emigrated from Dreen around 1816. The thatched house is open to visitors during the summer months.

REPUBLIC OF IRELAND

County Donegal in the extreme north-west borders Northern Ireland and many delightful thatched cottages may be found scattered there. The Doagh Visitor Centre at Inishowen has a variety of traditional Irish thatched cottages all gathered together and at the same time relates the suffering and starvation endured by their former occupants, with the onset of the Irish famine in 1845 when the potato crop failed. It also tells the story of their stark fear when later eviction orders were served. At the time of the eviction, whole families stood by to watch gangs of men demolish the humble thatched homes where they had lived in appalling conditions. Even bleaker poverty lay before them and only the sky was left as shelter. Eventually, many had to take refuge in the workhouse, whilst others sought a new life in Australia. The Doagh Visitor Centre is open to visitors between Easter and October. Even at the end of the nineteenth century, the poorest families who remained in Donegal could still only afford to live in cabins made of peat.

On a more pleasant note, a beautiful thatched group of ten cottages nestles beside the beach on Cruit Island, Kincasslagh in west Donegal and holiday makers who would like to sleep under a thatched roof can rent any of them. The gabled thatched cottages all have plain ridges that were historically preferred throughout Ireland, rather than the raised block type. A bridge joins Cruit Island to the mainland and nearby is the Glencolombkille Folk Village, a museum of rural life. This contains three small cottages, with bare-earth floors that depict the very basic living conditions endured by the occupants from the eighteenth to the early twentieth centuries.

In County Galway, thatched cottages also abound and a few display ornamental block ridges with points. The charming old town of Oughterard, near Galway City reveals at its centre a pretty row of houses lining the curving street, some of which are thatched and all of which have painted façades. The Irish have a long history of painting the façades of houses and cottages, and unusual combinations of dark greens, browns and pinks were often used. Each household traditionally mixed their own paints and chose the colours to harmonize with those of their neighbours. Oughterard, although small, is still the largest town on the western side of Lough Corrib and is well known for its fishing.

North of Oughterard the picture-book village of Cong sits on the narrow isthmus between Lough Corrib and Lough Mask. A mixture of pretty thatched cottages and old farmhouses are scattered throughout the village. Incidentally, the film *The Quiet Man* starring John Wayne as an Irish prizefighter, was filmed there in 1952. Fifteen miles (24 km) south of Galway City lies the village of Kinvara and on its outskirts may be found a lovely waterside thatched cottage called Moran's of the Weir. It is a seafood restaurant but it has also been the home of the Moran family since 1760. For visitors wishing to stay at a nearby thatched hotel, the whitewashed Merriman Inn nestles on the shores of Galway Bay.

For leisure seekers, a group of nine traditional Irish thatched cottages may be found in the picturesque village of Tullycross, also in County Galway, and each is available for renting. The gabled properties with their plain ridges stand in a long picturesque row along the street, with

A crofter's cottage at Rossaveal on the western coast of Eire

their thatched roofs protruding to shelter their doorways. The beautiful mountains of Connemara National Park provide wonderful scenery with trekking nearby. Connemara, although a largely barren coastal region, contains thatched cottages with their roofs anchored down with nets.

In County Limerick, the lovely thatched village of Adare, on the banks of the River Maigue near Limerick City, merits a visit. Its pretty stone thatched cottages arranged along a wide main street, resemble the model villages created by wealthy landowners in

England. Rustic timbers support overhanging thatched porches on some of them. A few sell traditional Irish crafts and one, opposite the Dunraven Arms, has been converted into a restaurant. In a similar way to estate villages in England, the local Dunraven family designed the ordered plan for the village in the nineteenth century, making it one of the most attractive in Ireland. The nearby manor house and its grounds are now used as a luxury hotel, called Adare Manor.

In Limerick City, an excursion to the Bunratty Castle and Folk Park rewards a visit. The castle, which was restored in 1954, houses a fine collection of paintings and furniture from the fifteenth and sixteenth centuries, whilst the adjacent Folk Park contains some charming nineteenth-century one-storeyed thatched cottages, with their traditional roofs tied down with ropes. Demonstrations of thatching are also available, together with other traditional craft skills.

County Kerry, south-west of Limerick, also has many thatched cottages. Breathtaking scenery, including lakes and the lofty mountains of Macgillycuddy's Reeks surround the town of Killarney, which has several lovely thatched cottages. Block ridges cut with points adorn some of the roofs.

In the south-east of Ireland, County Wexford contains many well-kept thatched cottages scattered around its countryside of low hills and river valleys. On the coast lies Kilmore Quay, about 14 miles (22.5 km) south of Rosslare. This is a peaceful village of thatched and white-washed cottages, which is very popular with anglers. The pretty village of Ballyhack is located a few miles to the west and contains several thatched cottages that are much admired by photographers and painters.

Many cottages can also be seen gathered together at the Yola Farmstead Folk Park at Tagoat, Rosslare. The complex contains thatched cottages such as the Commodore Barry Cottage and various other thatched vernacular farm buildings dating from the beginning of the eighteenth century. It also has a church, a forge and one of the country's few working windmills. It is open to visitors at varying times between March and October.

The adjoining county of Kilkenny has the Lory Meagher Centre at Brod Tullaroan. This boasts an unusual two-storeyed seventeenth-century mansion with a long thatched roof. The centre is open to the public and also contains the County Hurling Museum, displaying items from the traditional Irish game, played with sticks and a ball between two teams of fifteen players.

In County Waterford is Dunmore East, at the head of Waterford Harbour. Many thatched cottages are dotted along the single street of this delightful fishing village, with its attractive lighthouse.

John Nash designed a magnificent rustic *cottage ornée* which overlooks the Suir River at Cahir, in County Tipperary. The Swiss Cottage, as it is called, was built in 1810 and has quaint thatched eyebrow windows. Small thatched extensions abut at right angles from the long main stretch of thatch, which has square chimneys rising from its ridge. A separate tiled lean-to roof, supported by rustic timbers, lies just below the eaves of the thatch and runs the full length of the building. Admission to the house is gained only by joining one of the guided tours, held at various times during the year. Incidentally, John Nash also designed both the Church of Ireland church at the northern end of the town and the former school adjoining the church grounds.

As the name implies, Carrick-on-Suir also lies close to the River Suir and at nearby Ballynoran stand two adjoining thatched cottages which have been converted into a showroom for glass products from the Tipperary Crystal Factory.

A completely different type of display may be seen at the folk village at Cashel, also in County Tipperary. This displays a number of eighteenth- to early twentieth-century houses and shops. Lovely thatched roofs cover some of the buildings and several display elaborately decorated block ridges. The village is open to visitors daily from March to October.

No description of thatched buildings in Ireland would be complete without mentioning a small selection of thatched pubs. One of the most picturesque and authentic is Scanlon's of Kilberry, situated at Kilberry Cross, a few miles north of Navan in County Meath. The long immaculate thatched roof, extending over the gabled stone-built single-storeyed building, has a block ridge ornamented with a single point at its centre. The thatch flows outwards over the doorways to shelter the entrances. Another pub, one of the oldest in Ireland, dating to 1780 with the licence always held in the Treacy family, may be found at Portlaoise in County Laois. It is aptly named Treacys of the Heath, being located on the Great Heath of Portlaoise. Again built with stone in a single storey, its roof has a plain ridge and the floors inside are slated.

Another thatched pub, the Holycross at Butlerstown, in County Waterford, in contrast has a straight block ridge, with a square chimney in the centre. The gabled building also has a large restaurant, reputed to be one of the very best in the county. The Twelve Pins at Barna village, in County Galway also has a thatched roof, but with a block ridge ornamented with points. However, the restaurant attached to it has a solid roof. The Golden Thatch at Emly, in County Tipperary, is worth a mention because the Mulhall family has run it continuously since 1879; it was formerly called the Higgins Hotel. Finally, the Narin Inn at Portnoo in County Donegal does not have a thatched roof but there is a thatch over the bar in the interior.

Postscript

Although this book has been devoted to thatched cottages and buildings in Britain and Ireland, in conclusion it is worth mentioning that thatching is not only the oldest building craft in the world but also the most common method of roofing. This is because thatch is a sustainable natural product and various forms are widely abundant worldwide. In comparison to England's relatively small number of 50,000 or so thatched properties, India alone possesses well in excess of 30 million, with Africa not far behind. However, the average life span of their roofs is usually only about two to five years. Most of the houses consist of flimsy bamboo-framed round huts, thatched with coconut palm leaves tied directly onto the bamboo structure. In Africa, sheet tin metal or concrete is occasionally used to reinforce ridges, whilst in India the builders sometimes smear a bituminous mud over the thatch in the ridge area. This improves stability, increases resistance to rain and in the event of a fire slows down the rate of ignition.

Thatch in the form of coconut palm leaves is also found widely throughout the Pacific Islands, the West Indies and Bali in Indonesia. Visitors to these and other tropical islands will also be very familiar with thatch in their holiday resorts for roofing restaurants, bars and many smaller items such as beach umbrellas, shelters and even showers. There are huge numbers of thatched houses in South America and many other developing countries around the world. For example, both the Marsh Arabs of Iraq and the Uro-Indians of Lake Titicaca, in Southern Peru have for

Thatched summerhouse, Antigua, West Indies

273

centuries, not only constructed their homes with huge water reeds but have also erected them on artificial reed islands built in the marshes.

In addition to Britain and Ireland, other countries that produce durable thatch, lasting several decades, are North West Europe, South Africa and Japan. The standard of workmanship in these countries is high and the thatchers employed are not only highly skilled craftsmen but know the importance of only using the best-quality thatching materials available. In South Africa, Cape reed (dekriet) and Transvaal thatching grass are much favoured. Visitors to the country have probably seen such thatch on the many lodges located in the various game reserves; similar buildings may also be found in Botswana. In Japan, rice grass reed is the most widely used thatch material.

As discussed earlier, the ridge is the most vulnerable part of a roof and some European countries use various methods of strengthening it, although a plain traditional British type straw or sedge ridge will always remain the most pleasing to the eye. For instance, in Denmark and Sweden, thatchers first construct the ridge with loose straw before covering it with wire netting and then finally securing a series of small oak logs on top. The thatchers first fix a log each side of the ridge slope in an inverted V-shape, with the tops secured together. The process is then repeated along the full length of the ridge until each side is covered at intervals with logs. There are many examples and, in addition to cottages, farmhouses with such ridges may be found in South Denmark, at Lolland, which also has a few thatched holiday homes.

In Holland, water reed predominates as the favoured thatch material for the roofs but the ridge is often constructed with half-round burned clay tiles, concreted into position. Interestingly, many of the large pantiled barns in the Netherlands have the hip extremities thatched with reeds to limit wind damage. The use of clay ridge tiles is also common in Germany. Sometimes, burned clay tiles are also substituted for the thatch on the first lowest course, producing straight firm eaves, potentially of higher strength than a straw or reed one. In Germany, many homes bordering the North Sea and situated on the islands off the coast have thatched roofs, and some delightful farmhouses can be found in the marshland of Altes Land, between Stade and Hamburg. They have decorative timber framing, with brick infillings below their luxurious thatched roofs. Even larger properties with huge thatched roofs may be found in the Black Forest. Many builders prefer thatch in this area because of its excellent insulation properties. An interesting design feature entails many of the houses having a small unthatched roof area immediately over the back door, to allow for escape in the event of a fire; it reduces the danger of burning thatch debris falling on people leaving the house.

In northern France and particularly in Brittany and Normandy, iris corms plastered in thick mud are spread over the ridge. When flowering, the plants not only decorate the ridge but it is claimed they also prolong its life as the roots stabilize it by binding the straw together. In some industrialized countries, including France, grass roofs have gained in popularity, with the grass actually growing in soil on top of the roof to produce a lawn or meadow grass appearance. Sometimes the occasional goat may even be seen grazing on it, especially when the house is built on a steep slope!

Earth-sheltered buildings have recently assumed some prominence, the two main types being above ground and partially below ground. There is even a most unusual 'suspended' green roof over the International School at Lyons, in France; this suspended membrane structure claims to be the only one of its kind in the world. In England, the Chase Community Centre in St Ann's, Nottingham, boasts an 'above ground' pitched turf roof. Another one, of Swedish design, covers the Kew Building at the Horniman Museum, in south-east London. The turf roof, with flowers, housed the ecology display at the museum for an experimental period of ten years. Now that the experiment is completed, the building is used as offices for educational purposes. A series of vents protrude through the turf roof to control the air circulation, in order to maintain a constant temperature inside the building throughout the year. The future for thatch in its various forms, including the centuries-old use of turf, therefore appears to be bright.

Bibliography

AA Illustrated Guide To Country Towns and Villages of Britain (Drive Publications Ltd, 1985)

Billett, M. G., *Thatched Buildings of Dorset* (Robert Hale, 1984)

Billett, M. G., *Thatching and Thatched Buildings* (Robert Hale, 1988)

Book of the Countryside (Times Newspapers Ltd, 1980)

Brabbs, D., *English Country Pubs* (Weidenfeld and Nicolson, 1986)

Brown, R. J., *The English Country Cottage* (Robert Hale, 1979)

Brunskill, R. W., *Houses and Cottages of Britain* (Orion Publishing Group, 1997)

Brunskill, R. W., *Illustrated Handbook of Vernacular Architecture* (Faber and Faber, 1978)

The Dorset Model, Thatched Buildings: New Properties and Extensions (Dorset Local Authorities, 1998)

Greeves, L., *Country Cottages* (Pavilion Books, 1995)

Nash, J., *Thatchers and Thatching* (B. T. Batsford, 1991)

Reid, R., *The Book of Building* (Michael Joseph, 1980)

Reid, R., *The Shell Book of Cottages* (Michael Joseph, 1977)

Shell Guide to England (Michael Joseph and Rainbird, 1970)

Smith, O., *English Cottages and Farmhouses* (Thames and Hudson, 1982)

Smith, P., *Houses of the Welsh Countryside* (HMSO, 1975)

Stulz, R., and Mukerji, K., *Appropriate Building Materials* (SKAT and IT Publications, Switzerland, 1981)

Thatch – A Guide to Fire Safety in Thatched Dwellings (Dorset Fire and Rescue Service, 1999)

Thatch and Thatching: A Guidance Note (English Heritage, 2000)

Thatched Living magazine (Impromptu Publishing Ltd)

The Thatcher's Craft (Rural Industries Bureau, 1977)

West, R., *Thatch* (David and Charles, 1987)

Useful Addresses/Contacts

Country Insurance Services Ltd
2nd Floor
Exchange House
Worthing Road
HORSHAM
RH12 1SQ
Tel: 0345 660063

English Heritage
23 Savile Row
LONDON
W1X 1AB
Tel: 020 7963 3000

The Listed Property Owners Club
Lower Dane
HARTLIP
Kent
ME9 7TE
Tel: 01795 844939

National Council of Master Thatchers' Associations
Tel: 07000 781909

National Society of Master Thatchers
Secretary and Treasurer (Mrs Jayne Miller)
20 The Laurels
Tetsworth
Thame
Oxfordshire
OX9 7BH
Tel/Fax: 01844 281568
Mobile: 07803 250972

Period Property UK (web site)
www.periodproperty.co.uk

Stonecraft (Thatch Spark-arresters)
Burgh Road
AYLSHAM
Norfolk
NR11 6AR
Tel: 01263 733322

Thatched Living (web site)
www.thatchedliving.co.uk

Thatched Property Association (TPA)
2 Acorn Centre
Chestnut Avenue
BIGGLESWADE
Beds
SG18 0RA
Tel: 0800 2984379
        0500 824660 (For thatch insurance)

Thatching Advisory Services Ltd
Faircross Offices
Stratfield Saye
READING
Berkshire
RG7 2BT
Tel: 01256 880828 (General)
        0845 6030521 (For thatch insurance)
        0845 0706050 (For thatch advice and details of your local master
                thatcher)

The Thatched Owners Group (Insurance)
19 High Street
Offord D'Arcy
HUNTINGDON
Cambridgeshire
PE18 9RT
Tel: 01480 812600

Glossary

APRON

The thatch layer under chimneys and windows set in the roof. Also, completing a block-cut ridge finished with spars and liggers.

BACKFILL

A thin layer of thatch laid on top of the battens on a new roof. It allows further courses to be laid and slid into position without catching on the rough timbers.

BARGE

See GABLE.

BARGE-BOARD

A piece of timber to cover the ends of the horizontal roof timbers. It follows the thatch line at the gable end.

BASE COAT

A firm layer of the original thatch on which new thatch can be laid.

BATTEN

A horizontal wood strip onto which a new thatched coat is attached.

BED

A prepared heap of straw, sedge or rye which, after wetting, is pulled to remove unwanted material and to arrange parallel stems. Also long straw drawn from it and bundled into yealms.

BEETLE

See LEGGETT.

BIDDLE

A short roof ladder secured into the thatched roof with spikes or curved prongs.

BOTTLES

Small tightly tied bundles, used for starting the angle needed for setting eaves and gables and continuing the action of the tilting fillet. Also known as WADS.

BOULTING

A bundle of straw or reed.

BROTCHES or
  BROACHES

See SPARS

BROW COURSE

First course up from the eaves bundles.

BUNCH/BUNDLE

Bundle of water reed approximately 24 inches (60 cm) in circumference at the tie.

BUTT

The lower end of a bundle of straw or reed.

BUTTING	Dressing the butt ends by tapping them onto a hard surface.
COAT/COATWORK	The complete surface of a thatched roof; overcoating refers to putting a new coat over existing firm thatch.
COMBED WHEAT REED	Wheat straw that has been passed through a reed comber.
COURSE	A horizontal layer of reed or straw thatch.
CROOKS	An iron rod of ¼ inch (6 mm) diameter and varying in length from 8 to 12 inches (20–30 cm), pointed at one end like a nail and with a right-angle hook at the other to hold the sway.
CROSS-RODS	Split hazel rods used for fixing and decorating between liggers.
DEVON REED	Combed wheat reed.
DRAWING	See BED.
DUTCHMAN	A rounded wooden tool with holes in the surface to hold the butts of the reeds. It is used for forming valleys in thatch and to dress and round off corners of eyebrow windows.
EAVES	The horizontal overhang of a roof from the wall face.
EAVES HOOK	Tool used for cutting the eaves to shape.
FATHOM	Bundle of Norfolk reed with a circumference of 6 feet (1.8 metres), when measured 1 foot (30 cm) from the butt end. Consists of five or six smaller bundles of reed laid together.
FLECKING	A woven mat of water reed used as an alternative to battens; now rarely used.
GABLE	The finished edge of the thatch overhanging the gable end. Also the vertical triangular wall at the end of a building.
GADS	Trimmed bundles of hazel or willow ready to be made into spars.
HOOKS	See CROOKS.
LEGGETT	A wooden bat about 1 foot (30 cm) square with a grooved flat surface, used for dressing combed wheat reed or water reed into place.
LIGGERS	Long lengths of split hazel or willow that are pegged down with spars into thatch. Used on the ridges of water reed and combed wheat reed roofs to

secure and decorate them. Additionally employed on long straw roofs to hold in and ornament the eaves and verges.

LONG STRAW   Threshed wheat straw prepared by hand after wetting.

MARSH REED   See WATER REED.

NAILS   See CROOKS.

NEEDLE   A straight or curved needle, usually of metal, for sewing with twine the base coat of thatch onto the battens.

NITCH   A bundle of combed wheat reed weighing approximately 28 pounds (12.7 kg).

NORFOLK REED   Water reed grown in the region of Norfolk.

PINNACLE   The raised end of a ridge, gable or top point of a hip formed into a peak.

RIDGE   The apex of a roof capped with an additional layer of straw or sedge. The main types are:
a) Plain. Flush to the roof surface with minimal decoration.
b) Decorated. Also flush but decorated with cross-rods or a herringbone pattern.
c) Straight Cut Block. 3–4 inches (10-20 cm) thick above the roof surface and cut in a straight line below the bottom ligger.
d) Ornamented Cut Block. As above but with the bottom edge cut into scallops and points or other patterns.

RODS   See LIGGERS and SWAYS.

ROLL or DOLLY   A sausage-shape roll of reed or straw, approximately 4–8 inches (10-20 cm) in diameter and of varying length, used to build up the top of the roof to a sharp apex prior to capping.

RYE STRAW   Threshed and now mainly used for ridging.

SCREW FIXING   A screw attached to a stainless steel wire that is secured into the rafter and the wire fastened to the sway.

SEDGE   Used for ridge construction on a water reed roof.

SHEARING HOOK   Hook used for shearing protruding ends of thatch to give a tidy finished appearance.

SIDE RAKE   A combing tool for tidying the surface of a long straw roof.

SKIRT	See APRON.
SPAR	A split hazel rod, pointed at each end and twisted in the centre into a U-shape which, when thrust into thatch over a ligger or sway, holds down one layer on another.
SPAR BILL HOOK	A keen-edged tool used for splitting and sharpening spars.
STRAW ROPE	A continuous length of rope made from twisted straw.
SWAY	A long rod made of hazel, willow or now often steel, laid across a course to secure it to the rafters. Sways are fixed with hooks driven into the rafter or attached with screw ties or tarred twine. The sways are hidden when the next course is laid over them.
SWEEP	The forming of a valley.
TARRED TWINE	Strong cord impregnated with Stockholm tar. Used for tying thatch to battens and rafters.
THRAVE	A bundle of straw or reed.
TILTING FILLET	Timber used at the eaves and gable to start the roof at the correct angle to ensure correct tension throughout the thatch roof; also known as arris rail.
VALLEY	The sloping junction of two inclined roof surfaces.
VERGE	See GABLE.
WADS	See BOTTLES.
WATER REED	A wetland plant used as thatch material.
WHIMMER or WIMBLE	A tool for making a straw rope by twisting stems together.
YEALM	A prepared layer of long straw formed by drawing straw from a bed of threshed material, approximately 16 inches (40 cm) wide and about 5 inches (12.5 cm) thick.
YEALMING	The practice of preparing long straw on the ground by wetting, drawing and forming yealms.

Index